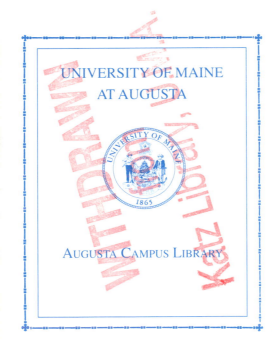

THE FOOD
INDUSTRY WARS

THE
FOOD INDUSTRY
WARS

Marketing Triumphs
and Blunders

Ronald D. Michman
Edward M. Mazze

QUORUM BOOKS
Westport, Connecticut • London

Library of Congress Cataloging-in-Publication Data

Michman, Ronald D.
    The food industry wars : marketing triumphs and blunders / Ronald
D. Michman, Edward M. Mazze.
        p.   cm.
    Includes bibliographical references and index.
    ISBN 1–56720–111–3 (alk. paper)
    1. Food industry and trade—United States.   2. Food—Marketing.
I. Mazze, Edward M.   II. Title.
HD9005.M44   1998
664'.0068'8—dc21   97–32992

British Library Cataloguing in Publication Data is available.

Library of Congress Catalog Card Number: 97–32992
ISBN: 1–56720–111–3

First published in 1998

Quorum Books, 88 Post Road West, Westport, CT 06881
An imprint of Greenwood Publishing Group, Inc.

Printed in the United States of America

The paper used in this book complies with the
Permanent Paper Standard issued by the National
Information Standards Organization (Z39.48–1984).

10 9 8 7 6 5 4 3 2 1

To the memory of Ruth Krefting Michman

To my wife, Sharon Sue Mazze

CONTENTS

TABLES

PREFACE

Success comes when managers act on their organizations' specific capabilities and advantages. Today's managers need to look beyond financial statements to ensure profitability. A strategy that is proclaimed and then not executed is worse than no strategy. Essentially, the role of management is to manage changes that might affect its organizations. Increasingly, a proactive rather than a reactive approach to events is warranted. In order to accomplish these objectives, organizations need to understand past history and practices so that mistakes can be avoided. Managers must determine what they can do either differently or better than the competition. Facing intense competition, marketers are confronting different types of challenges and need to comprehend complexities and interrelationships in a volatile economic environment. For example, in the breakfast cereal industry, with the marketing of cereal bars such as Kellogg's Nutri-Grain, there is competition not only within its own industry but with the snack food and candy industries as well. Thus the food industry wars are growing fiercer.

Key variables have been identified for ensuring the success of food marketers. These variables include: innovation, target-market segmentation and image, physical environmental resources, and human resources. In considering the successes, failures, and mistakes of food marketers, the challenge is to discern whether successful food marketers received high grades using all of the variables or was success determined by using some of the variables in an exceedingly capable manner. Correspondingly, it would be interesting to discern if failure or mistakes can be attributed to either the lack of use of all variables or just the ineffective use of some variables.

This volume evolved from many years of observing the business environment, teaching courses in marketing strategy, and closely monitoring the literature in the public domain. As a result, a distinctive framework has been developed emphasizing how food marketers use key variables such as innovation, image and target-market segmentation, the physical environment, and human resources. How the management of these variables brings about a successful exchange between a firm and its customers is the central focus of this book. The process of developing this framework required extensive analysis of marketing successes and mistakes in the food industry. Emphasis is on how to adapt key variables in a volatile economic environment. The result is an approach to marketing management that should prove beneficial to executives and students.

To avoid cumbersome references within the text, the authors did not use footnotes since the material was available in public, corporate, and governmental publications. Those interested in pursuing specific topics should refer to the selected bibliography.

The last decade of the 20th century is as critical as it is unique. It is critical because of the extreme pervasiveness of environmental and technological change affecting the structure of the food industry. The course that these changes follow and the end results during the 1990s will lend direction for the early decades of the 21st century. This decade in history is unique inasmuch as sophisticated technological changes along with social changes have created many more opportunities for firms to develop differential advantages. A differential advantage is at the heart of a firm's performance in competitive markets. Differential advantages are the unique characteristics in a firm's marketing program that cause consumers to purchase its product and not the competitor's. Differential advantages can be achieved by the development of a distinctive image, targeting a precise market segment in a special way, and employing physical and human resources with great proficiency as well as with the ability to innovate.

This volume has been divided into ten chapters. The first chapter presents an overview of food marketing and distribution by analyzing the supermarket industry. Subsequent chapters depict the following industries: fast food, ice cream, soup, breakfast cereal, baby food, ethnic food, candy, snack food, and soft drinks. Many of the accounts of failures in the food industry have focused upon the shortsightedness of management executives. This work offers a much broader perspective by providing a historical examination of ten institutional formats in the American food marketing and distribution structure. Each chapter analyzes the inter- and intraenvironment competition challenging a sector of the food industry and investigates five key factors in food-marketing success: innovation, target-market segmentation, image, physical environment resources, and human resources. The fundamentals for sustaining competitive dominance in the food industry are identified. It is hoped that managers and students, by focusing in particular on these fundamentals, will now be equipped with a more powerful tool for duplicating success and avoiding failure. The gap between successful, failing, and merely surviving food organizations is widening each day. The point is this—food marketers live in a world of galloping change. Adjustments to the world of change and anticipation of change is vital in order for food marketing operations to progress smoothly. This work provides a starting point for executives to obtain more appropriate insights in order to understand the complexities and interrelationships in marketing food products. Hopefully, these insights will prevent mistakes and allow companies in the food industry to take greater advantage of market opportunities.

ACKNOWLEDGMENTS

Every book owes its knowledge, personality, and features not just to the authors but to a team of hardworking individuals behind the scenes. A great debt is owed to our research assistants, Cavan Harris, Ashley Tison, and Megan Barber Allende, who helped pull together information from numerous sources. Special recognition is extended to LaVonda Hayes, who typed all of the chapters and helped with many organizational aspects of this project. The senior author would like to thank Laura Michman Dessel, who contributed many insights to the chapters on the fast-food, breakfast cereal, snack food, and candy industries. Even though a team effort is cited, any errors of omission or commission are our responsibility.

CHAPTER 1

FOOD MARKETING AND DISTRIBUTION

Strategies in a Mature Market
- Use advanced technology aggressively
- Capitalize quickly on new opportunities
- Use a proactive rather than a reactive approach
- Use new distribution formats
- Use geographical market segmentation
- Differentiate from national, regional, and local requirements
- Shift to non-price variables
- Financial productivity ratios
- Customer focus

Distribution Mistakes
- Status quo mentality
- Poor brand differentiation
- Slow reaction to entry of non-food retailers
- Slow to identify local distribution requirements
- Slow to promote a partnership approach

The distinctions between the marketing and the distribution of food products reflects a single concept. Marketing begins with an idea and a potential market, and distribution does not commence until there is a product to distribute. Management in marketing food products considers such variables as the competitive framework, innovation, resourcefulness, the target market, the firm's existing physical and human resources, brand development, potential areas of conflict and cooperation among institutions, and total customer satisfaction. Distribution, in contrast, is concerned with the flow of the product, namely the selection of distribution channels and the performance of specific distribution activities.

The marketing of food products rests on four pillars: market focus, customer orientation, coordinated marketing, and profitability. All the pillars are aimed at generating customer satisfaction.

A company cannot operate in every market and satisfy every need. Therefore, a market focus needs to be developed. For example, past studies reveal that General Foods' Maxwell House ground coffee is made stronger for consumers in the West than for consumers in the East, and families in the South spend more than the national average on products such as sugar, sweets, and beverages. Campbell Soup sells a spicier nacho-flavored cheese soup in California and Texas in order to accommodate subcultural differences.

A customer orientation requires the company to define customer needs from the customer's point of view. For example, a supermarket on the Navajo reservation in northern Arizona stocks not only conventional grocery items but also distinctive items, such as skinned sheep heads and other items that are desired by residents of the area. Some food marketers, such as Campbell and Stouffer, have appealed to the "singles" market. Campbell has a line of Soups-for-One and Stouffer has promoted frozen entrees to single people.

A coordinated marketing effort involves the internal and external integration of various marketing functions such as sales, product management, promotion, research, and physical distribution. To illustrate, in the past, Coors Beer was attempting to penetrate national markets. The external strategy was to locate dealers who would remove Coors Beer from the shelves in thirty days to prevent the taste from fading. This was necessary because unlike most beers, Coors is not pasteurized. Dealers must use refrigerated warehouses, since the beer must be maintained under 40 degrees Fahrenheit. A joint promotional plan with dealers was also vital for Coors to be successful. Internally, Coors had to coordinate marketing research information about potential customers and competitors, develop agreements on price and other terms, and arrange for ordering and reordering procedures.

In considering food marketing and distribution successes and failures, even the most successful organization can make mistakes. Survival depends on factors such as innovation, target market, image, timing, physical environmental resources, and human resources. Historically, Kellogg was the first to sell cereal from packages rather than barrels, and Gerber was the first to sell baby food already prepared in jars. More recently, soft drink manufacturers have developed new products such as diet colas and colas without caffeine.

Campbell Soup has been able to adjust its product mix to serve different target markets in diverse geographical areas. Quaker Oats has used a trademark of a Quaker, and this has been a positive image for the company for a number of years. Both A&P and Kroger have used vertical integration to strengthen physical environmental resources. The Gerber merchandising representatives who have stocked the supermarket shelves have been well known for their expertise through the years. Positive characteristics of food marketing and distribution include the aggressive use of advanced technology and a customer focus. Negative characteristics of food marketing and distribution include a lack of speed to ease stock-out conditions and the failure to capitalize on unexpected new opportunities.

Profitability is an important goal of marketing. The goal is to find a profitable way to satisfy a target market segment. Marketers are highly involved in analyzing the profit potential of different marketing opportunities. For example, to be more responsive to ecological concerns, StarKist (a division of H. J. Heinz) adopted a "dolphin-safe" policy. StarKist does not buy tuna from fishers who trap dolphins in tuna nets, and has placed a "dolphin-safe" logo on all its cans in order to achieve a competitive advantage. Thus profitability and consumer satisfaction go hand in hand.

DISTINCTION BETWEEN TRADITIONAL
MANAGEMENT AND STRATEGIC MANAGEMENT

A traditional management orientation focuses on short-term objectives, usually during a given financial year. The quarterly and the annual profit results are paramount. While this is an important management concern, decisions that are relevant for a much longer time frame also need to be examined. Therefore, the market is considered dynamic and constantly changing. Forecasting is related to strategic and contingency planning, whereas traditional management places less emphasis on environmental analysis and contingency planning.

Management has traditionally concentrated on marketing research. A newer approach is to utilize a marketing information system that reveals consumer buying characteristics in each particular market and for the food store in each neighborhood. This orientation should make a bottom-up decision-making approval more of a possibility, rather than the traditional top-down perspective. Emphasis is upon integrating the organization on horizontal and vertical levels rather than the traditional functional approach.

Leadership style is viewed with a proactive perspective, with a high degree of creativity. The traditional approach emphasized a reactive perspective, with a maturity and control orientation. The selection and motivation of participants in marketing and food distribution was based on the needs and characteristics of the target market and the development of product, price, promotion, and distribution strategies. A newer approach is to focus on the organizational vision and mission, objectives, and reduction of strategic gaps.

Only a small number of companies have been able to plan strategy for more than five years. Nestlé has been able to shift its marketing strategies from short-term to long-term, enabling it to transfer successful products and marketing methods from one country and culture to another.

This ability to plan strategically means that Nestlé has been able to absorb high short-range costs while patiently building market share. This marketing strategy has been largely responsible for revitalizing a once lethargic Swiss chocolate firm.

Strategic planning differs from short-term planning in the following ways:

- More uncertainties and environmental changes must be investigated for long-term than for short term implications.

- Corporate objectives and strategies may require greater restraint.

- Investment payoff and the time needed to recover costs are of greater concern.

- Anticipated future earnings need to be adjusted for inflation as well as adjusted to a present-value basis because of the interest factor.

- Long-term financial projections should be more concerned with cash flow.

As a changing market environment has caused business decisions to grow more complex, strategic planning has become a more crucial part of the corporate system. The distinction between traditional management and strategic management broadens the vision scope of marketing management. For example, a decade ago, General Mills marketed consumer goods and services in such areas as consumer foods, restaurants, toys, fashion, and specialty retailing. This resulted in a lack of direction. General Mills was committed to a strategy of diversification, aggressive consumer marketing, and positioning within each industry group. Overdiversification resulted in an unclear organizational mission and poor financial results. After a careful review by management, General Mills decided to concentrate in the consumer food and restaurant industries with such well-known names as Cheerios cereal, Betty Crocker foods, Gold Medal flour, Gorton's frozen seafoods, and Red Lobster and Olive Garden restaurants. A proactive approach that anticipates rather than reacts to a changing marketing environment is an important determinant of success as the food wars intensify.

RETAIL DISTRIBUTION

The supermarket was the first large-scale retail institution to sell merchandise by using strategies of impulse buying, promotion of national brands, and customer self-service. Eventually, the supermarket was able to develop its own private label brands in competition with national, regional, and local manufacturers' brands. Private-label or store brands were once regarded as somewhat inferior in quality to national brands, but they have made extraordinary inroads in market share in the 1980s and 1990s. Innovation in the supermarket industry occurred years ago when Piggly Wiggly introduced self-service and King Kullen, scrambled merchandising. The introduction of new business formats such as superstores, warehouse stores, and box stores, as developed by Jewel T and Aldi, and convenience stores, as developed by 7–11, have served as viable innovations.

Target-market and image factors have been sharply developed by Food Lion, Weis, and Giant Food. Food Lion has developed a cost-focus approach and is perceived as a discounter by its target market. Weis serves midsize cities and carefully selects locations where it can dominate the trading area. Giant Food was the first large chain to provide unit pricing, open dating, and fish labeling, and is perceived as a consumer-oriented chain by its target market.

In the early days of supermarkets, both A&P and Kroger used vertical integration to strengthen physical environmental resources. Even though A&P has stumbled, its physical integration, which manifested itself with the development of store-label brands, has sustained this organization. The use of new technology has helped American Stores, especially with their Jewel and Lucky Store divisions, to maintain a competitive advantage. The ownership of physical manufacturing resources has a great impact on retail distribution. For example, Kroger has thirty-seven food processing facilities that supply private-label products to its supermarkets. Facilities include a dairy, bakery, and grocery-product divisions. Such items as private-label milk, ice cream, bottled water, bread, peanut butter, jellies, and a host of other products are distributed.

The concept of differential advantage explains much of the dynamics of the supermarket industry. Through operating efficiencies, Food Lion is able to control costs. So far, this strategy has enabled Food Lion to be an above-average performer in the industry. Safeway assumed a cost-leadership strategy through economies of scale and superior management of new, specialized departments, and these tactics helped to neutralize the strategies of A&P and American Stores.

New types of institutions have emerged in the retail-food industry, such as the superstore, a combination supermarket and drugstore. The environment, again, has promoted the growth of this new retailing format. As consumers become more time pressured, the convenience offered by superstores in the food trade creates a competitive advantage over traditional supermarkets. The emergence of new types of institutions changes the nature of competition because new opportunities for growth are present. However, in a negative sense, new institutional changes may foreshadow decline and demise.

In the past, manufacturers tended to dominate relationships between wholesalers and retailers because they had better market coverage and recognition, and wholesalers and retailers were small and localized. The growth of large national wholesale and retail chains accompanied by large purchase volume and the popularity and acceptance of private-label brands has shifted the balance of power to wholesalers and retailers. For example, the A&P private-label brand of Eight O'clock Coffee is supplied widely to other retailers and might really qualify as a national brand. Moreover, A&P's American Choice entries, have been equated in product quality with that of national brands and available at lower prices. The forces of power, conflict, and cooperation are present in the retail distribution of food products, and manufacturers, wholesalers, and retailers need to reconcile objectives so that compatible objectives of service and profitability are accommodated.

Food-store selection by manufacturers is dependent upon qualitative and quantitative profitability factors, the required number of resellers, and services that need to be performed. If the manufacturer is powerful in the industry, such as Kraft in refrigerated dairy cases, then there are many choices available. However, if the food store is dominant, then the manufacturer needs special inducements to motivate the reseller to stock the manufacturer's line or brand.

The manufacturer generally considers factors such as the sales strength of the food chain, the average order size, customer concentration, the perishability of the product, the distance from the market, and the seasonability of sales. The retailer, in making a decision to either retain the product or add to its inventory, generally considers that degree of brand recognition, potential sales volume, profitability, and the amount of promotional support. Manufacturers also contemplate the types of middlemen needed for market coverage, such as food brokers, cash-and-carry food wholesalers, and drop shippers.

When selecting food stores, the food manufacturer or wholesaler carefully evaluates market opportunities and threats with regard to overall organizational objectives. However, there are situations when the food store selects the food marketer as a distribution partner rather than vice versa. Strategic management objectives in selecting food stores include coverage of important resellers. These important resellers might be situated in key volume markets or in new developing markets, or they may be vital in penetrating competitive markets.

A second objective for food marketers involves coverage within the retail outlet itself. Shelf position is an important impetus for impulse buying. Slotting allowances for the introduction of new products is another managerial aspect; this involves payment to the supermarket for shelf position.

A third objective is the coverage of specific geographic markets. These locations may not only be situated in key areas but might involve key neighborhoods. Food products within the line might be substituted depending upon precise neighborhood buyer behavior characteristics.

A fourth objective is effective selling by resellers. This managerial dimension involves the use of point-of-purchase materials, shelf stocking, location in the store, and inventory management by the food store.

Finally, promotion is an important consideration. Price management, using specials and cooperative promotion, is an effective strategy for ensuring profitability. However, it must be acknowledged that in recent years the power pendulum has shifted in favor of the food store. Food marketers are frequently placed in the position of explaining why their brands should be stocked and giving increasing incentives to motivate resellers to stock their brands.

MARKET STRUCTURE

The market structure of food stores is concentrated but highly diversified. Food sales are concentrated among national, regional, and local supermarket chains. Convenience stores, such as the 7–11 chain, complement the competitive structure. Ma-and-pa stores are not an important part of the market structure except in vacation or rural areas. Scrambled merchandising, the selling of merchandise not related to the retail institution's primary mission, has increased significantly in recent years and will probably become even more important in the future. In particular, discount stores such as Wal-Mart and drug stores such as Walgreens have successfully entered the market by selling detergents, paper products, soft drinks, and snack foods such as potato chips and pretzels. This type of product line sold by discounters and drug stores will be more comprehensive in the future.

A conventional supermarket consists of approximately 20,000 square feet, offers about 10,000 items, and has sales around $1 million or more a year. Competition in the food industry is causing supermarket organizations to adopt new strategies. One challenge to the supermarket industry is that it is oversaturated with competitors, such as Safeway, A&P, Kroger, American Stores, Winn-Dixie, Giant Food, and Weis. Another challenge is that various types of institutions (hypermarkets, deep-discount drugstores, supercenters, warehouse stores, category killers, gourmet shops, health-food stores, and convenience stores) are taking away market share.

In the 1930s, wholesalers organized groups of independent retailers into unified groups known as wholesaler-sponsored voluntary chains. The best known wholesaler-sponsored voluntary groups in the food field are the Independent Grocer's Alliance (IGA), Super Value, and Foodland. In the food industry, many independent grocery stores could not compete with such national chains as A&P. These independent food stores desired reseller label or store brands in order to compete with national, regional, or local supermarket store brands. The wholesaler not only satisfied this need but put together a packaged program of services as an inducement for independent retailers to join the chain. The wholesaler-sponsored voluntary group may furnish consultants who aid the small merchants with accounting procedures, inventory control methods, display, advertising, and numerous other services.

Some supermarket organizations have reduced costs and emphasized low prices by offering more store brands, generic products, bulk packs of non-perishables, and fewer customer services. Other supermarket organizations have expanded their store size and product assortments by offering more nonfood merchandise lines, targeting ethnic groups with special food lines, and offering service departments such as pharmacies, florists, and banking services. Take-out food departments have been expanded, and snack bars already exist. Supermarkets are now renting videocassettes and selling paperback novels, greeting cards, low-price watches, flowers, plants, and a wide range of over-the-counter drug items. Some drug and discount stores are selling snack and food items, which increases intertype competition. It is conceivable that in the future new types of food operations will increase their market shares, to the detriment of supermarkets.

Discount department stores and drugstores have used scrambled merchandising to their advantage by selling more packaged foods. Many fast-food restaurants continually increase the variety of foods they offer, to the satisfaction of their customers. Wholesale clubs have also taken on a new dimension and have become effective at competing with conventional supermarkets. Competitive dimensions related to merchandise offerings concern the freshness and quality of meats and produce and the availability of branded grocery items.

A number of other types of food stores have eroded the market share of supermarkets. The aim of the superstore is to provide one-stop shopping by offering a wider range of goods and services. For example, television sets may be carried. Moreover, such merchandise lines as wine and gourmet foods are generally added. Pathmark exemplifies such an operation. Skaggs-Albertson's operates combination stores that sell food and drug items and are based principally in Florida, Louisiana, Nebraska, South Dakota, and Texas. Jewel T and Aldi operate box stores, where lower prices are offered on private-label brands and consumers furnish their own bags or do their own bagging.

Supercenters operated by Wal-Mart and Kmart carry products that are well defined by brand, allowing customers to easily identify product features and uses; heavily supported by national advertising, so that customers are presold and informed about products before entering retail stores; and purchased with great frequency, enabling customers to develop brand preferences.

The basic strategy of a convenience store is to offer fill-in and impulse merchandise, to help shoppers avoid long supermarket lines, and to remain open in the very early and late hours when supermarkets are closed. A convenience store is a modern-day version of the ma-and-pa grocery store, ranging from 1,000 to 4,000 square feet compared to 15,000 to 20,000 for a supermarket. Many product lines feature staple merchandise that needs frequent replacement, such as dairy and bakery products. Leading convenience stores are 7–11, Minit Markets, Jiffy, Mumford, and Quik-Pik. Although their prices are generally higher than those of supermarkets, convenience stores have seized a sizable market share away from supermarkets.

Although other food-store formats are eroding the market share of supermarkets, supermarket organizations have fought back by developing other formats. For example, Jewel has developed Jewel T, and A&P has developed Superfresh. Safeway and Kroger have both developed superstores. American Stores has invested heavily in new technology to counteract new types of food-store competition.

Table 1.1 shows the number of store units and sales for the top supermarket systems in the United States. At one time A&P, and subsequently Safeway, had the most store units, but first place is now held by Kroger. The acquisition of Vons, with its 320 store units, by Safeway in 1996 has established Safeway as the second-largest supermarket chain in the United States. This acquisition reflects a trend toward consolidation in

Table 1.1
Top Supermarket Chains, 1996

Company	1996 Sales	Number of Stores in 1996
The Kroger Co.[a]	$25,170,909,000	1,356
Safeway Stores[b]	$17,269,000,000	1,052
Albertson's	$13,776,678,000	841
American Stores	$13,420,000,000	813
Winn-Dixie	$12,955,000,000	1,178
Ahold USA (Royal Ahold)[c]	$11,244,000,000	800
Publix Super Markets	$10,400,000,000	548
A&P[b]	$10,089,014,000	1,022
Food Lion	$ 9,005,932,000	1,112
Vons Companies, Inc.[d]	$ 5,407,000,000	320

Source: Derived from corporate reports.

[a]Reflects total company operations
[b]Includes Canadian operations
[c]Includes convenience-store operations
[d]Acquired by Safeway Stores in December 1996

a fragmented industry, as companies need size and financial resources to operate modern stores with multiple departments and high-tech systems. The two organizations, for the most part, do not overlap geographically, and Safeway will continue to operate its new division under the Vons and Pavilion brand names. Even though Food Lion was started in the late 1950s, it is the fastest-growing supermarket chain in the United States. Most of the other chains, such as Albertson's and Winn-Dixie, have grown at the expense of Safeway and A&P.

Food distribution is highly competitive and subject to pronounced changes. In the early 1990s, new entrants such as Wal-Mart's Sam's Club and Kmart's Price Club have increased their market share. Supercenters developed by Wal-Mart and other organizations will have a profound impact on food distribution in the future, and much turbulence is anticipated. Moreover, in an industry that is plagued by extreme fragmentation and too many stores, a rational strategy can be made for further consolidation.

MARKET CONDUCT

Market conduct consists of the practices and strategies by which firms attract customers, respond to each other's competitive policies and strategies, innovate, and satisfy customers. Significant types of conduct from the viewpoint of marketing are innovation, target-market segmentation, the use of physical and human resources, brand management, and the positive aspects of conflict and cooperation among institutions, aspects that lead to customer satisfaction.

The history of triumphs and blunders needs to be traced in order to develop managerial insights through historical perspectives. A changing competitive framework needs to be traced in order to understand how successful strategies have evolved and to attempt to use this knowledge to develop future strategies. Sound fundamentals need to be identified for the sustenance of competitive dominance and the establishment of firms in new or particular markets. In this way resources can be effectively allocated.

Prior to the development of the supermarket concept in the early 1930s, consumers made daily trips to the neighborhood grocery store to purchase small quantities of groceries and to replenish such items as milk and bread. Purchases were made through a sales clerk who suggested specific items and obtained the merchandise from the shelves for the customer. Small stores might offer credit and home delivery. In sharp contrast, the supermarket eliminated such services and offered lower prices.

Present-day supermarkets are planned for maximum efficiency. The sales and profitability of each item are analyzed from checkout scanners, and floor space is allocated accordingly. Supermarkets have continued to evolve, and new forms of supermarkets are now present.

One of the most significant changes in market conduct has been the development of store brands over the years. Market share of store brands has been increasing from decade to decade. Private or store brands account for approximately 15 percent of U.S. supermarket revenues and about 20 percent of supermarket unit sales. Refrigerated and frozen foods have the highest private-label grocery products sales. The chief private-label food categories are milk, fresh bread and rolls, cheese, ice cream, frozen vegetables, carbonated beverages, juices, cold cereals, chips and snacks, and cottage cheese. Dairy products seem to predominate, and consequently refrigeration and technology may be factors instigating against national brands. As prices of national brands increase, it is expected that store brands will make further inroads into market share.

A historical examination of food marketing and distribution reveals that in the 1920s there was a need for less food preparation time, which led to the growth of the food-processing industry. Canned fruits and vegetables were preferred to the fresh variety, and frozen salads turned messy food into neat, icy squares. Immigrants from Italy opened many small restaurants, and Italian food became popular. Zucchini, broccoli, squash, and tomatoes gained in popularity as Italian food gained momentum.

After the end of World War II, new stoves and refrigerators were installed in the soaring housing industry. Because consumers had been deprived of meat during the war, meat sales accelerated. Sales of dairy products also increased significantly; however, margarine decreased the overall consumption of butter.

In the 1950s the trend toward eating more meat continued, along with backyard barbecues and the introduction of TV dinners. In the 1960s McDonald's became popular, and America's sweet tooth sweetened. Dining out still meant meat, baked potatoes, and iceberg lettuce salads.

In the 1970s health food began to make its mark, but so did vegetables smothered in sauces. Favored appliances were blenders, food processors, microwave ovens, and crockpots. In the 1980s health food became increasingly popular. Sales were one and a half times greater than in the 1970s. Foods with fiber and oat bran became popular. Red meat consumption declined, and chicken consumption significantly increased.

The 1990s stressed low-fat foods and Thai cuisine, Pan-American cooking, and the blending of cuisines from different countries. The winners in the early 1990s were turkey, pizza, and frozen entrees. Rice, microwave popcorn, diet ice cream, frozen yogurt, diet beverages, and low-fat and skim milk also gained in popularity. The losers in the early 1990s were meat, cheese, fried potatoes, regular ice cream, and whole milk. The trend toward more healthy eating in the 1990s marches on into the twenty-first century.

Firms in the food industry use various forms of competitive advantage to beat their competitors, and to offer greater perceived customer value than their competition. For example, Food Lion places emphasis on buying at a lower cost, to charge customers low prices. Lance develops low-fat products for a narrow-market segment to offer products with a unique appeal. Ben & Jerry's offers ice cream products that have a broad appeal, but also have unique features at a higher price.

FOOD LEGISLATION: A REFLECTION OF MARKET CONDUCT

The consumer has benefited from government action to improve the quality of information and provide protection from misleading selling tactics. Early food marketing was plagued with sanitary violations, and therefore much legislation was passed for health reasons. Generally, food legislation was passed to prevent unfair competition by corporations, to protect consumers from unfair business practices, and to protect the interests of society.

The laws that are designed to prevent unfair competition are enforced by the Federal Trade Commission and the Antitrust Division of the Attorney General's Office. For example, the Sherman Antitrust Act of 1890 prohibits attempts to monopolize or restrain trade. The Federal Trade Commission Act of 1914 empowered this body to issue cease and desist orders and to investigate unfair methods of competition.

The protection of consumers from unfair business practices has become more paramount in recent years. Historical food legislation concentrated on sanitary practices. For example, the Federal Food and Drug Act of 1906 forbids the sale of adulterated, labeled foods in interstate commerce. This was later amended by the Food Additives Act in 1958. The Fair Packaging and Labeling Act of 1966 provides for the packaging and labeling of consumer goods. More recent legislation specifies that the percentages of fat, sodium, and other ingredients be precisely spelled out on food labels.

A third purpose of government regulation is to protect the interests of society and to make certain that firms take responsibility for the social costs of their products. The National Environmental Policy Act of 1969, the Consumer Product Safety Act of 1972, and the Magnuson-Moss Warranty/FTC Improvement Act of 1975 have expanded powers over unfair or deceptive practices in order to protect the interests of society.

Public interest groups have also grown to protect the interests of society. The most notable has been Ralph Nader's Public Citizen group, which was instrumental in the passage of the Wholesome Meat Act of 1967. Consumerism has become a major social force and has led to legislation involving item price removal and unit pricing. Giant Food of Washington, D.C., has assumed leadership in the supermarket industry for furthering consumer interests, and was the first chain to initiate unit pricing.

Public policy toward food distribution has been concentrated on acquisitions by large food chains and on competitive tactics in buying and selling. There has been opposition by local communities to the large size of food chains based upon the assumption that these chains will exercise power by either predatory pricing in local markets or in bargaining with manufacturers or wholesalers. However, these fears, though in some cases justified, are mostly unfounded. Grocery chains, with their private labels; large-scale, coordinated operations; and low margins, deserve special praise for maintaining low prices. Moreover, intense competition from discounters, wholesale clubs, and no-frills operations have served consumers well.

The Robinson-Patman Act of 1936 served to inhibit price discrimination and to protect small food retailers from the giant chains. Since the power in the food line has shifted away from manufacturers to supermarket chains, consumers have benefited. Generally, concessions and allowances are one-shot affairs, and therefore dangers to the system are minimized. Inefficiencies and inequities are traceable mainly to increased concentration. The food-distribution industry seems to have performed quite well.

Although there has been criticism of food supermarkets for not locating in low-income neighborhoods and for charging higher prices in these areas, this criticism may not be warranted. Insurance costs for fire and theft are extremely high in these neighborhoods and may account for some of the increased costs.

Although a great preponderance of legislation affecting food marketers was passed in the 1980s, label laws will continue to challenge the existing status quo of food companies. For example, the Nutrition Labeling and Education Act of 1990 took effect in 1994, and food manufacturers must now disclose what is in their products in a uniform manner. For consumers, this is a plus and may even lead to a healthier diet. For food marketers, this has become a costly and frequently confusing process. Labels must list not only a product's total fat content but also the amount of saturated fat and the number of calories derived from fat. Firms must also reveal information on cholesterol, sodium, carbohydrates, and protein, among other requirements.

Third-party endorsements from groups such as the American Heart Association are also permitted. Kellogg, a leader in creating nutritious cereal, is elated over the prospect of third-party endorsements. Quaker Oats has formed a task force to oversee labeling changes on an estimated 1,700 food packages. Pillsbury, on the other hand has filed more than two hundred pages of inquiry with the government. Further legislation affecting nutrition and health will probably occur in the future as consumer advocates maintain and increase their militancy.

INNOVATION

Innovation is often directly linked with product design and changes in marketing and manufacturing; thus it should become fully integrated in marketing planning and strategy. Innovation is an uncharted area that has great inherent risk for both the firm and the entrepreneur. Innovation can be associated with new technology, the introduction of new products, or the establishment of products through different channels of distribution. For example, operations like Kmart's Price Club and Wal-Mart's Sam's Club have changed the buying habits of Americans. These wholesale clubs, where consumers buy food and household products in bulk, are breaking the grip supermarkets once had on the food industry.

Historically, Kellogg was the first to sell cereal or cornflakes from packages rather than barrels. Gerber was the first to sell baby food already prepared in jars. Clarence Saunders, the founder of the Piggly Wiggly chain of food stores, pioneered the concept of self-service in the early 1900s. Self-service has meant that products must be easily identified by the customer and presold before they are placed on the store shelf. These changes have caused manufacturers to increase their promotional outlays, wholesalers to push the movement of known brands, and retailers to develop their own brands with strong store identification.

Innovation is often a determinant of profit or survival in the food industry. After some years of directing its product to young people, Kellogg is now also directing appeals to the adult market. Demographics such as the "baby bust" necessitated a change in strategy. Market opportunity is closely tied to the innovative process. Market opportunity refers to potential demand and encourages innovation. Market opportunity also determines strategies that food firms develop to effectively reach target markets.

Innovation can be a source of competitive advantage. Product innovation can be embedded in the minds of consumers so that the innovator has the benefit of being the standard of comparison and thus the most distinctive product in the group. A second advantage of being the innovator is that the pioneer can charge a higher price or achieve greater sales than later entries. The second entry generally must offer a lower price or increased benefits for consumers to be compensated for the perceived risk, especially if the innovator has satisfied customer needs. A third advantage to the innovator is that the product, during a certain period of consumer adoption, will produce profits that will never be available to followers. A fourth advantage to the innovator is that if positioning strategy has been implemented correctly, it is difficult for competitors to copy. It is better for followers to differentiate their products, since it is extremely difficult to be as successful as the innovator.

A proactive strategy may be rewarding, since in most cases a substantial market share is achieved by the first entrant in the market. Hopefully, sales volume and economies of scale will be realized. Heavy expenditures on advertising and promotion by later entrants in the market might moderate the situation. It is also possible that a "second but better" strategy might overcome the early lead of the innovator. In general, however, the innovating firm sustains a competitive advantage and higher profits, thus making the risks feasible.

The market leaders should recognize when there is a need for change and respond creatively. New opportunities should be identified and targeted and reasonable risks encouraged. The organization needs to be innovative in basic technology, product design, production, distribution, advertising, selling, promotion, and service. The most challenging task of innovation is to satisfy the needs of a target-market segment better than its competitors. The ability to innovate and innovate well is an important determinant of success.

Risk taking is a component of marketing innovation. Successful marketing executives have the ability to evaluate their firms' abilities and the marketing environment and accurately evaluate the risks involved. A high degree of risk may be present, but efforts can be made to decrease them to manageable proportions. Generally, only those risks are undertaken that offer a positive anticipated return. Meaningful strategies are then developed in terms of criteria such as return on investment and company growth.

Milton Hershey undertook a risk when he sold a successful company that made primarily caramels to develop a firm producing chocolate candy. Hershey believed that caramels were a consumer eating fad but that candy would be an enduring product. Another risk Hershey took involved the purchasing of equipment from the French that was on display at the 1893 Exposition in Chicago. This allowed Hershey to produce a candy not previously sold in the United States. A trip to Denver also gave Hershey the idea of adding fresh milk to the product in order to increase shelf life.

The Gerber Company started as a wholesale grocery business but changed its direction because of an innovation. When left to baby-sit, someone in the firm developed the idea that it would be much more convenient for parents if the baby food was already mashed and prepared in a jar. Thus, Gerber became a manufacturer of baby food rather than a grocery wholesaler.

Risk is an integral part of innovation. Successful entrepreneurs do fail. Hershey failed three times before succeeding. However, at the root of a successful organization is the calculation of the degree of risk and the efforts to minimize that risk. Innovation does not simply happen; it must be brought about by the interaction of individuals and organizations. The trick is to be first, hopefully insuring the widest profit margins, and to secure a favorable position in the market when competition is not a serious threat.

MARKETING STRATEGIES

The development of marketing strategies deals with the delineation of target markets and the determination of product, place, promotion, and price policies for those market segments. Most firms implement more than one strategy at a time. Generally, the business organization aims at several target markets and formulates different marketing strategies for each one. A sound strategy should identify marketing's contribution to the achievement of corporate objectives and serve as a primary source of integration for the firm.

Product management involves consideration of brand, packaging, product additions, product deletions, and other strategies. For the food marketer, brand strategy is one of the most important ones. When consumers are asked which brand comes to mind if potato chips are considered for purchase, usually there is a ready answer. The same is true if consumers are asked about colas, cereal, baby food, candy bars, or hundreds of other mass-marketed products. A firm's brand name in this world of products with only slight product differentiation is the only thing a competitor cannot copy. When brand awareness is carefully developed, hopefully brand loyalty will follow.

The powerful impact of brand loyalty was perceived in 1985 when Coca-Cola dropped its old formula in favor of the "New" Coke. A large number of loyal Coke consumers clearly communicated to Coca-Cola that no substitute would suffice. Because of brand loyalty, Coca-Cola reintroduced the original brand as Coca-Cola Classic. Generally, however, the brand with the lower price, higher quality, or better performance will have the brand loyalty edge. Exceptions include brands such as Gerber's baby food or Kellogg's Corn Flakes, which have loyal consumers mainly due to the fact that the firms were innovators and established themselves early in many buyers' lives.

Although brands and brand loyalty are important factors in purchasing, admittedly many consumers are fickle, and brand loyalty can easily vanish for many reasons. Coca-Cola, Pepsi-Cola, Gerber, and Kellogg are exceptions. For the most part, national manufacturers have not developed strong brands in food distribution, and therefore have lost market share to store brands. This situation is becoming increasingly dangerous as nonfood retailers such as Wal-Mart have entered the food marketing environment.

Place or distribution strategies are developed to ensure that products are available in the proper quantities at the right time and place. Distribution decisions involve modes of transportation, warehousing, inventory management, and selections of distribution outlets. For example, White Castle, a hamburger chain of three hundred restaurants, added another distribution outlet to its system when it decided to sell a frozen version of its bite-sized hamburgers in supermarkets. White Castle hamburgers are small and inexpensive, and in supermarkets they are sold in packages of six and positioned as a snack food.

Promotional strategy deals with advertising, sales promotion, public relations, and personal selling. For example, General Mills sells microwave popcorn nationwide under the trademark Betty Crocker Pop Secret brand name, using its own sales force and distribution system. The popcorn is sold direct to mass-merchandise chain accounts. General Mills also sells the popcorn through its own sales force to supermarkets. By advertising through national television commercials, General Mills supports its distribution outlets.

Pricing can also be an important part of marketing strategy. Price refers to all the terms of the purchase, including discounts, handling and shipping fees, credit card charges, and even trade-in allowances. When Pepsi-Cola marketed Slice as a fruit juice, initially coupons and in-store promotions were used to influence consumers to try the brand. In-store displays were coordinated with a national advertising campaign to create immediate brand recognition in the store. Food manufacturers, particularly in the ready-to-eat cereal industry, continue to confront an extremely challenging operating environment. Price-oriented grocery shoppers of the 1990s are making it difficult for food manufacturers to increase their selling prices. The 1980s, in contrast, was a period when average inflation in packaged food prices was the norm. Although current pricing pressures can vary by category, it is anticipated that these pressures will continue well into the 21st century.

Marketing strategies blend many different elements into a coordinated program designed to achieve the firm's marketing objectives. Although both Hershey and Godiva are chocolate snacks, the integration of price, distribution, and promotion causes them to aim at different markets and accomplish different marketing objectives. Manufacturers like Frito-Lay promise delivery within 24 hours to ease stores' stock-out conditions. Other manufacturers and wholesalers cannot implement this policy. Similarly, Campbell Soup has successfully tracked local requirements and implemented a market-segmentation strategy on a geographical basis. Again, many manufacturers are unable to duplicate Campbell's successful strategy, and consequently, store brands continue to make inroads on the market.

CONFLICT AND COOPERATION

The attempt by manufacturers and supermarkets to gain wider acceptance of their respective brands is an example of competition, but it can easily lead to conflict. For example, manufacturers desire as much shelf space as possible to stock their brands, but supermarkets try to restrict space in order to feature their own store brands and thereby obtain the largest dollar return on shelf space.

Cooperation can take place between manufacturers and supermarkets when they properly allocate their resources. To illustrate, an ice cream manufacturer decides to sell the premium brand while the supermarket sells the store brand, which is targeted to the middle and lower end of the market. The ice cream manufacturer then produces both the store brand and the premium brand, thereby benefiting both institutions. In this way conflict can be either eased or avoided, since private brands would not be promoted or displayed at the expense of the manufacturer.

Conflict can have a destructive impact on operations between manufacturers, wholesalers, and retailers, so it is necessary to secure cooperation among institutions. One means is through a firm that assumes a definite leadership role. Kraft, in the refrigerated dairy case, administered a program that coordinates, directs, and supports supermarket retailers. Kraft has a strong consumer image, and as a result there is confidence in its brand.

In recent years, manufacturers and food retailers have tried to go one step further than cooperative relationships and promote a concept of a distributor-partnership approach. This is not a partnership in the legal sense of the term, but suggests a supportive relationship. The end result is a mutual understanding of the role expectations and the commitment of all of the parties to fulfill the roles and objectives of the long-term relationship. For example, McDonald's has highly developed distribution programs for motivating its franchised members. A cooperative relationship can result in an on-again off-again, relationship, but a partnership approach lends stability and much more permanency to the relationship.

Manufacturers and retailers have also formed advisory councils to provide information and obtain market feedback. Lastly, strategic alliances have been developed, such as Kroger Company with Corning Glass Works, to utilize biotechnology to produce commercial food products from dairy products.

Manufacturers also join with other manufacturers to form strategic alliances. For example, despite Sara Lee's acceptance in the frozen-baked-goods market, the company seems to lack the resources to market fresh-baked items. Frito-Lay, on the other hand, already delivers cookies, crackers, and other items along with potato, tortilla, and corn chips. The two firms have made an arrangement in which Sara Lee makes and advertises its line of fresh-baked items and Frito-Lay sells and distributes them.

CONSUMER BEHAVIOR

The marketing environment has had a profound impact on the development of new types of food organizations and new marketing strategies. Such trends as poverty of time, dual-income families, more women in the work force, more men doing the shopping, an increase in the singles market, and a new prominence placed on ethnic foods affect the shape of existing and new types of institutions. There is also a need to monitor economic trends, since shopping behavior is changed or modified by both adverse and favorable economic conditions. Moreover, new nutritional guidelines have renewed consumer interest in healthy eating.

One noticeable trend is the increase of male grocery shoppers. Males now account for more than 40 percent of the grocery shoppers in the United States. Many of these men are shopping in convenience stores such as the 7–11. They are part of two income families and do not desire to stand in long supermarket checkout lines. Manufacturers have changed their promotional strategies, given that men are less likely to use coupons, to make a shopping list, or to check different supermarket advertisements. Men are more likely to purchase impulse items, to spend more on food shopping, and to purchase certain types of food, especially snacks and convenience products.

The singles market has increased by some 15 percent since 1985. Single-serving packaged foods, soups, desserts, and frozen entrees are appropriate not only for the singles market but also for families who have different work schedules and do not eat together. Supermarkets are also preparing items and competing with restaurants with expanded take-out food departments. Emphasis is placed on foods that just need to be warmed up or are already prepared for immediate eating.

Ethnic food, especially Mexican and Cajun specialties, has become more popular in mainstream America. Mexican food has been targeted for hamburger and roast-beef franchise restaurants, and Cajun food for certain upscale restaurants. Manufacturers target supermarkets with Chinese food, Jewish rye bread and frozen bagels.

Economic conditions have contributed to the growth of new business formats such as no-frills grocery stores and box stores. The emergence of Sam's Club, a warehouse discount store operated by Wal-Mart, has made inroads into supermarket market share. In 1990, Sam's Club updated existing units with bakery, fresh meat, and produce departments. Pace, Price, and Costco are main competitors, and these organizations usually generate 20–30 percent of sales in food products.

CHANGING TECHNOLOGY

Over the last decade, significant technological innovations or advances have been applied in food marketing. Video-cart computer screens attached to shopping carts provide marketers with a customer tracking system showing the length of time that customers spend in different sections of the supermarket, and the information is transmitted to in-store computers.

Information Resources Inc. (IRI), via its BehaviorScan service, monitors the viewing habits and shopping behavior of thousands of households in many markets. Microcomputers are attached to household television sets and record all programs and commercials viewed.

Consumers also shop in supermarkets and drugstores equipped with scanning registers. Checkout cashiers enter each consumer's identification code, which is electronically keyed to every item purchased. Computer analysis then proceeds to match such demographics as age and income.

Frito-Lay, the snack food division of PepsiCo that markets such brands as Fritos, Ruffles, and Doritos, has a marketing information system that tracks more than 100 different products sold through 400,000 retail stores. The data include prices, special store promotions, and the number of stale and returned items by store. Since the data are reported on regional and local levels, Frito-Lay is able to discern whether a promotion is more effective in a suburban versus a rural location, whether large-sized bags of chips sell well in low-income areas, and how well its brands sell relative to local brands. This information allows Frito-Lay to determine the impact of its strategies on key accounts and in specific regions, as well as to assess competitors' market shares.

Due to advanced technology, Campbell Soup has been able to develop many successful regional brands. Campbell sells its spicy Ranchero beans in the Southwest, creole soup in the South, and red-bean soup in Hispanic areas. Moreover, Campbell found that northeasterners prefer their pickles very sour and established Zesty Pickles for this market. Campbell has divided its market into twenty-two regions for the purposes of target marketing. Gone are the days when a company can effectively mass-market a single product using a single advertising campaign across the country.

Advancing technology has also extended to credit card systems. The rise of debit cards for point-of-purchase transactions is now aggressively pushed by both Visa and MasterCard. The question arises as to why retail food stores should be receptive to the use of debit cards. First, the debit card is affiliated directly to the customer's checking account. They are essentially electronic checks, and are a guaranteed form of payment. Unlike paper checks, the retailer assumes virtually no risk. Secondly, retailers benefit from the lower costs of debit card transactions. The use of debit cards is much faster at point-of-purchase than checks and a better audit trail than cash, preventing pilferage. Supermarkets without heavy check-handling environments significantly reduce office expenses. Third, by accepting debit cards, food stores are able to offer customers more payment options. In California, such supermarket chains as Safeway and Lucky Stores offer comprehensive payment plans including debit and credit cards. Retailers believe that offering as many payment options as possible helps to provide the highest level of customer service and satisfaction.

Kroger, the Cincinnati-based supermarket chain, has introduced MasterCard in its stores in Texas, Michigan, and Louisiana markets. The most commonly accepted credit cards in supermarkets are MasterCard and Visa, which are followed by Discover. However, credit cards and debit sales currently account for only 2 percent of transactions. Over 10 percent of supermarkets accept debit cards, and this is a fast-growing method of payment. Some customers do not like to carry cash or find payment by checks slow at point-of-purchase. Debit cards offer shopping convenience, and usage will increase significantly in the future.

TOTAL CUSTOMER SATISFACTION

Large retailers such as Safeway and Kroger now offer many consumer services to their customers. Supermarket chains have allowed banks to locate branches on their premises or provide automatic teller machines. Giant Food of Washington, D.C., sells more flowers and plants than traditional florist retailers. Pharmacies have also been established in supermarkets. Take-out food departments also compete with restaurants. Wal-Mart, which sells some food products, has established food restaurants with limited menus on their premises.

Customer satisfaction rests on three fundamental bases. First, the product or service must perform as expected and be backed by guarantees. Second, the product should have social reinforcement expectations. Third, the product or service should satisfy consequential experience expectations.

The problem with manufacturer or wholesaler and food-retailer relations is that there must be a trade-off between distribution costs and customer satisfaction. Maximizing retailer food-store service may require larger inventories to avoid stock-outs, speedier transportation to ensure on-time reliability, and more warehouses or distribution centers. All of these services increase distribution costs. Frito-Lay has made a pledge to retailers that their shelves will be restocked within 24 hours even if it means that Frito-Lay will incur an additional expense to avoid the stock-out. Entenmann replaces baked goods from supermarket shelves in order to guarantee freshness, and in turn sells them in their own thrift stores. One reason why just-in-time and other automatic inventory-control systems are a source of competitive advantage is that they are cost-efficient in improving customer service and thereby serve to ensure customer satisfaction.

Customer convenience is used by supermarkets as a basis for both competitive advantage and customer satisfaction. Supermarkets are competitive victims because the market is oversaturated. Low margins, the high cost of new technology, and high labor rates have contributed to supermarket problems. But more than anything else, the competition from discount stores, convenience stores, new business formats, and supermarkets themselves has caused contraction in the industry. As competition has intensified, the struggle for mere survival has become a challenge.

The food industry has performed quite well over time. Those inefficiencies and inequities that persist are traceable mainly to the increasing concentration of large national chains. Oligopoly, a market dominated by a few sellers, will continue to be dynamic and noncollusive as long as ease of entry remains relatively easy. The growth of scrambled merchandising and the entry of new business formats into food retailing should also inspire the performance of the food industry. Consumers in the future will be increasingly pleased with the performance of food marketers.

At the core of total customer satisfaction is the effective use of human resources and the development of consumer-friendly programs. For example, Giant Food has adhered to safety standards of age-labeling toys, that are beyond those required by government agencies, and provides money and equipment to schools. Giant Food was the first large chain to offer unit pricing, open dating, and fish labeling.

HOW FOOD STORES TRY TO OVERCOME PAST MISTAKES

Food stores in the past perceived their marketing mission within narrow limits, and this mistake unfortunately has caused turbulence in the industry. The marketing mission is a long-term vision or purpose of the firm, which provides direction for the achievement of objectives. There is a need to define core concepts rather than surface-level goals. A narrow definition of the organizational mission can lead to myopia in relation to potential opportunities. Retail food stores must develop a mission statement to guide strategies at the corporate level. Essential questions must be asked: "What business are we in?" "What business would we like to be in?" The purpose of the supermarket, as first conceived, was to sell a broad range of food items to satisfy household needs. Later the supermarket conceived of itself as distributing a broad range of goods and services to satisfy household needs. Services such as banking and nonfood items like greeting cards and mops and brooms were added.

Supermarkets and food stores have broadened their marketing mission to include prepared take-out foods in order to reduce the threat posed by fast-food restaurants. This broadened mission acknowledges environmental changes in the basic nature of the target market. This strategy has been successful, and the food-store market share of the replacement home meal market has significantly increased. Food stores are also emphasizing the freshness of their salads and marketing a "salad in the bag." Food stores have a differential advantage in selling the freshness of these perishables. Thus a broadened marketing mission has placed food stores on a more competitive footing with competitors. Food stores need to remember that their primary objective is total food distribution and services related to distribution. The selling of nonfood items and services is secondary and not primary.

Another mistake of food stores is the tarnishing of their image by allowing prices to get out of control. Consumers, either justly or unjustly, have complained about high food prices. Certainly higher prices on milk, bread, and paper products seem to remain fixed in the minds of consumers. Discounters such as Wal-Mart sell detergents, paper products, and snack foods for significantly less than food stores.

Organizations such as Food Lion have fought back, but these firms are in the minority, not the majority. Food Lion is the fastest growing supermarket chain in the United States and also one of the most profitable. The strategy at Food Lion is to compete on a cost-leadership basis with no-frills stores and low prices. Strong price competition can be advanced only as a positive strategy if there are economies of scale or pronounced competitive differentials.

Supermarkets are endeavoring to decrease their costs and become more competitive by centralizing their operations and developing more private-label products. Another strategy has been to expand and remodel stores, thereby deriving more sales per square foot of space; this has yielded higher profitability. Chains such as Giant Food and Jewel have advanced such consumer-oriented policies as unit pricing, open dating, nutritional labeling, and the creation of educational informational booklets relating to food management. These chains have developed strong customer-oriented images. While this is a step in the right direction, food stores need to do more in this area.

Food stores will eradicate some past mistakes by emphasizing store positioning in the future. For example, A&P was able to revitalize itself because of successful store positioning in small towns even though its reception was unfavorable in suburban communities. As more and more chains attempt to promote a strong regional base, store positioning may take the form of upscale and discount food stores targeted to precise consumer segments. Moreover, food stores must develop proactive rather than reactive strategies and adhere strictly to financial productivity ratios.

Successes in Food Marketing and Distribution

- Development of technology with emphasis on packaging, refrigeration, inventory control, and information systems
- Target-market segmentation in diverse geographical areas
- Positive and identifiable trademarks and trade characters
- Effective use of distribution centers for logistic purposes
- Development of high-quality store brands that convey value for the price
- Innovation linked to packaging design, self-service in supermarkets, and the development of wholesale-sponsored brands and stores
- Scrambled merchandising, with drug and discount stores selling food and food-related products
- Effective use of vertical integration by supermarket chains
- Innovation in the form of new distribution formats such as super-centers, box stores, and combination stores

Mistakes in Food Marketing and Distribution

- Overdiversification outside the food industry in the breakfast cereal industry
- Departure from cost focus approach by some supermarket chains
- Manufacturers allowing store brands to make market inroads
- Slow response on the part of some supermarket chains to population location shifts
- Manufacturers and distributors slow to promote a partnership approach
- Slow to develop a competitive differential based upon such social-movement trends as unit pricing and open dating
- Supermarket chains slow to add such new departments as flowers, pharmacy, gourmet foods, and natural food centers

MANAGING CHANGE

The evolution of A&P demonstrates the role of managerial vision. First, A&P branched out from its pre–Civil War product line into a wide variety of food lines. Second, there was the move into economy stores prior to World War I. Third, during the Depression, thousands of A&P stores were closed, and A&P was transformed into a supermarket chain. Unfortunately the lack of comparable management vision by succeeding management diminished the effectiveness of the A&P chain.

The supermarket industry must respond to such forces as slow market growth, the growth of branded goods, increasing costs, and new forms of food institutions. Food retailers are confronted with increased competition from similar stores and from other types of stores that sell the same merchandise. Even take-out food sold at restaurants has taken away market share from the supermarket industry. Food retailers should focus on competition at the local level when designing marketing strategies. Price, location, store atmosphere and service are areas for food retailers to differentiate to gain a competitive advantage.

National manufacturers are repeatedly engaged in the battle of their brands versus store brands, generic brands, and the brands of local and regional manufacturers. There is a constant attempt to gain a greater market share, control over marketing strategy, consumer loyalty, shelf space and locations, and a larger share of profits. The extent of the battle can be illustrated in the cereal industry. Store-brand cereal and cornflake sales sold in the United States have doubled since 1987. Ralston Purina, which is fifth in United States cereal sales, has benefited greatly, since it makes most of the private-brand cereals. Kellogg's Corn Flakes may sell for about $3.00 a box, but on an adjacent shelf, the private label sells for only half that price.

The largest national brands, such as Kraft, Coke, Pepsi, Campbell, Budweiser, and Minute Maid, have continued to hold their own, but inroads have been made. For example, Kraft Singles cheeses, a few years ago, were about 50 percent more expensive than private-label rivals, and now they sell for only about 35 percent more. Kraft has added additional varieties of cheeses to take advantage of increased microwave use by consumers.

Store brands have made inroads into such areas as milk, fresh bread and rolls, cheese, ice cream, carbonated beverages, canned vegetables, and refrigerated juices. The most recent advances have occurred with the sales of private-label cigarettes, bottled water, baby diapers, and laundry detergent. The growth of private-label sales represents a striking shift in consumer behavior and is a danger signal for manufacturers. For example, diet cola is experiencing declines in sales as consumers switch to bottled waters and teas. In response to the private-label competition, more manufacturers are doing private-label work. Examples are Keebler with cookies, Ralston Purina with cereals, H. J. Heinz with soup, and Borden with pasta.

Markets have changed, as Del Monte has discovered. Unit sales of canned fruit and vegetables peaked in 1969 and then began a slow decline. Del Monte considers fresh produce rather than frozen vegetables its chief rival. It is trying to target the baby boomers and their children, who are convinced canned vegetables are only for older people. However, upscale and sophisticated buyers prefer fresh vegetables; canned vegetables could become more popular during poor economic times.

Changing dietary habits have caused manufacturers to reevaluate their marketing strategies. Nutritionists have recommended diets rich in fruits and vegetables, cutting back on fats, eating whole grains, and limiting smoked and salt-cured foods such as bacon, ham, and lox. Accordingly, many snack food manufacturers and dairy producers have endeavored to produce either no-fat or low-fat products. As the baby boomers age, the health and diet mania will continue and bottled water will be the fastest growing beverage.

Nutritional awareness has changed the culture as consumers change their dietary practices and beliefs. Supermarket chains like Kroger are competing with health food stores in an effort to satisfy the growing market for organic and natural foods. Safeway, in California, has added natural-food centers to over 400 stores, featuring such high-sales-volume products as unfertilized eggs, pomegranate juice, and seaweed. Many supermarket chains have added salad bars and are increasing the store space devoted to selling vitamins. Fresh meat sales have declined, and the future appears to be in prepared foods and in lighter fare and healthier foods.

MANAGERIAL INSIGHTS

The balance of power has shifted dramatically toward grocery retailers. Large national supermarket chains have gained control of the marketing process as more and more manufacturers' products compete for limited shelf space and scanners give food retailers greater leverage with market information. Giant manufacturers, such as Pillsbury, Campbell, Kraft, and General Foods, can no longer dictate terms and policies.

Mistakes have been made in food marketing and distribution. For example, national manufacturers have not been able to promote brands in a way that could withstand the competitive threat of store brands. Wholesalers, with the exception of Fleming Companies, have not fully developed their own brands. Supermarkets have allowed their costs and prices to increase, thereby opening a door for companies like Sam's Club to enter the food industry. Many manufacturers have been unable to duplicate Campbell Soup's ability to target local markets and Frito-Lay's ability to accelerate delivery.

Manufacturers, for the most part, are not vertically integrated on the retail levels. The candy industry, with retail stores owned and franchised by Fanny Farmer, Lofts, Barricini, and Barton's is an exception. The supermarket organizations that have vertically integrated have done so by purchasing and owning controlling interests in dairy farms and coffee-roasting plants. For example, Kroger manufactures dairy products, baked goods, ice cream, and other items. Giant Food owns its own dairy, a plastic-milk-container factory, and beverage and ice cube plants. Fleming Companies and Wetterau are two grocery wholesalers who own some of their production facilities and provide a wide range of services to independent retailers. In many cases, vertical integration results in lower costs.

Among food suppliers there is relatively little concentration among dairy or meat manufacturing firms. There is, however, concentration in the dry grocery area. Manufacturers compete by offering cents-off coupons and free samples to consumers and promotional support to food retailers. The battle of the brands, particularly among manufacturers and food retailers, can be quite fierce. Suppliers have undertaken producing private-label brands for food retailers, thereby eliminating the need for food retailers to own manufacturing plants for various dry grocery items. Manufacturers have been willing to do so because it has assisted them in obtaining valuable shelf space, making use of idle plant capacity, increasing total income, and shifting promotional costs to the retailer. In the past, there was reluctance by food manufacturers to contract private label work, but there is little evidence of this presently.

There have been profound changes in food distribution in the twentieth century. Self-service, scrambled merchandising, the growth of technology, and the growth of large chains have had a significant impact on food marketers. The flexibility to adapt with changing marketing strategies has distinguished the marketing champions from the losers.

Food marketing lives in a world of galloping change. Adjustment to and anticipation of change is vital for manufacturers, wholesalers, and retailers in order to develop successful marketing strategies. There are times when even successful marketers suffer from lethargy. To illustrate, from the period 1989 to 1992, Kellogg lost an estimated 2 percent market share to General Mills. Each share point is valued at about $60 million in sales. Consumers are reading the labels, and desire something healthy like oats and bran. As a result, changing consumer lifestyles altered the competitive breakfast cereal market. Consequently, new health awareness concerns threatened Kellogg's market share and created new opportunities for General Mills and other competitors.

Factors such as innovation, target-market segmentation and image, brand management, marketing strategies, and the challenges of coping with power, conflict, and cooperation among institutions seem to determine success or failure in food marketing and distribution. Moreover, physical environmental resources like the degree of vertical integration and the human resources involved play a crucial role in the determination of customer satisfaction. All of these elements need to operate in harmony in order to achieve desirable results.

CHAPTER 2

THE
FAST-FOOD
INDUSTRY

Environmental Changes
- Fierce intratype and intertype competition
- Health and dietary changes
- Ethnic population changes
- A maturing population
- Popularity of take-out food
- Popularity of family restaurants

Responses to Environmental Changes
- Maintain low price strategies
- Maintain cost-focus approach
- Broaden menu offerings but also delete unprofitable items
- New product innovations
- Offer fast, superior customer service
- Use value approach strategies
- Position image and product offerings to distinguish offerings from competition
- Use different restaurant formats in new markets
- Increase location availability

Although franchising in the fast-food industry has attracted considerable attention since the 1960s, the concept actually began in 1851 when the Singer Company established franchised sewing machine outlets. Franchising was also introduced by General Motors in 1893 and by Rexall in 1902. As franchising has evolved, even major producers and suppliers have entered this exciting industry. For example Tricon Global Restaurants controls Pizza Hut, Kentucky Fried Chicken, and Taco Bell. Darden Restaurants, Inc., a once wholly owned subsidiary of General Mills, controls Red Lobster, and Grand Metropolitan of Great Britain administers Burger King. At one time or another organizations such as United Fruit and Pillsbury owned fast-food chains.

There have been a number of favorable consequences of franchising for the economic environment. Franchising greatly increased the opportunities for individuals to become independent business people. Franchise businesses in the past have had lower failure rates than other types of business. Economic concentration decreases by providing a viable alternative to completely integrated vertical chains. Minority-group members are provided with opportunities to own their own businesses. Consumers are able to buy standardized products and services.

The unfavorable consequences of franchising include the fact that it can constitute an anticompetitive system of distribution. To illustrate, it is very difficult for an independent individual to compete with a McDonald's or, for that matter, a Subway. Franchise agreements are one-sided in favor of protecting the prerogatives of franchisers, and some franchisers may employ questionable techniques in selling franchises.

A larger and growing percentage of retail sales volume is conducted through franchise systems in the fast-food industry. Organizations such as McDonald's, Wendy's, Red Lobster, and Taco Bell own some retail units, but they usually franchise the majority of their units to help obtain wider market coverage. Franchisees are expected to conform to standardized contractual rules and regulations and to pay compensation for the privilege of using the franchise name. The franchiser provides some or all of the following services: location analysis; store development, including lease negotiations; store design; aid in equipment purchasing; management training; promotion assistance; centralized purchasing; financial assistance in the establishment of the business; an exclusive territory; and the goodwill and identification of a known corporate name. In return, the parent organization or franchiser receives from the franchisee an initial franchise fee, an operating fee based on gross sales, rental or lease fees for facilities and equipment, and management fees for rendered services and assistance.

Three decision trends loom large for the 21st century. First of all, the menus for many fast-food establishments have been broadened. For example, Domino's Pizza now offers buffalo wings in some locations, Kentucky Fried Chicken offers turkey, Wendy's offers chicken, and Hardee's offers roast beef. Even White Castle, which has avoided change, added a chicken sandwich in 1987 and a cinnamon roll in 1992. The fundamental concept of profit through volume is still inherent, and there are attempts to be first in new menu additions. Second, although many consumers desire healthy food, the fast-food customer may say one thing and do another. McDonald's, which is the most successful fast-food organization, fries its hamburgers. However, Wendy's has successfully offered the baked potato. Salad bars have been introduced by many fast-food organizations. One trend as we move toward the future will be to experiment with the introduction of healthier food. Dairy Queen already provides nonfat ice cream. Second, more educated consumers will demonstrate concern over their children's eating habits and food preparation, and a low-fat diet will become more appealing. Third, fast food will become more available. Business organizations operating restaurants for employees will desire fast-food organizations to assume a greater part of the task of feeding employees. Fast-food chains are located in airport, bus, and railway terminals and in large department stores and supermarkets. School districts have solicited bids from fast-food organizations to service their needs. Tricon Global Restaurants, with its control over Pizza Hut, Taco Bell, and Kentucky Fried Chicken, are in a favorable position to satisfy a variety of menu requirements. Some other organizations, such as Hardee's, serve hamburgers, roast beef, and fried chicken as well. The institutional and corporate markets may demand ever greater menu diversification.

In considering the successes and failures in the fast-food industry, many mistakes have been made, and the organizations that remain viable are only those that were able to make constant adjustments with such variables as innovation, target-market segmentation and image, physical environmental resources, and human resources.

Innovations took place when McDonald's developed the concept of the assembly-line hamburger with french fries and when Wendy's became the first hamburger chain to offer salad bars and baked potatoes nationwide. Pizza Hut has continued to innovate with new product introductions, and Domino's revolutionized the pizza industry with a promised 30-minute home delivery.

McDonald's earned high marks for image identification with its golden arches and for its trade character, Ronald McDonald, which has become almost as well known to children as Santa Claus. Wendy's has been successful in targeting the female market, and Hardee's has successfully targeted the small-town market.

Hardee's has used physical environmental resources well, with vertical integration of a bakery operation, a food-processing firm, and a construction firm. Tricon Global Restaurants, with ownership of Pizza Hut, Kentucky Fried Chicken, and Taco Bell, combines some units into a single store, thereby providing customers with greater selection. Checkers provides only drive-through service and does not have eat-in space, and McDonald's emphasizes a smaller café-style restaurant in some locations.

McDonald's has cultivated human resources well by the establishment of Hamburger University, which trains owners or franchisees. This learning center stresses the teaching of the standardized procedures that are essential to a successful operation. Dave Thomas has humanized the appeal of Wendy's by projecting his own personality in advertisements. While this use of human resources has not been as influential as Lee Iacocca with Chrysler, it has still been effective.

Failure in the fast-food industry has occured as the result of ineffective relationships with franchisees. This has been true with Kentucky Fried Chicken, Church's Fried Chicken, Popeye's and Burger King.

Burger Chef did not innovate and was unable to effectively control product quality or service and therefore could not match the efficiencies of McDonald's or Burger King. Burger Chef lacked a distinctive image and was unable to successfully target a specific market segment. Mistakes were made in selection of locations, diminishing the impact of physical resources. Burger Chef also expanded too quickly and lacked uniform franchise operational efficiencies.

As competitive threats intensify from pizza, ethnic food, and family mid-price establishments, the hamburger industry will become more cost conscious. Already, McDonald's, once known for its successful franchise relationships, is experiencing discord in its organization. Indeed, there are ominous dark clouds on the horizon for the hamburger industry.

MARKET STRUCTURE

The fastest growing form of competition in the retail fast-food industry is intertype competition—direct confrontation in a specific food category between different types of restaurants. Competition between hamburger chains, referred to as intratype competition, is intense, but is not growing as fast as intertype competition. Intertype competition occurs when hamburger chains sell chicken and roast beef sandwiches, and conversely, when roast beef organizations sell hamburgers. Although fast-food restaurants have specialized in different foods, broadened menu offerings have pitted different types of fast-food restaurants against each other.

The fast-food industry has been marked by competitive turbulence. Chains such as Popeye's Famous Fried Chicken, Church's Fried Chicken, Long John Silver, and Burger Chef have fallen upon financial hard times. Subway and midprice family restaurants are making startling inroads into the fast-food industry.

The level of promotion in retailing is generally low except for the leading fast-food franchises. McDonald's spends nearly $700 million in advertising every year, and Burger King spends about $300 million. This amounts to about 4 percent of these organizations' total sales. In contrast, supermarkets typically spend between one-tenth and two-tenths of 1 percent of sales on advertising. Locations for fast-food restaurants vary. Fast-food restaurants that target lunchtime crowds seek locations near busy commercial areas. Those that target travelers are situated near highways, airports, and tourist sites. Finally, another group of fast-food restaurants locates in neighborhoods in which many families with children tend to reside. The specific population segment targeted will to a large extent dictate location policy. For example, McDonald's tends to serve families with children, whereas Wendy's serves primarily the adult market.

A franchise system pools resources and coordinates product and marketing activities to make a greater market impact and to obtain operational economies of scale, which are more difficult for the unaffiliated business person to achieve. The capital and entrepreneurial spirit of the franchisee is combined with the strength of an established, more experienced franchiser organization. An important advantage in becoming a franchisee is the program of research and development that is designed to improve the product or the service. Wendy's and McDonald's do research to identify new menu additions that could improve profitability and satisfy customer tastes. Local market entry is also much easier with an established market identity.

Table 2.1 shows the top franchise restaurant systems in the United States. Subway is near the top of the list, although the chain began franchising in 1974, while in comparison, McDonald's, Burger King, and Dairy Queen began franchising in 1955, 1961, and 1940 respectively. The Subway units can be established only with a modest investment, compared to other leading chains. The growth of Subway was an overnight sensation in the 1985 to 1995 period. What is also remarkable about Table 2.1 is the impact of pizza establishments and Taco Bell, which sell ethnic food. Boston

Table 2.1
1996 Top Franchise Restaurant Systems

Restaurant	1996 U.S. Revenue	Number of U.S. Restaurants
McDonald's	$16,370,000,000	12,094
Subway[a]	$ 3,200,000,000	11,081
Pizza Hut[b]	$ 9,110,000,000	8,950
Burger King[a]	$ 9,000,000,000	7,166
Taco Bell[b]	$ 9,110,000,000	6,890
Kentucky Fried Chicken[b]	$ 9,110,000,000	5,079
Dairy Queen	Not Available	5,035
Wendy's[a]	$ 4,784,077,000	4,369
Domino's Pizza	$ 2,800,000,000	4,300
Hardee's	$ 4,000,000,000	3,200
Denny's	$ 1,257,000,000	1,571
Red Lobster	$ 1,900,000,000	729

Source: Derived from corporate reports.

[a]Reflects company's worldwide system.
[b]Includes Pizza Hut, Kentucky Fried Chicken, and Taco Bell.

Market, which began franchising in 1992, is another success story and has approximately 800 units. Once known as Boston Chicken, its name was changed to Boston Market to include a broader menu, with items such as turkey. This success story reflects the strategy of following the current trend for consumers to maintain low-fat diets. A future trend will be the increase of family-style midprice restaurants such as Denny's and Shoney's.

The fast-food industry over the years has reacted to a changing environment, which is also vital for future success. Along with adaptation, the factor of management vision must be present. A proactive rather than a reactive management style is essential for the 21st century. The hamburger industry, especially with McDonald's, Burger King, Wendy's, and Hardee's, will be under attack by other sectors of the fast-food industry.

MARKET CONDUCT

The fast-food hamburger industry is moving toward more diversified menus, including salad bars, poultry, roast beef, baked potatoes, and ice cream. Breakfast has become an attractive growth market. A shift to ethnic foods such as tacos and burritos is increasing. Significant development of foreign markets will continue during the next decade. Europe and Canada continue to be attractive markets for fast-food organizations, and South America and Asia are deemed potential high-growth markets. Hamburger organizations, which have experienced tremendous growth over the past two decades, have reached a plateau as a result of both direct and indirect competition in the United States. Convenience stores, gasoline stations, and supermarkets are just some of the places where the consumer can purchase a hamburger. However, the most rapidly growing fast-food category is Mexican. Ethnic foods from Asia and Italian favorites are other growth areas.

The issue of maintaining fast customer service and satisfaction in a maturing industry that has broadened its menu offerings must be considered. Additional items such as fish, or chicken, or pizza slow customer service. The very real challenge of maintaining high customer-service standards confronts the fast-food industry. Not only is the quality of menu items an important consideration, but also issues of ecology and nutrition have pushed their way to the forefront.

Fast-food operations have been successful because their focus has been a narrow product range, an emphasis on division of labor, standardization of tasks, and extensive short-interval measurement of performance levels. Sales of nonhamburger fast foods have grown, while sales for the hamburger industry have remained constant. Chains such as Pizza Hut and Taco Bell hold dominant positions in the fast-food categories of pizza and Mexican food.

Overall market conduct has been directed toward emphasizing time savings, value, and convenience. One way to satisfy consumers with time constraints is to offer delivery service, and this has been done by pizza establishments. Free delivery especially targets the double-income family, which is time oriented. The importance of value has been reflected in low prices. Hamburger organizations such as McDonald's, Wendy's, and Hardee's have stressed value meals. By comparison based upon price and quantity of food, the competition has found the value appeal hard to beat. Pizza Hut has satisfied the convenience demand by developing the Pizza Hut Express Kiosk. The Kiosk is a small, self-contained unit capable of preparing Personal Pan Pizza at a rate of up to 240 per hour. Pizza Hut can now more effectively serve cafeterias, airports, schools, and stadiums.

Since projected birthrates indicate a decline in the teenage market, Pizza Hut already has designed new menus and advertising campaigns to cultivate the 25-to-34-year-old market rather than teenagers. Booths have been added to give Pizza Hut restaurants a more intimate atmosphere, and the gaudy red interiors are being replaced by more subdued wood tones. Not only have demographics played a role in market conduct, but so has social class. For example, there is a tendency for the middle class to eat in Wendy's and for the working class to prefer Denny's. Consequently, subtle associations reflected in decor, color, menu offerings, and other factors are employed.

A shift in consumer preference that could have an impact on fast-food restaurant sales is the trend toward eating healthier foods. Consumer awareness of proper diet and nutrition is reflected in menu selections and, ultimately, in the cost of a meal. Sales of salads, pasta, baked potatoes, and "lighter foods" have increased at the expense of meat entrees.

In particular, pizza and ethnic food sellers have offered delivery to consumers. Mobile food wars in the future may become increasingly important—competition in providing food at construction sites and other places of high-population density. Moreover, gourmet restaurants are making specialty dishes to be eaten at home, generally at customary prices.

CASE STUDIES

McDonald's: A Pioneer in Image Development

McDonald's was founded by Ray Kroc, one of the pioneers of the modern franchise organization format, in 1955. Ray Kroc was a salesman of malted-milk machines who observed that one of his customers, a hamburger restaurant operated by Maurice and Richard McDonald, had developed the concept of the assembly-line hamburger with French fries. There was also a large sign in front of the restaurant displaying two golden arches. Kroc became enchanted with this fast-food concept and talked the McDonald brothers into allowing him to sell the franchise rights nationwide. By 1961 there were some 228 franchise units, and Ray Kroc had completely bought out the McDonald's brothers' interests. Ray Kroc strongly believed in the concept of systems. Quality, service, and cleanliness served as the basic goals for the system. The system also stressed physical standardization. While the hamburger industry in the 1950s had a reputation for slovenly conditions, Kroc emphasized clean surroundings, including personnel, equipment, and, most conspicuously, rest rooms.

McDonald's situated itself in suburban locations, cultivating the vast population movement of the late 1950s and 1960s. In contrast, many fast-food firms chose to remain in the central cities and ignored suburban growth. In the 1970s, McDonald's expanded into the cities and into some small towns.

In 1968, McDonald's established Hamburger University, which was to serve as a teaching and training model for the hamburger industry. The success of this learning center is attributed to the teaching of the standardized procedures that are vital to a successful operation. All franchisees must attend and also receive retraining at specified time intervals.

The trade character Ronald McDonald, first played by Willard Scott, a well-known weatherman, has become almost as well known to children as

Santa Claus. The work of the Ronald McDonald houses, mainly located adjacent to hospitals, which serve the purpose of housing ill children and their families, has earned international respect and praise.

High volume, low prices, and a concentration on low costs has characterized the successful operation of McDonald's. The willingness to innovate, for example, by offering breakfast, has been another important pattern for the successful organization. The golden arches, a wholesome environment, low prices, and fast, quality service are all factors in image development and success.

In 1996, McDonald's had 12,000 units in the United States and is adding additional store units, although the heavily promoted Arch Deluxe obtained disappointing reviews, and sales are not as robust as in previous years. Other fast-food chains, from Taco Bell to Hardee's, are experiencing sales-volume problems as well in a mature industry, but McDonald's is investing heavily in more units. This investment in growth may mean short-term margin pressure, but corporation objectives are also geared toward expansion. More than half of the new store units in the United States have drive-through windows and thereby less seating capacity. Joint venture alliances with Chevron and Amoco, and an arrangement with Disney have been made to promote each other's brands.

The guiding objective of McDonald's is to shift from a focus only on individual store sales and profits to a focus on market share. According to McDonald's, increasing market share means adding more store units in order to increase the number of transactions per capita in its market. As a result of this objective, the number of per-capita transactions varies proportionately with penetration into a particular market. Consequently, competitors will stay out of that specific market and would have the net impact of precluding competition. Costs and the impact of diminishing returns can be easily overlooked in the haste to preclude competition. Overexpansion is an important factor in the decline of organizations, and it remains to be seen if there are already too many McDonald's units. A yellow waving light is flashing for the future.

Burger King: Second Best

Burger King was founded in 1954 by entrepreneurs who believed there was a consumer demand for hamburger restaurants that would serve reasonably priced quality food quickly and in attractive, clean environments. In 1967, the Pillsbury Company acquired Burger King but in 1988 sold it to Grand Metropolitan, a British firm considered to be a world leader in the food, retailing, and beverage businesses. Currently, Burger King is the second-largest fast-food hamburger restaurant in the United States, with more than 7,000 retail units.

Burger King has been beset with problems since the late 1970s. These problems were partially caused by management changes, strategy modifications, and ineffective advertising campaigns. An attempt to broaden menu offerings with pizza and veal parmigiana sandwiches has also been unsuccessful. Burger King, however, has had some success with its salad bars.

Burger King, like McDonald's, targets the family market, and also like McDonald's, has segmented the adult market by serving breakfast. Burger King is considered a clone of McDonald's, with only slight differences that set them apart. Consequently, Burger King is vulnerable to competitive attacks by Hardee's, which has acquired Roy Rogers and is aggressively leaving its small-town base. Like Burger King, Hardee's caters to the breakfast segment of the fast-food market. Burger King broils its burgers, uses promotional campaigns to its advantage, and has developed new location formats.

Wendy's: An Innovator

Wendy's was founded in 1969 by R. David Thomas, who was previously a regional operations director for Kentucky Fried Chicken and a vice president of operations at Arthur Treacher's Fish and Chips. Thomas's marketing strategy development was greatly influenced by Colonel Harlan Sanders, the founder of Kentucky Fried Chicken. By 1975, Wendy's had opened its one hundredth restaurant. Wendy's now has over 4,000 units operating in the United States.

Wendy's differentiates its offerings through product quality. Wendy's hamburgers are 100 percent ground beef, and its chicken sandwich is made from a skinless breast of chicken pressure-fried in vegetable shortening. Whereas McDonald's hamburgers are fried, Wendy's hamburgers are broiled on a grill. Wendy's was the first hamburger chain to offer a salad bar and baked potatoes nationally. Wendy's offers the most diverse menu compared to McDonald's and Burger King, and has the largest proportion of female customers.

When Thomas first opened his restaurants, Wendy's depended upon word-of-mouth communication to spread the word about high-quality food, friendly service, and a pleasant dining atmosphere. But as the chain developed, Wendy's in 1973 turned to local television and radio advertising, and in 1977, Wendy's turned to national televised commercials. In 1981, R. David Thomas was featured in the company's national advertising campaigns, which emphasized a personalized appeal to customers. In 1984, Wendy's achieved sales success with its "Where's the beef?" television-ad campaign that rocked the ad world and became a household phrase. Wendy's has also profitably targeted the adult market and a more discriminating customer. Its interior decor, with Tiffany-style lamps, bentwood chairs, and carpeting, is geared to please discriminating customers.

Higher-priced hamburgers of quality are the core of Wendy's marketing strategy.

Hardee's: Small-Town Market Segmentation

Wilbur Hardee opened the first unit of his restaurant chain in 1961 in Rocky Mount, North Carolina. This first restaurant served as a prototype for many others, with a uniform design that would include ceramic tile, aluminum, and glass, and approximately $25,000 in equipment. An outstanding feature was a water-purifying system that floated away grease and kept the charcoal free from impurities. This was one of the few broilers of this type operating in the United States at that time.

In 1962, Hardee's formed its own manufacturing and distribution group, now known as Fast Food Merchandisers, which services nearly all of its retail outlets. The hexagonal, pagoda-style building was introduced in 1963. Hardee's first international unit opened in Heidelberg, Germany, in 1965. Vertical integration became an important characteristic of the Hardee system; a bakery operation, a food-processing firm and a construction company were acquired in 1967. Five years later a 200-unit fast-food chain in the Midwest, Sandy's, merged with Hardee's.

In 1981 Imasco Ltd., a Canadian conglomerate, purchased Hardee's and was able to better finance future expansion. Consequently, in 1982, more than 700 restaurants of the Burger Chef organization were acquired from General Foods. The Burger Chef acquisition gave Hardee's a midwestern orientation, but Hardee's was still focused on developing retail units in small towns. The objective was to serve markets not dominated by such chains as McDonald's and Burger King. Hardee's also acquired Roy Rogers, and now has over 3,200 units.

In 1997, Carl's, Jr., a California chain, acquired Hardee's. Hardee's was a victim of overexpansion, lack of product innovation, and lack of aggressive public relations. Hardee's had failed to position its image and product offerings to distinguish its offerings from the competition's.

Burger Chef: Marketing Mistakes

Burger Chef's approximately 700 retail units were acquired by General Foods Corporation in 1967. The chain was substantially expanded to some 1,200 outlets by 1970. Two years later, Burger Chef was in financial difficulties. Key personnel had left Burger Chef for a variety of reasons, and new management was not effective. Consequently, the chain incurred heavy losses. Expansion had been launched too quickly, and mistakes were made in selecting locations and controlling quality of product and service.

The demise of Burger Chef can be attributed to a combination of factors. Burger Chef lacked a distinctive sign such as McDonald's golden arches, the outlets themselves were poorly constructed, and there was little uniformity in design among the franchised operations. Another factor was that its 700 outlets at the time of the Hardee's acquisition in 1982 were thinly dispersed and spread over thirty-nine states. A better strategy may have been a slower geographical expansion based upon market-by-market development.

White Castle: Fierce Brand Loyalty

White Castle was established in 1921 and is generally considered the original fast-food hamburger chain. Its loyal patrons are sometimes referred to as part of a fanatic cult. White Castle has preferred not to franchise and retains complete control and ownership of its units. White Castle is a small chain with 300 units situated in ten states. Wider market coverage was achieved through mail-order and telemarketing operations and the sale of packages of its hamburgers and cheeseburgers in the frozen-food sections of supermarkets.

Each hamburger contains a square beef patty with five holes punched in it for faster frying, a pickle and a dollop of grilled onions wrapped in a plain, white-bread bun. Singer Frank Sinatra once had White Castle ship him frozen hamburgers at a concert site. White Castle avoids franchising and features expansion without taking on additional debt. These characteristics have spelled success.

Checkers: High Image Identification

Checkers features a black-and-white checkered building with a large red sign showing its name in bold white letters. Checkers targets the drive-through market and does not provide premises in which to eat. The industry features a double drive-through concept, along with the largest chain, Rally's, and others including Central Park, Beefy's, and Fast Track. Checkers restaurants have a limited menu, with a 1950s diner and art deco theme. Because of its limited menu, Checkers is able to serve patrons faster and charge lower prices than the large hamburger chains.

Pizza Hut: Continued Product Innovations

Pizza Hut has changed from primarily an eat-in restaurant to an organization that concentrates on distribution and home delivery. Pizza Hut is situated in fifty-four countries and is a leader in forty-six of these markets. Approximately 25 percent of revenues is derived from distribution. In 1977, Pizza Hut was acquired by PepsiCo. Since Pepsi announced in 1996 that it would spin off Kentucky Fried Chicken, Taco Bell, and Pizza Hut,

Pizza Hut has floundered, a victim of aggressive competition. Local pizza restaurants appear to be servicing customers better, and Pizza Hut needs to improve its products. Pizza Hut is failing the taste tests, but this is possibly a temporary setback, and it should be able to correct this condition.

Pizza Hut is experimenting with a drive-through-only kiosks and locations in 7–11 stores. Pizza Hut has also developed a franchise agreement with Washington, D.C.–based Marriott Corporation in which Marriott placed 900 kiosks in its own contract food locations, including airports, colleges, and hospitals. Hand-tossed traditional pizza was added to the product line in 1988, and now accounts for about 20 percent of total sales. In the 1980s the 5-minute personal pan pizza was introduced and positioned against the traditional fast-food hamburger industry by offering a similarly quick preparation and serving time. Pizza Hut is the largest pizza chain, with almost 8,000 units, half of them owned and operated by franchisees. Pizza Hut continues to innovate with new product introductions, such as the Triple Decker pizza, which consists of two crusts and an extra layer of cheese.

Domino's Pizza: A Logistics Innovator

Domino's Pizza Distribution Corporation supplies stores with dough and other ingredients to make pizzas in addition to equipment and promotional materials. Over 95 percent of the unit stores purchase food supplies and equipment from the Distribution Corporation.

Domino's Pizza is the third-largest pizza chain, with more than 4,300 unit stores. Efforts are made to maintain a simple menu with only two sizes of pizza, eleven toppings, and only one choice of soft drink—a cola. Standardization would appear to keynote a successful operation. Domino's revolutionized the industry with a promised 30-minute home delivery. However, it had to drop its 30-minute guarantee due to liability problems caused by zealous drivers. The reduction of transactions to a routine has been a successful method of operation for Domino's.

The company's strategy in the past has been to locate in university towns or towns near military bases because of the market potential, then expand into nearby residential areas. Obviously, with military bases contracting in size and even closing, this past strategy will need reexamination.

Taco Bell: Ethnic Food Segmentation

The fastest growing fast-food category is Mexican. Taco Bell is the foremost fast-food restaurant chain in the Mexican food category, with more than 6,800 units. Approximately 40 percent of these 6,800 outlets are franchised. Ninety percent of Taco Bell's restaurants are freestanding, but the company is investigating alternative formats.

Taco Bell has broadened its menu base by introducing Steak Fajitas, Chicken Fajitas, and the Meximelt, a tortilla with melted cheese. Wendy's and McDonald's have also entered this market, but Burger King and Hardee's have not joined in as of yet. Taco Bell has offered a line of reduced-fat tacos and burritos that are called Border Lights and are designed to attract health-conscious consumers.

Kentucky Fried Chicken: Overcoming Marketing Mistakes

Although Kentucky Fried Chicken (KFC) has experienced a host of managerial problems in the past, PepsiCo management has improved the situation, and the chain now has more than 5,000 units. Its original founder, Colonel Harlan Sanders, was noted by the press to have exclaimed that his original recipe had not been followed by all retail units and that the changed recipe tasted "like sandpaper." New product offerings, such as Chicken Little sandwiches and grilled chicken, were introduced in the late 1980s. In addition to the freestanding stores, new outlets have opened in shopping malls, and the chain has experimented with home delivery. In the past, KFC was plagued by a lack of new-product introduction and a lack of innovation. The increased popularity of healthier foods created an urgent need for new product introduction. Home delivery might also open up new markets.

PepsiCo is experimenting with the concept of combining Pizza Hut, Taco Bell, and Kentucky Fried Chicken into one store. The objective is to provide customers with a greater selection. These combination stores have been established in at least ten locations.

Subway: A New Competitor

Subway was founded in 1965 and began franchising operations in 1974. Subway specializes in sandwiches made with bread baked daily at each store. Potential start-up costs are less than $100,000, compared to more than $1 million for some of the hamburger chains. This low cost has resulted in more than 13,100 franchised units in 1998 which, in size, surpasses most hamburger and pizza chains.

Midprice Family Restaurants: Cost-Focused Strategy

Midprice family restaurants such as Cracker Barrel, Shoney's, Denny's, Red Lobster, and Sizzler are providing growing competition for fast-food chains. Prices at these midprice establishments average no more than three or four dollars more than at most fast-food outlets. Moreover, surroundings are comfortable and attractive, and there is table service. It is anticipated that baby-boomer, two-income couples and the increasingly older population will patronize these midprice restaurants to the detriment of fast-food establishments. Steak houses such as Ponderosa and Bonanza have also made inroads into the fast-food industry by selling burgers, chicken, and fish.

The market structure of the fast-food industry has been one of continuous change. Off-premise dining characterized by home delivery and supermarket sales has made exciting inroads. Drive-through restaurants have increased market share, but this small segment will probably stabilize. Midprice family dining, illustrated by Shoney's, Bob Evans, and Cracker Barrel, will take away some market share from the fast-food industry. Continued innovation related to menu planning and catering to health concerns will be required in the future. If costs can be controlled effectively, further inroads into the fast-food industry will be made.

INNOVATION AND OTHER STAGES OF THE RETAIL LIFE CYCLE

The initial decision by Ray Kroc of McDonald's that a large consumer segment would be very receptive to eating hamburgers in a clean and wholesome environment was an exciting innovation. David Thomas of Wendy's and others were to add to this innovation, and the hamburger industry, comprised of McDonald's, Burger King, Wendy's and Hardee's has become an American institution. This American institution has spread overseas and become a valuable export. But the hamburger industry no longer innovates the way it did years ago. There are some exceptions. A small chain, known as White Castle, made exciting inroads by shipping hamburgers around the country and selling frozen packaged hamburgers to supermarket chains. Checkers, another small chain, has innovated by using distinctive decor, returning to the original basic menu of hamburger chains, and establishing a drive-through restaurant without eat-in capacity.

As consumers mature, they tend to frequent family-type restaurants rather than fast-food single establishments. It might make sense to house under one umbrella a restaurant that offers hamburgers, chicken, pizza, and ethnic food. Tricon Global Restaurants, with ownership of Kentucky Fried Chicken, Taco Bell, and Pizza Hut, will have the capacity to offer such a diversified menu. Strategic alliances between hamburger and pizza organizations might also prove advantageous.

Domino's Pizza, with its innovation of home delivery, has made significant inroads into the hamburger industry market. This innovation has encountered roadblocks, such as outsiders deliberately trying to delay the promised 30-minute delivery, but for the most part it has been successful. Deliveries made by fast-food enterprises to business organizations could prove fruitful. This would have the impact of employees remaining for lunch on their employer's premises.

The fast-food industry is in the maturity phase of the retail life cycle. The retail life-cycle theory asserts that all retail institutions pass through a series of four life stages: innovation, accelerated development, maturity, and decline. The first stage in the retail life cycle is innovation. An innovation usually represents some marked departure from existing norms. The jumbo size of the hypermarket and its food and discount merchandise combination is one example of a retail institution in the innovative stage that resulted in failure. Domino's home delivery succeeded.

The second stage, accelerated development, is characterized by geographic expansion and the market entry of new competitors. For example, Hardee's has emerged from its small-town southern roots to established units in the mid-Atlantic states and has also, by means of acquisition, gained entry in the Midwest. Pizza Hut also sought to gain entry in small towns.

Market maturity is marked by intense competition and therefore must be carefully managed. To illustrate, Burger King has returned to a more functional organization, which increases central control, reduces substantial overhead, and increases opportunities for coordination. There is more attention to costs and customer service and less attention to new-product introduction versus refining existing ones.

The final stage in the retail life cycle is the decline stage. During this stage industry sales and profits begin to decline, and a shakeout occurs. Burger Chef, for example, had to consolidate its resources, and it closed many of its units before it was acquired by Hardee's. Adaptation is essential toward the end of the cycle, as the chains place more emphasis on nonfat and leaner products to satisfy changing consumer health preferences. Decline can be postponed by repositioning the institution. Maturity is brought on by the entry of a great many competitors, but by serving new markets, decline can be either postponed or avoided.

MARKETING STRATEGIES

Strategy is marketplace driven. The objective is to develop a competitive advantage in creating value for customers. A competitive differential may stem from precisely serving a target market or from some adjustment to the use of product or to promotion, price, or distribution strategies. These strategies may develop through the planning process or through functional departments of the firm. Frequently, environmental forces drive competitors to develop strategies to combat varying intensities of competition.

The mass market for the fast-food industry is large and diverse in its tastes and preferences. Marketers desiring to serve the mass market endeavor to be all things to all people with a single, undifferentiated marketing program. In most product markets, however, it is likely that undifferentiated marketing will cause some consumer needs and wants to go unsatisfied. To better serve diverse customer preferences, and to potentially strengthen their competitive position through more focused efforts, marketers in the fast-food industry usually employ market-segmentation and product-differentiation strategies.

Related to the strategy of market segmentation is the process of dividing the mass market into groups of consumers with similar combinations of needs, wants, demographics, lifestyles, and behavior. McDonald's, for example, originally targeted lunch and late-snack customers. Following careful research and analysis, the decision was made to target other market segments, such as consumers who desired a quick breakfast on the way to work. New product offerings were added to the menu, such as the Egg McMuffin, and new promotional campaigns were developed to announce the offering.

Unlike market segmentation, which focuses on consumer differences, a product differentiation strategy focuses on developing and promoting differences among products that compete with one another within market segments or in the mass market. For example, consumers within the market segment that likes hamburgers as part of a meal or snack can choose from McDonald's fried burgers or Burger King's flame-broiled variety. In this situation, the product is differentiated, but it is aimed at the same market segment, consumers who like hamburgers. Thus, two or more marketers attempt to serve the same market segment or the mass market with differentiated products. Pizza Hut differentiated its product by introducing pan pizza in 1980 and hand-tossed pizza in 1988. Vegetarian pizza is an attempt to both segment and differentiate the product. Segmentation is achieved by targeting a market concerned with dietary health habits, and differentiation is achieved by providing another variety of pizza.

Wendy's marketing strategy has focused on market-segmentation strategies. Wendy's in the late 1980s experimented with appealing to the family, weekend, and dinner markets. Moreover, drive-through restaurants and take-out menus were added. Wendy's positioned itself as a hamburger chain at the higher end of the fast-food spectrum. Because of the recession in the early 1990s and Wendy's desire to broaden its customer base, low-priced, value-oriented menu items were launched. In an effort to further segment the market, a Wendy's "kids' meal" was added; it consists of a smaller hamburger, smaller order of French fries, and a small Frosty (much like a milkshake) or a small soft drink. Another new item added was the taco salad, which capitalized on consumer interest in ethnic food, a growing, viable market that other hamburger chains have largely ignored.

McDonald's has successfully used a differentiated market segmentation strategy by targeting the family unit, and particularly children, with their "happy meals" and low prices. McDonald's has traditionally offered lower prices than other hamburger chains, thus winning the patronage of larger families. The location of its outlets has been instrumental in making McDonald's very successful. It was the first hamburger chain to expand into the suburbs and into the crowded downtown areas of large urban cities.

McDonald's marketing strategy has focused upon menu diversification, site location extension, improving public relations, and price discounts in a recessional period. In the 1980s and early 1990s, McDonald's introduced the chicken biscuit sandwich, McNuggets, prepackaged salads, McRib, and breakfast burritos. The McChicken sandwich which was also introduced during this period was a failure. McDonald's decision to open new retail outlets in airports and hospitals have proven to be successful. Its promotional message has advanced goodwill with the annual Charity Christmas Parade in Chicago and its Ronald McDonald House exposure. McDonald's has worked with school administrators to promote reading programs among children.

Burger King's marketing strategy concentrated on product differentiation in the 1980s by offering a more diversified menu. Chicken Fingers, Chicken Tenders, Fish Tenders, and a salad bar were introduced. Burger King was the first hamburger chain to cater to nutritional trends by publishing a guide that included information on the calorie, fat, salt, and protein content of menu items. Efforts were made to attract new market segments by including broiled chicken on the menu and by offering Häagen-Dazs ice-cream bars. Promotional efforts were weak, and Burger King's advertising campaigns appeared to have missed their mark in many instances.

Burger King, with its market share at its peak in 1985 at 8.7 percent, had a number of promotional campaign flops. The "Search for Herb" campaign concentrated on an eccentric nerd and unfortunately associated the Burger King image with a "nerdy" personality. In 1988, the promotional campaign focused on flame broiling, but the message was confusing and demonstrated bad humor and poor acting. The "BK Tee Vee" promotion featured MTV personality Don Cortese and targeted teenage males. Unfortunately, parents and others found the commercials irritating.

Since the middle 1980s, Burger King has had difficulty developing a distinct target market and image that can compete with its competition. Many customers think of Burger King as second to McDonald's. Wendy's and Hardee's were successful in developing their own separate and distinct target markets. Burger King now has about a 6 percent market share, which is only slightly ahead of the 4.5 percent market shares of Hardee's and Wendy's. However, both Hardee's and Wendy's sales are increasing more rapidly than Burger King's. McDonald's remains supreme in the hamburger industry, with approximately a 15 percent market share. Burger King has been further hampered by an inefficient franchise system that was finally, in 1977, entirely remade based on the McDonald's model and took some time to successfully implement.

Burger King has successfully introduced a number of innovations to the fast-food industry, but more recently innovations have been in response to innovations by competitors. An early innovation was the continuous-chain broiler, which gave fast-food customers an alternative to the fried hamburger. Burger King also pioneered drive-through window service and provided inside sit-down eating for what had previously been all take-out food. However, in 1983, Burger King introduced a salad bar in response to Wendy's salad bar and a one-third-pound hamburger in response to other chains that increased the size of their hamburgers. Burger King has located on military bases, but with base closings and reductions in force, this move may not be advantageous. Burger King has also located itself in Woolworth retail stores, but Woolworth stores have fallen upon hard times. Burger King would seem to live in the shadow of McDonald's; it did not introduce its Kid Club until 1990. There may be ominous, striking similarities between Montgomery Ward's existence in the shadow of Sears and Burger King's possible image as a me-too McDonald's.

The marketing strategy of Hardee's has focused upon expansion through acquisition. In 1982, Hardee's acquired Burger Chef's 650 units from General Foods Corporation, giving the firm market coverage in the Midwest. In 1990 Hardee's added to its 3,110-unit chain some 650 stores from the Roy Rogers chain in key markets such as Washington, D.C., Baltimore, Philadelphia, and New York City, making Hardee's the number three hamburger chain just ahead of Wendy's and expanding its southern base. The strength of Hardee's in the breakfast market, which represents about 30 percent of sales, complemented Roy Rogers's success with dinner items, such as fried chicken, thus broadening the chain's customer base.

Although the Roy Rogers acquisition was synergistically sound, Hardee's encountered difficulty in convincing Roy Rogers's 287 franchisees to convert into Hardee's outlets. Market research conducted after the acquisition confirmed that consumers in the Northeast—where Hardee's had no brand recognition—preferred the Roy Rogers name and wanted it back. Consequently, in 1982 Roy Rogers was relaunched as its own chain, and those 363 company-owned Roy Rogers outlets that had been converted to Hardee's were switched back.

The Roy Rogers conversion failure and plunging profits—from $118 million in 1989 to $40 million in 1991—contributed to Hardee's decision to scale back plans to turn the regional chain into a nationwide fast-food company. Finally, Hardee's decided to sell its Roy Rogers outlets. Overexpansion and the failure to develop a burger to compete with the McDonald's Big Mac and the Burger King Whopper are blamed, among other reasons for difficulties. Menu diversification with fried chicken may have blurred Hardee's image with consumers.

White Castle's marketing strategy is unique among the hamburger chains in that direct mail is used to reach a broader customer base. Some market segments are intensely loyal and place orders by mail, since White Castle does not have retail outlets situated nationally. White Castle uses as a product preparation method the steaming of hamburgers, which is unique in the hamburger industry. This preparation method produces a much easier-to-eat and more moist product, which is especially preferred by children. By early 1996, White Castle had 300 retail outlets in only ten states, but its average sales per unit is the highest in the industry, exceeding even that of McDonald's. Supermarket distribution has been another marketing strategy employed by this chain. White Castle has established itself as a small but innovative leader in the hamburger industry, one that has survived in an industry populated by financially stronger hamburger chains.

CONFLICT AND COOPERATION

Tensions do arise between franchisers and franchisees. Since the franchisee is not an employee but an independent owner, franchiser controls can be viewed as too rigid. The franchise agreement frequently contains a buy-back clause, and franchisees might fear that the franchiser will exercise this option because of higher profit potential. Another source of conflict is that restrictions on product purchases might cause franchisees to believe that franchisers are charging higher prices and that product assortments are too limited.

Many franchisers own a number of their outlets, and some of these units compete with those owned by franchisees. Efforts are made to avoid the problem of dual distribution, but these attempts are not always successful. Moreover, the reaction to field services and operating controls is not always positive. Franchisers have tended to rely on field representation to reconcile any differences, but these field representatives are not only responsible for field service and liaison with franchisees, but also must recruit additional franchisees. Consequently, franchisees may complain that field representatives pay too little attention to franchisees' management problems.

Although in 1971 Kentucky Fried Chicken was acquired by Heublein, Inc., a producer and distributor of alcoholic beverages, Colonel Sanders was retained in a public-relations capacity. Colonel Sanders became furious over quality-control issues and restaurant cleanliness. Expansion was too rapid, stores were not being remodeled, and service quality was declining. Unfortunately, much of this conflict between Colonel Sanders and Heublein became public, to the detriment of Kentucky Fried Chicken. New construction was discontinued and cleanliness and service were emphasized, but it was not until 1982 that these problems were fully corrected.

In the 1970s Burger King had problems with Chart House Inc., one of its franchisees. Unlike many other franchisees, Chart House owned the land

and building of each restaurant. Chart House had grown so large that it was competing for territorial expansion with Pillsbury, the owner of Burger King at the time. Subsequently, the franchise agreement was changed so that the new franchises could not infringe upon Burger King. This was accomplished by modeling the franchise agreement after that of McDonald's.

Potential negative franchiser actions include agreement termination, the reduction of promotional and sales support, insufficient territorial protection, and poor business practices. McDonald's and Tricon Global Restaurants dominate the fast-food industry, so their standardized, routine practices can be rigidly enforced. This may not be so true with franchiser-franchisee relationships in other industries.

Church's Fried Chicken and Popeye's, famous for its spicy chicken and Cajun food, also had conflicts with franchisees. Church's eventually sought protection under the bankruptcy act. The evidence, as demonstrated by conflicts in organizations such as Kentucky Fried Chicken, Burger King, Church's, and Popeye's, reveals that conflicts arising when both franchisers and franchisees believe they have been wronged are a serious detriment to future success. Some amount of conflict can be constructive, since it can lead to a more dynamic adaptation to a changing environment. On the other hand, too much conflict is dysfunctional. The problem is not one of eliminating conflict but of managing it better.

CONSUMER BEHAVIOR

Consumer eating habits changed noticeably in the 1980s. There is now more concern about health and about fat and sodium content of foods. Moreover, adults are monitoring their weight. Consumption of poultry products such as chicken and turkey has increased, while consumption of red meats has declined. Lean meats with lower cholesterol content are a significant consumer preference. To illustrate, there is interest in buffalo meat and buffalo burgers, which are much lower in cholesterol. The method of food preparation—whether food is broiled or fried—has become another concern.

As a result of consumer interest in the nutritional and caloric value of foods, McDonald's has reduced the sodium content in its foods about 15 percent since 1983. Moreover, vegetable shortening is now used to fry its chicken and fish. Wendy's offers baked potatoes as an alternative to french fries, and both Burger King and Wendy's maintain extensive salad bars, while McDonald's offers prepackaged salads.

There is a danger that consumers will say one thing and do another. Consumers demonstrated little enthusiasm for Hardee's low-fat burger, called Lean One, and for McDonald's McLean Deluxe burger. After five years, McDonald's has decided to discontinue the McLean Deluxe burger.

Kentucky Fried Chicken failed with Skinfree Crispy, skinless chicken cooked with a pressure-frying method.

Although chicken is a popular menu entry, a number of chains have had poor results in selling it to consumers. Fast-food analysts have concluded that Church's Fried Chicken was the worst fried chicken in America. The chain was plagued with other problems, but its unique southern-style fried chicken was one of its biggest problems. Popeye's, another chicken fast-food chain, derived its strength from its spicy chicken and Cajun menu items. However, its prices were much higher than those of its competition, and the burger chains made penetrating inroads into Popeye's market share.

One might theorize that when consumers eat out they desire to indulge themselves. However, it would be a mistake for the fast-food chains to discontinue testing healthful entrees. The baby boomers are growing older, and this trend in itself may make consumers more health conscious.

Aging baby boomers, now in their forties and more established financially, are demanding higher-quality and higher-priced entries in the fast-food industry. Many baby boomers are part of double-income families, which eat out more frequently and desire to upgrade their restaurant selection. Such chains as Mr. Steak and Red Lobster have targeted this more upscale market.

Some consumers, because of small children or for other reasons, find it more convenient to eat at home. Take-out and home-delivery services have rapidly emerged in the fast-food industry. Pizza restaurants have used home delivery as a competitive strategy. Chinese restaurants have also stressed their take-out food service. Even supermarkets have tried to compete, offering take-out food service, deli sandwiches, and salads.

The hamburger industry, confronted with slow growth and the competition from family restaurants, has diversified its menu. Some hamburger chains have added salad bars, and nearly all offer some varieties of chicken, roast beef, and fish. Wendy's and McDonald's are also offering some Mexican foods. McDonald's is testing pizza, which is an industry that is experiencing greater growth than hamburgers. The hamburger industry has switched from beef tallow to 100 percent vegetable oil in the preparation of fries and hash browns. Ice cream has been replaced with low-fat yogurt. In contrast to both Wendy's and McDonald's, Burger King has not made a special effort to target the fast growing Hispanic market.

The pizza industry, with the leadership of Domino's, has targeted the take-out consumer, who for various reasons desires to eat at home. Deliveries to travelers in hotels and to business establishments, especially at lunch time, have become very popular. The pizza industry has also differentiated the product for consumers' tastes by increasing the different types of pizzas and toppings. Other ethnic restaurants, such as oriental ones, have also developed the take-out market. Significant in size, the take-out market has seized market share away from the hamburger industry.

CHALLENGES CONFRONTING THE FAST-FOOD INDUSTRY

Challenges confronting the fast-food industry threaten its equilibrium. Burger King and Wendy's are nibbling away at the market share of McDonald's, and indirect competitors have improved their marketing strategies and products so that hamburgers are no longer supreme. McDonald's, once referred to as the "golden arches," is now cited by some as the "fallen arches." Sales have been flat since 1995, franchises are in rebellion, and consumer tastes are changing. To make matters worse, a deep-discount program called Campaign 55 (the company was founded in 1955), failed.

Consumers seem to like Starbucks and Einstein Brothers for coffee and bagels in the morning and are patronizing Boston Market more for dinner. Furthermore, supermarkets and food stores with take-out meals are taking away significant market share from the fast-food industry. Taste tests demonstrate that consumers like Burger King hamburgers better than McDonald's and that Wendy's has a better menu. Carl's Jr. has disturbed the fast-food equilibrium on the West Coast.

Franchisees of McDonald's are not only cranky but mad. Franchisees are cranky because profit margins are eroding and Campaign 55 failed. Many franchisees predicted that Campaign 55 would not do well and now believe that the company disregarded their input. Franchisees are mad because the McDonald's expansion program has infringed upon trading areas, and established franchises are competing with new McDonald's units.

Bottom-up marketing has hit some snags in the McDonald organization. Bottom-up planning involves assembling information from field personnel relating to products, operations, timetables, and objectives. Despite a system of regional managers, information was difficult to transmit back to headquarters because of numerous management layers in the corporate structure. A more effective policy was to combine bottom-up with top-down marketing planning, with senior executives establishing overall objectives and policy, and sales, advertising, and product personnel establishing plans for implementing the policy. What was needed by McDonald's was an integrated operational plan.

McDonald's is still McDonald's, with one of the most powerful brands in the United States, but it must confront the reality of having direct and indirect competitors. The indirect competitors are the supermarkets, pizza restaurants, and midprice restaurants which provide varied menus at moderate prices.

Meanwhile, Hardee's has fallen upon hard times. Hardee's last served its charcoal-broiled burger in 1985, switching to fried, a change that may have caused its downward trend. The charcoal-broiled burger was part of Hardee's image, and that image was altered. Consumers who are health conscious might be more comfortable eating at Burger King or Wendy's. CKE Restaurants, the owner of Carl's Jr., a largely California eatery, has made an offer to acquire Hardee's from Imasco. In 1996, CKE acquired Casa Bonita, Inc., an operator of taco and other restaurants, and purchased an interest in Rally's Hamburgers Inc.

Burger King increased its share of the adult fast-food audience with advertisements that its Whopper outweighed McDonald's Big Mac; it also introduced a grilled chicken sandwich years before McDonald's. Wendy's continues to offer everyday value and diversify its products without engaging in a price war.

Among other challenges confronting the fast-food industry are an uncertain environment due to changes in PepsiCo strategy and the development of new theme restaurants. PepsiCo divested itself of Pizza Hut, Taco Bell, and Kentucky Fried Chicken. This move will disrupt the balance of the fast-food industry. Some firms may be strengthened and others will be weakened as a result of this divestment. Another challenge is the development of theme restaurants. Theme restaurants have made a marked impact in the past few years. Themes range from sports to the macabre, or restaurants may be designed around a Polynesian or rain-forest theme. Elaborate themes could also be based on everything from roaring Harley-Davidsons to indoor tropical rainstorms to some type of music, such as early rock. Supermarkets and food stores are also challenging the fast-food industry with take-out meals, and discount stores such as Wal-Mart may construct more eateries within their stores.

Marketing Successes in the Fast-Food Industry

- The McDonald's image identification, with its golden arches and its trade character Ronald McDonald
- The innovation of home delivery by Domino's
- The development of Hamburger University to train personnel by McDonald's
- Humanizing the appeal of Wendy's by projecting the personality of David Thomas, its founder, in advertisements
- The emphasis on a systems approach by McDonald's
- Innovation in menu assortment by Wendy's
- Target-market segmentation of small towns by Hardee's
- White Castle's marketing innovation of mail-order and supermarket distribution
- Pizza Hut's emphasis on new-product introductions
- The success of Wendy's in targeting the adult market.

- The poor relations with franchises of Kentucky Fried Chicken, Church's Fried Chicken, Popeye's, and Burger King
- Burger Chef's selection of store sites
- Burger Chef's lack of a distinctive image
- Kentucky Fried Chicken's lack of product quality control
- Slow response to consumer concerns for low-fat food
- Slowness in reducing sodium content of foods

MANAGING CHANGE

Many of the triumphs and blunders of the fast-food industry stem from the indigenous nature of franchising. There must be a high degree of brand identity and adherence to rigorous operational and quality standards. McDonald's has met these two criteria, and this basically accounts for its phenomenal success. In contrast, Burger Chef failed because it did not exercise tight operational controls and had a weak brand identity. Quality standards were inconsistent in Church's Fried Chicken stores, and this was one of the reasons for its financial difficulties.

The lessons learned from success and failure in the fast-food industry include the following:

- Organizational concentration is vital for segmenting markets. Hardee's concentrated its operation in small towns in regional locations, thus avoiding direct competition with McDonald's, in its early stage. Burger Chef units were thinly spread over thirty-nine states. A strong market identification can be promoted and rigid operational controls implemented if the organization can group its forces in smaller geographical areas.
- Product quality and diversification is essential in a mature market. Service is still tied to customer satisfaction. Services such as order filling, preparation, and speed of generating a final product must be standardized and controlled from unit to unit. In this way services maintain high standards in all locations and a quality image can be maintained. Taco Bell is experimenting with new technology that actively engages customers. Customers use computer terminals to place their own orders and in turn receive a number; they repeat that number when paying a cashier. Boston Market is using a computer program that tracks the sales of every menu item on an hourly basis and establishes cooking schedules. From the computer printout, Boston Market can then determine how much chicken to cook, when to place it in the rotisserie, and the exact time it can

be served. Domino's Pizza has established 30-minute delivery service, an innovation that is the envy of the fast-food industry.

- Social movements dictate strategies. The social and cultural trend toward better nutrition has had a profound impact on menu changes, spawning the addition of salads and potatoes. Wendy's has had huge success in targeting the female market with the introduction of baked potatoes. This social movement has also had an impact on cooking methods. Fast-food organizations selling pasta and some types of oriental food have prospered.

- Continuous experimentation and long-term planning are necessary to maintain success. New-product offerings such as ethnic food and pizza are needed in a mature market confronted with new competitive and environmental threats. Store size and locational convenience in schools, corporate restaurants, and other sites will need continuous monitoring. Popeye's, for example, known for its spicy chicken and Cajun-style menu items, failed with its new-product introductions. An important reason was that franchisees complained that a growing number of new products were created not so much to improve their businesses as to provide the franchiser with higher profit margins. Moreover, franchisees had no assurance that higher advertising fees would be returned to local markets. Continuous experimentation is necessary for growth, but the total organization must operate in consort to be successful.

The competitive structure in the industry must be understood. McDonald's and Wendy's have achieved success with a differentiated cost-leadership strategy. McDonald's has distinguished itself with superior customer service and product consistency while offering low prices and high value to consumers. It has also chosen to target families and children. Its distinctive golden arches constitute a symbolic trademark and are memorable. One possible caveat is that as the baby boomers mature they may become less inclined toward fried hamburgers and more favorably disposed to broiled hamburgers. Wendy's has offered a product assortment and services that have been viewed by an adult market as distinctive. White Castle has used a focused strategy in the product offering, cultivating a very small and distinct market with unique services. Burger King has not developed a clear strategy and as a result, has experienced below-average performance in the industry. Burger King appears to have followed a strategy of being second best, as a close market follower of McDonald's. The fast-food industry is oversaturated with competitors, and unless there is careful planning, a shakeout is on the horizon. Even supermarkets with take-out foods are eroding the market share of the fast-food industry. This shakeout will particularly strike the hamburger segment, with ethnic food and casual dining organizations the winners.

Both Church's and Popeye's Fried Chicken have had organizational snags. Burger King was also handicapped by this sort of problem in its early days. If the fast-food industry with its franchise system is to succeed, there must be clear lines of communication and standardized operating procedures.

CHAPTER 3

THE
ICE CREAM
INDUSTRY

Successful Strategies
- Brand positioning
- Knowledgeable sales personnel
- Product differentiation with assorted flavors
- Market segmentation strategies
- Environmental orientation
- Health and diet orientation
- Strategic alliances for location and distribution strategies
- Image development

Marketing Mistakes
- Reliance on past brand loyalties
- Lack of strong trademark recognition
- A blurred image
- Lack of product differentiation
- Slow response to changing consumer behavior preferences
- Use of market-driven rather than customer-driven strategies

Every company that survives in a competitive business environment must search for consumer needs and either be the first to satisfy them or satisfy them better than its competition. The problems of the ice cream industry have changed since the aftermath of World War II. In the past, ice cream was purchased from a neighborhood drugstore or confectionery and was packed by hand. Local manufacturer's brands dominated the industry. Today, most ice cream purchases are made through supermarkets by consumers, and ice cream counter arrangements are based on the amount of space allocated to national and regional manufacturers' brands; private-label brands; quality items, such as French ice cream; and segmented market items, such as dietetic ice cream and novelties.

It is uncertain when ice cream first arrived from Paris and was eaten in the United States, but it is known that both George Washington and Thomas Jefferson enjoyed ice cream. Dolly Madison served ice cream at her husband's second inauguration in 1812, and this did much to increase popularity. The first commercial ice cream plant in the United States was established in 1851, and Bassett's Ice Cream, introduced in 1861 in Philadelphia, is the oldest brand still on the market.

The commercial production of ice cream was facilitated by improvements in technology. The homogenizer, which gave ice cream its smooth texture; freezers; mechanical refrigeration; electric motors; packaging machinery; insulation methods; and the motorized delivery van made wide distribution possible. A major problem in the ice cream industry was and is distribution. Frequent deliveries to retail stores increase costs and maintain a level of high prices. Due to improvements in refrigeration and technology, deliveries have been reduced considerably. This will probably have an important bearing on performance of the ice cream industry in the future. Dramatic increases in production have resulted: from approximately 5 million gallons in 1899, to 30 million gallons in 1909, to over 150 million gallons in the 1990s.

Ice cream novelties such as bars, sticks, sandwiches, ice milk, and sherbet originated in the 1920s. By 1922 Eskimo Pie ice cream sold roughly about a million bars each day, and the Good Humor bar on a stick followed in 1924. Ice cream became a typical American food in the 1920s. By the 1960s, the bulk of ice cream sales had shifted from drugstores to supermarkets. Many supermarket chains introduced their own private-label or store brands of ice cream. These store brands were usually lower in butterfat, artificially flavored, higher in air content, and lower priced than the national, regional, or local brands.

In considering the shortcomings of ice cream manufacturers, even the most successful manufacturer has made mistakes. However, these mistakes can be overcome as long as factors such as innovation, target market, image, physical environmental resources, and human resources are positive. These ice cream manufacturers did not necessarily obtain high grades using all variables, but some of the variables were used and implemented in a capable manner. Especially noteworthy has been Häagen-Dazs's penetration of a high price market and Kraft's use of human resources. Baskin-Robbins's innovation in developing an assortment of flavors deserves high grades. Ben & Jerry's stands out in the development of image and target-market segmentation.

None of these successes have been able to overcome the market impact of private-label store brands. Ice cream manufacturers have not been able to build strong brands to limit the market penetration of store brands. No longer is there a stigma attached to buying private labels. Ice-cream manufacturers need to reevaluate their marketing strategies and the threat of private-label brands. Both Borden and Kraft (with Breyers and Sealtest), long entrenched in a fragmented ice cream industry, have found survival difficult. The ice cream wars have heated up with the sale of Kraft's ice cream division to Unilever, Borden's decline, and the increasing strength of Ben & Jerry's and Dreyer's Grand/Edy's. Dreyer's, Ben & Jerry's, and Unilever have marshalled their forces to increase the competitive wars with private labels, wars that in the past have not been successful.

Throughout the period from the 1970s to the 1990s, the production of ice cream in the United States remained essentially flat. However, a very lucrative superpremium ice cream market averaging over 15 percent annual growth developed. Häagen-Dazs was the trailblazer, and subsequently many local, regional, and national ice cream companies endeavored to capture a segment of this highly prized premium market. New fat substitutes such as frozen yogurt also grew appreciably in sales.

MARKET STRUCTURE

The ice cream industry includes a few large multiplant firms with nationwide or regional coverage, some smaller, local multiplant firms, and a large number of single-plant firms. The industry is moderately concentrated, with national manufacturers having a relatively small market share of the entire industry. There is ease of entry for small, local manufacturers and independent retail ice cream stores.

Such terms as "national," "regional," "private-label," and "local" have been used in the ice cream industry to describe different types of firms. The term "national" refers to such brands as Sealtest and Borden, which have countrywide distribution. The term "regional" generally has been used to describe those firms that market their brands in a limited geographical area, such as Dairylea or Hood's. "Private-label" refers to the brands made by manufacturers for distributors such as A&P, Safeway, and Winn-Dixie. Local brands are marketed by manufacturers either to target a particular city or an area no larger than one or two states. Larger ice cream corporations began to acquire smaller organizations as improvements in refrigeration techniques made it possible to transport ice cream longer distances. Previous to these acquisitions, most dairy producers viewed ice cream as a sideline of selling milk and other dairy products.

Kraft, a prominent dairy company, has distributed Sealtest, Breyers, and Frusen Glädjé on a national basis, although sales strength is primarily in the Northeast. Borden (including Lady Borden) is another national organization and distributor, with sales strength largely in the Southeast and Southwest. Allied-Lyons North America distributes Baskin-Robbins products on a nationwide basis. Grand Metropolitan, Ltd., distributes Häagen-Dazs products on a national basis, but sales strength is concentrated primarily in the New England, mid-Atlantic, and California areas. Integrated Resources distributes Steve's in New England and the mid-Atlantic regions and Swensen's in South Florida, Texas, Arizona, and New England. Dreyer's Grand Ice Cream sells its products in the Midwest and Western United States. Ben & Jerry's Homemade ice cream has made a significant penetration in the New England market and gains in the national market through franchising. Table 3.1, An Overview of the Ice Cream Industry in 1996 shows the mergers and acquisitions in the ice cream industry. Häagen-Dazs represents one of the great success stories of the 1970s.

Restaurants have also been important distributors of ice cream. Friendly's Restaurants and Howard Johnson have been noted for the sale of quality ice cream. While some restaurants have developed their own brands, many are supplied by Sealtest, Borden, and other regional and local manufacturers.

Since there has been a history of mergers in the ice cream industry, it is

Table 3.1
An Overview of the Ice Cream Industry in 1996

Manufacturers	Brands
Unilever (Kraft)	Breyers, Sealtest, Light 'n Lively, Frusen Glädjé, Good Humor, Klondike, Popsicle
Borden	Lady Borden
Grand Metropolitan, Ltd.	Häagen-Dazs
Ben & Jerry's	Ben & Jerry's
Dreyer's Grand/Edy's	Dreyer's, Edy's
Integrated Resources	Steve's, Swensen's
Allied-Lyons North America	Baskin-Robbins (Retail Franchise)
Dairy Queen	Dairy Queen (Retail Franchise)
Private Labels	Significant Market Share for Store Brands

Note: Reported are major brands of some national significance. Brands that are primarily regional are not reported.

especially important to preserve the distinction between competition and concentration. For example, in the 1980s Häagen-Dazs was purchased by Pillsbury and Integrated Resources purchased Steve's Ice Cream. Kraft also acquired Frusen Glädjé. Philip Morris acquired Kraft, which marketed the Sealtest brand. Integrated Resources has also acquired Swensen's. Although Pet, Inc., controls the Great Ice Creams of the South, and manufacturers such as Campbell Soup have marketed ice cream under their logos, brand-name competition in the industry is generally on a local rather than a national basis.

Despite the market penetration attempts of Kraft and Borden, no brand of ice cream has commanded more than 15 percent of the market. The perishable nature of the product and the route delivery method commonly used limits the distance reached from ice cream plants. Although a few large sellers control a large share of each local market, regional and local competition is intense. Since Unilever has acquired Kraft's ice cream brands of Breyers and Sealtest, added to previously acquired brands of Good Humor, Klondike, and Popsicle, an array of well-known brands is now available to compete with both manufacturers' and private-label brands.

A major problem confronting the market structure of the ice cream industry has been the development of private-label brands. Manufacturers are challenged with the problem of supplying their own brand, finding shelf space in freezers, and also producing private-label brands for corporate grocery chains and groups of affiliated independent grocers. This has necessitated a reassessment of corporate objectives. Should the ice cream manufacturer decide to promote its own brand and produce private-label brands as well, then the program should be viewed not as competitive but as complementary. The total strategy encompassing pricing, promotion, and product development should be planned in consort.

The chief barriers to entry are finding available shelf space and the promotional outlay to penetrate a market. Many local entrepreneurs sell their ice cream directly to the public and are quite successful in this respect. However, distribution through food stores and drugstores is difficult to achieve.

MARKET CONDUCT

According to the *1994 Statistical Abstract of the United States*, per-capita consumption of ice cream in pounds reached a high of 18.6 in 1975 and tapered off to 16.4 in 1992, indicating a significant decrease in consumption. The retail price of a bulk, prepacked half gallon of ice cream was $2.54 in 1988 and $2.59 in 1993. Inflationary prices do not seem to be a serious factor in the purchase of ice cream.

National manufacturers of both ice cream and milk are confronted with diverse, competitive market elements. The manufacturer of milk operates within a market structure of pure competition, whereas this same manufacturer assumes a position of a differentiated oligopolist in a national ice-cream market. However, there is ease of entry on local levels, and therefore a perfectly competitive market structure prevails. National manufacturers have a very small percentage of the ice cream market. Kraft has approximately 15 percent, Häagen-Dazs 6.6 percent, Dreyer's Grand/Edy's 6.4 percent, and Ben & Jerry's Homemade 5.1 percent. Private store brands constitute 32 percent of the ice cream market, and a very large 34.4 percent falls under the other or miscellaneous category in 1994. The big surprise has been that the public has favored the premium and superpremium market in spite of pressure to eat low-fat foods.

The vanilla flavor has the largest share of the ice cream market, with 28 percent. Subsequently, fruit flavors command 15 percent, nut flavors 14 percent, candy mix-in flavors 13 percent, chocolate 8 percent, and Neapolitan 7 percent. The leading frozen novelty brands of ice cream are Weight Watchers, Klondike, Häagen-Dazs, Popsicle, Eskimo Pie, and the Dove Bar. Again, even in the area of frozen novelty ice cream, private-labels have two or three times the market share of national brands. The vast majority of soft-serve desserts are actually ice milk. Dairy Queen and Tastee Freeze are the leading sellers of soft-serve products. There is a consumer willingness to try new flavors, and Baskin-Robbins now offers more than 500 flavors to its retailers.

Food critics have proclaimed various brands of ice cream as the best tasting over the years. Howard Johnson's, Swensen's, Häagen-Dazs, and Baskin-Robbins ice cream have won assorted taste tests. Schrafts, Friendly's, and

Howard Johnson have been rated as excellent, while Baskin-Robbins, Louis Sherry, Sealtest, Dreyer's, and Breyers were rated very good by various media; the private labels of Safeway, A&P, and Kroger were judged as good.

Competitive rivalry among ice cream processors has been directed to quality—or at least the image of quality—variety, and price. In 1961 Häagen-Dazs entered the market as a superpremium ice cream. Although superpremium ice cream was not an overnight success, the 1960s did bring a proliferation of ice cream shops, such as Baskin-Robbins shops, featuring high-quality products. It was not until the 1980s that consumer enthusiasm for superpremium ice cream products soared dramatically. In the 1990s, superpremium brands accounted for a sizable 13 percent of the ice cream market. Surprisingly, superpremium brands, despite their high butterfat content and the health concerns that have hurt the ice cream business, have reported higher sales than other ice cream market segments. Häagen-Dazs and Frusen Glädjé, with their European-sounding names, have had commanding market shares of the superpremium market. Campbell Soup entered the market with Godiva chocolates and Pepperidge Farms, Pet, Inc., Land O'Lakes and others have also penetrated this potentially lucrative market. Meanwhile, Kraft, which sells Breyers and Sealtest products, has increased its advertising budget substantially. Manufacturers have achieved the goal of consumer satisfaction in serving this market segment.

CASE STUDIES

Kraft: Effective Use of Human Resources

Philip Morris purchased Kraft in 1988, and with the subsequent merger of Kraft and General Foods, it became the largest food manufacturer in the United States and second in the world. Kraft has produced some of the best-known food brands in the United States, such as Kraft, Velveeta, Parkay, Miracle Whip, Philadelphia, Cracker Barrel, Sealtest, Light 'n Lively, Breyers, and Breakstone. Most of the products produced by Kraft fall into five broad categories: natural and processed cheese; ice cream and other frozen desserts; cultured dairy products, including cottage cheese, sour cream, and yogurt; salad dressings, mayonnaise, and margarine; and other products, including frozen foods, confections, and condiments.

At the time of the acquisition, ice cream accounted for less than 5 percent of the sales of Kraft's food division. Brand names such as Sealtest, Breyers, and Frusen Glädjé were well known. Breyers was one of the best-selling premium ice creams in the country, and Frusen Glädjé was the number two brand of superpremium ice cream behind Häagen-Dazs. Sealtest was distributed not only to consumer outlets, including supermarkets and drugstores, but to industrial markets including hotels, restaurants, and business-organization employee cafeterias. Breyers had expanded its coverage by marketing to many western and southern states. Kraft's sales force called on both consumer and industrial markets, and was highly regarded in the dairy industry as one of the most sophisticated and best trained.

Added to the product line of ice cream have been sherbet, ice milk, frozen tofu, frozen gelatin bars, and other products, which have had varying degrees of sales increases and decreases throughout the years. Cited in the mission statement of Kraft is innovation, competitiveness, and an action orientation. Kraft with its ice cream division can be noted for its strength in strong brand recognition, packaging, and good customer relationships. The ice cream division is not especially noted for innovation or new-product development. Strategies seem to be more reactive than proactive. However, Kraft does a very competent job in developing brand positioning strategies. For example, Breyers was targeted at consumers who desired a premium, all-natural product. Sealtest was positioned for a market segment that was not attracted by the appeal of naturalness, but wanted something special. Thus was born the slogan, "The Supermarket Ice Cream with that Ice Cream Parlor Taste." Light 'n Lively was developed as a premium ice milk brand priced above other ice milks but below the two premium brands of ice cream.

Unilever: A New Player

Unilever acquired Kraft's ice cream business in September 1993. Notable brands such as Breyers, Sealtest, Frusen Glädjé, and Light 'n Lively were included in the transaction. Unilever is the world's largest marketer of ice cream products and the number one advertiser outside of the United States. Unilever has a reputation as an aggressive supporter of its ice cream products.

Unilever appears to have made a serious commitment to marketing ice cream in the United States. Early in 1993, Popsicle Industries and Klondike were purchased. Unilever is vigorously supporting its Good Humor brand with television and print promotions, and increased attention is being given to promoting the Good Humor trucks. Although Unilever has a good reputation for marketing ice cream abroad, its Breyers brand has lost market share to Dreyer's. It is still too early to tell what the future holds for Unilever. However, the ice cream business is extremely competitive, and Unilever will need all of its marketing expertise to survive. In addition, Kraft has sold its Entenmann's brand, Kraft marshmallows, and Parkay margarine in efforts to divert resources from weak performers. Turbulence would seem apparent.

Borden: Stumbling and Fumbling

Borden was founded in 1858 by Gail Borden, the inventor of condensed milk, and grew to become one of the United States' largest sellers of ice cream, cheese, and milk. Borden envisioned changes coming in the dairy industry and moved to meet them by diversification; the strategy was good, but execution was poor, and costs became uncontrollable. Small regional food companies were purchased, such as Meadow Gold Dairies, but the Borden distribution system was not implemented to coordinate with the purchase effectively.

The retailers who made up Borden's market had changed, desiring a highly focused, integrated approach. Yet Borden persisted until recently in operating eight sales and seven distribution organizations. This meant that multiple representatives from Borden called on a single nationwide retailer selling different brands.

The dairy division had a number of brands with strong consumer brand recognition and was an effective dairy leader in many regional markets. Lady Borden was the premium brand of ice cream and a market leader but eventually lost ground to Häagen-Dazs. Borden, Meadow Gold, Viva, and Lite Live milk and ice cream, as well as frozen desserts, process cheese, and Lite Live diet cheese products all had high consumer recognition. Borden was number one in sliced diet cheese domestically, and Elsie the Cow was one of the most recognized food trademarks. Elsie was created in 1936 but put out to pasture in the early 1970s.

The question is whether or not an updated version of Elsie on all its dairy products, in conjunction with a major television and print advertising campaign, can come to the aid of Borden. Elsie looks like an overmilked, underfed cash cow. Borden runs the danger of reminding only an older market segment of the popularity of a past brand but not reaching the younger consumer who must be attracted. One theory that has been expressed is that Elsie recalls a simpler era of wholesomeness and quality that even a younger generation will relate to favorably. Another theory that has been expressed is that Elsie's reappearance is an act of desperation. If the decision to withdraw Elsie was a wise one in the 1970s, then what has changed to revive it?

Borden's has also used a decentralized approach in advertising, and this is yet another reason for loss of consumer appeal. Borden, in the 1980s, acquired dozens of other food companies and retained practically all of their advertising agencies. It wasn't until the early 1990s that Borden decided to operate with just one advertising agency and discarded about nineteen agencies that were promoting different Borden food brands.

Even Lady Borden, with its high consumer recognition, slugs it out with private-label store brands, while Ben & Jerry's, Häagen-Dazs, and others have effectively seized this premium market. Borden was very slow to react to changes in the premium market. A proactive strategy has been lacking. Even in the regular ice cream market, the frozen yogurt market, and the frozen novelties market, Borden is not a significant player.

Borden needs to develop strategies that emphasize marketing volume and to upgrade ice cream quality. Volume has been lost through faulty pricing and trade practices and needs to be regained. Retailers appear to have lost confidence in Borden's marketing expertise. Improved distribution, better plant utilization, and lower overhead expenses need to be implemented in order to reduce costs. Promotion is still an important problem and needs to be addressed, and new flavors might prove helpful.

Kohlberg Kravis Roberts and Company in May 1997 reported that it had agreed to sell its Borden/Meadow Gold Dairies unit to Mid-American Dairymen Inc., a dairy marketing cooperative based in Springfield, Missouri. Borden also intends to sell its Realemon and Realime reconstituted juices as well as Creamora, a nondairy creamer. While it would be premature to assess the impact of this sale on the ice cream industry, the sale of an established company such as Borden will change the competitive environment. It is anticipated that Unilever (Kraft) and Dreyer's Grand/Edy's would be especially strengthened by this sale.

Dreyer's Grand/Edy's: Effective Use of Physical Resources

Dreyer's Grand Ice Cream distributes Dreyer's and Edy's largely in the Midwest and Western United States. Efforts have been made to widen this distribution pattern. For example, Publix in South Florida sells many of the brands marketed by Dreyer's Grand/Edy's.

Dreyer's spectacular growth has been due to the use of a refrigerated fleet of trucks with wider territory coverage, driven by sales representatives. These sales reps visit large grocery stores and maintain well-stocked freezers. Dreyer's, because of its distribution superiority, markets competing brands, including Ben & Jerry's, Mars's Dove Bar, ConAgra's Healthy Choice, and Nestlé's line of frozen treats. One-third of total revenues is generated from marketing competing brands and helps to defray the cost of operating refrigerated trucks. The sales reps, with the aid of hand-held computers, are able to report to headquarters about flavors and products desired in local markets. For example, senior citizens prefer more sugar-free products, while urban consumers desire coffee flavors.

Dreyer's has made inroads into Breyers's market, is almost even in market share, and is quickly gaining momentum. In a further move to gain strength, Nestlé has been made a minority partner, with about 22 percent of the stock. Dreyer's distributes Nestlé Drumsticks, Bon Bons, and other novelty products. Current strategy is for Dreyer's to aggressively compete with small independent companies in local markets. For example, Dreyer's has successfully gained 10 percent market share competing against Blue Bell, a well-known local brand in the Houston, Texas market. Dreyer's intends to build a strong brand image by using this strategy. In an effort to gain a more favorable brand preference, Edy's/Dreyer's turned to television advertising, and in a survey of the most popular television commercials in the United States, it was voted tenth by the advertising industry's 1995 annual survey.

Innovation has been a successful strategy for Dreyer's. Dreyer's and Edy's

Grand Light were the first premium light ice creams in the industry. Sophisticated research and technology combined to develop a product specifically targeted at an unmet consumer need. The launching of frozen yogurt in half-gallon and quart sizes also led the market. Moreover, distribution centers are situated in major metropolitan markets that reach more than 70 percent of the households in the United States. Competitors have been unable to match Dreyer's direct-store-delivery system in either size or market coverage.

Ben & Jerry's Homemade, Inc.: Environmental Activism

Ben & Jerry's produces superpremium ice cream, ice cream novelties, and light superpremium ice milk. The company was founded in 1978 and opened an ice cream parlor in Burlington, Vermont, in a renovated gas station. The history of Ben & Jerry's is part of ice cream folklore. Two hippies with a social mission created a delectable superpremium product. Ben Cohen and Jerry Greenfield never forgot their antiestablishment roots. Promotion policy was permeated with "stunts" that generated loads of free publicity. Ben & Jerry's quickly developed an image for producing delicious, unusual flavors. Eventually, one of their flavors was named Rain Forest Crunch, which was a manifestation of their social mission. Ben & Jerry's was delivering ice cream to grocery stores and restaurants by 1980, and *Time* magazine (August 10, 1981) hailed the company as making "the best ice cream in the world," consequently adding to further expansion. In a few short years, Ben & Jerry's had successfully linked a product mission to sell a high-quality ice cream with innovative flavors to a social mission that would improve the social life of the community. Success was to be measured by both financial and social performance.

Ben & Jerry's has established a foundation that contributes to the peace movement and to a nonprofit program that supports mentally ill people. The company has, in turn, influenced its suppliers to hire homeless people. Ben & Jerry's in 1989 created a position of environmental development to direct the company's environmental practices and spread its social mission. The end result was 60 percent of office papers and packaging materials recycled and employment by the recycling company of the physically and emotionally handicapped. Forty percent of the Rain Forest Crunch flavor profits are donated to preservation groups.

Ben & Jerry's has differentiated itself from competitors by placing pictures of the founders on all packaging materials and by making personal appearances to further their social mission. The "down-home Vermont" image is also placed on all packaging, sales material, and promotional materials. Ben & Jerry's avoids advertising in the more expensive mass media and instead sponsors community events, such as the Newport Folk Festival in Newport, Rhode Island, and various charity concerts.

Ben & Jerry's actively competes in the superpremium market. The principal competitors are Häagen-Dazs, Frusen Glädjé, Steve's Homemade Ice Cream, Dreyer's, Grand/Edy's and the novelty-segment firms such as Dove Bar. Ben & Jerry's continues to encourage franchising in order to penetrate new markets.

Ben & Jerry's sales plateaued in 1994 despite holding a 42 percent market share of the superpremium market, surpassing the lead of Häagen-Dazs. The consumers who purchase Ben & Jerry's superpremium ice cream are exactly the types that read the new government-ordered nutritional labels. Ben & Jerry's flavors contain more than 40 percent of the fat that an adult should consume daily. Steve's Homemade Ice Cream has acquired a majority interest in American Glacé, a manufacturer of fat- and cholesterol-free desserts. Moreover, Weight Watchers is a leading player in the frozen novelty ice cream segment. There is a danger that consumers who are concerned about fat will switch to Breyers, Sealtest, Dolly Madison, or Louis Sherry, which are perceived as more medium in price and richness. It is doubtful that consumers in the superpremium market, however, will switch to Light 'n Lively or the supermarket brands. In late 1997, Ben & Jerry's deemphasized lower-fat sorbets and yogurts in favor of its superrich ice cream products. The company also hired an advertising agency for the first time.

Häagen-Dazs: An Innovator

Founded in 1961 in the Bronx, New York, Häagen-Dazs was to become the superpremium ice cream phenomenon of the 1980s. The brand was purchased in 1983 by Pillsbury while there was dramatic consumer enthusiasm for superpremium ice cream products. Britain's Grand Metropolitan, PLC, bought Pillsbury in 1989, and by 1990 superpremium brands accounted for about 13 percent of annual retail sales of ice cream. Häagen-Dazs, in 1990, was the brand leader of the superpremium market and was selling its product through supermarkets as well as its own approximately 300 Häagen-Dazs Shoppes.

Häagen-Dazs was also the national distributor for Tofutti and Le Sorbet. Häagen-Dazs, Ben & Jerry's, Godiva, Frusen Glädjé, and Alpen-Zauber are perceived by consumers as expensive and very rich, or high in butterfat content. Breyers, Sealtest, Dolly Madison, and Louis Sherry are perceived as medium in price and richness. Weight Watcher's and Light 'n Lively are perceived as medium in price and have moderate butterfat content. Supermarket or store brands are perceived as low in price and modest in richness.

Häagen-Dazs was the innovator in the superpremium ice cream market, and other ice cream manufacturers followed its leadership role. Häagen-Dazs successfully targeted the self-indulgence of the "me generation" in the 1980s. Even though some consumers believed that they could not afford a new car or expensive stereo equipment, luxury ice cream was affordable. The Häagen-Dazs name with its foreign connotation conveyed quality and distinction. Consumers believed that Häagen-Dazs ice cream was a treat and something they deserved.

Häagen-Dazs, once an icon of an era of self-indulgence, is now scrambling to cope with the new cultural values of the 1990s. Nutrition and health are emerging concerns of the 1990s. This is closely related to the purchase of food products and is manifesting itself in more-educated consumers becoming more careful and discriminating in their eating habits. Ice cream consumption experienced a decline from 4 to 5 percent in 1990. Consumers concerned about fat and cholesterol began to turn away from superrich ice cream. Häagen-Dazs developed the promotional campaign with the theme, "Enter the State of Häagen-Dazs" in an effort to broaden its appeal. Ben & Jerry's overtook Häagen-Dazs in sales; the marketing of social causes seemed more successful than the Häagen-Dazs campaign.

There is a combination of reasons for the loss of market leadership of Häagen-Dazs to Ben & Jerry's. One reason is that Ben & Jerry's has been very successful with their cause-related marketing efforts. Moreover, Ben & Jerry's is very adept at gaining publicity from their various "stunts." Another reason is that conflict developed between Häagen-Dazs and its retailers. Owners of franchised Häagen-Dazs stores rebelled when confronted with a strategy to sell to supermarkets. Retailers claimed their marketing efforts were undermined and subsequently sales and profits reduced when Häagen-Dazs decided to sell its brand in supermarkets as well as in franchised stores.

Baskin-Robbins: The Flavor King

Baskin-Robbins was founded in 1946 and represents one of the outstanding marketing success stories in North America. Allied-Lyons purchased Baskin-Robbins from United Brands in 1973. Allied-Lyons North American Corporation is the London-based firm that also owns Tetley Tea. Baskin-Robbins is comprised of over 2,400 stores in the United States and more than 1,000 stores in foreign countries, and is engaged in the marketing of high-quality ice cream.

The success of Baskin-Robbins is attributed to its philosophy, which has been more closely related to products and product distribution than to formal mass-communication campaigns. However, the company has relied heavily on in-store promotion programs. When Baskin-Robbins entered the ice cream market, supermarkets were beginning to dominate sales and relied on price and shopping convenience. Prior to this period, the corner drugstore with its soda fountain and strategic location dominated retail ice cream distributors. An essential factor in motivating demand was the creation of an unprecedented variety of unusual ice cream flavors. Baskin-

Robbins has a rotating assortment of 31 flavors, with an extensive stock of more than 500 flavors. A 1984 Tastes of America survey voted Baskin-Robbins the favorite fast-food chain, and Baskin-Robbins has received a number of Gold Medal awards periodically over the years at state and county fairs based upon competitive judging.

In 1985 Baskin-Robbins decided to change its image somewhat by re-structuring the company in an effort to attract more adult customers without alienating its base of children. To cultivate the adult market, Baskin-Robbins replaced its pink, white, and brown decor with new store graphics, new furniture, increased seating capacity, and softer color tones. Baskin-Robbins also allowed franchise owners to tailor their store decors to fit in with shopping centers or malls. The numeral 31 was added to the Baskin-Robbins name to aid customer brand recognition and to improve trademark design. The new logo appeared not only in promotional campaigns but also on delivery trucks.

The image campaign for brand recognition has proven successful. Well-known characters and television shows demonstrated more flavors, such as Charley Brownie, Jolly Green Mint, and Jack Lemmon Ice Cream. Baskin-Robbins introduced such flavors as Yankee Doodle Strudel and Valley Forge Fudge to celebrate the bicentennial. Baskin-Robbins also noted that Häagen-Dazs and other superpremiums had failed to market frozen yogurt and other health-oriented desserts. Therefore, the company was the first retail operation to carry a 100 percent aspartame-sweetened dairy dessert when it launched its Low, Light & Luscious flavor in 1989. There has been some cannibalization of ice cream with yogurt. Baskin-Robbins has installed yogurt machines in many of its retail outlets, but Dairy Queen would seem to have a commanding market share of frozen yogurt in stores selling both ice cream and yogurt. TCBY is the largest frozen yogurt franchiser. McDonald's has also entered the frozen yogurt market.

Baskin-Robbins has borrowed from McDonald's inasmuch as comprehensive training is given to franchise owners for approximately one month, and the company publishes a three-volume set of Management Guides. No other franchise ice cream organization has ever produced such in-depth, comprehensive coverage of every phase of the store's operation in manual form. One volume is an employee-training manual with tested techniques that have proven successful. A second volume is a desserts manual with proven recipes and decorating suggestions. The third volume focuses on operations such as products and supplies, financial management, equipment and store maintenance, and selling and merchandising techniques.

Although Dairy Queen has almost 6,000 retail outlets, Baskin-Robbins does not compete for the same market. Dairy Queen has a predominantly small-town presence and also sells hamburgers. Moreover, Dairy Queen concentrates more on frozen yogurt than ice cream. In 1979 Hershey Foods purchased the Friendly's Ice Cream Corporation. While ice cream is served,

other types of food are also offered for sale. There is no doubt that
Friendly's and Howard Johnson restaurants will take away sales from
Baskin-Robbins, since these markets overlap with Baskin-Robbins. With all
of these considerations, Baskin-Robbins has indeed met the challenge of its
competitors.

The modification of a brand and company image calls for creativity that
should deliver emotional power. An image is the set of beliefs, ideas, and
impressions that customers maintain. Store decor of speckled walls and
pink-and-aqua color scheme served Baskin-Robbins well before the introduction of premium ice creams. Baskin-Robbins is now modifying its image
to compete with Starbucks, Jamba Juice, and TCBY. The new store decor
features bright three-dimensional replicas of drinks, straws, and birthday
candles—oversized design elements that children can easily identify. Dairy
Queen is no longer viewed as its main competitor. Currently, Ben & Jerry's
and Häagen-Dazs derive most of their revenue from supermarket sales.
Baskin-Robbins does not use this distribution channel and in the future this
may be a mistake.

Steve's Homemade Ice Cream: Franchise Diversification

Integrated Resources controls Steve's Homemade Ice Cream Shops,
Swensen's, and Heidi's Frozen Yogurt Shoppes. The company also owns
a controlling interest in American Glacé, Inc., which markets a no-
cholesterol, no-fat, low-calorie soft-serve frozen dessert mix to yogurt and
ice cream stores and also sells prepurchased pints to supermarkets and
other food stores, primarily in New Jersey, Connecticut, California, and
Florida. Integrated Resources offers prospective retail franchise stores a Triple Trademark franchise. Every franchisee would be able to offer each
branded line of Steve's, Swensen's, and Heidi's ice cream and, through a
special arrangement, David's Cookies in a single store for the price of a
single franchise. The store would be divided into three sections, with independent counter designs, signs, and products.

Steve's Homemade Ice Cream gained recognition for its mix-in concept,
whereby chunks of fruits, nuts, cookies and candies were mixed into its
superpremium ice cream. Steve's also distributed its mixed-in ice cream in
prepackaged pints to supermarkets, grocery stores, gourmet shops, convenience stores, and delicatessens. Moreover, over 100 ice cream stores have
been franchised.

Swensen's operates a number of stores, ranging from ice-cream-only
shops with no seats, to ice-cream-only stores with 25 to 30 seats, to limited-
menu restaurants with 80 to 100 seats. Swensen concentration is primarily
in Texas, Arizona, California, and New England. Swensen's retail stores
have a differential advantage inasmuch as ice cream was made in 20- or
40-quart batches by the operator of each store, either on the premises or

in a nearby location. This technique permitted each store to produce small quantities of an assortment of flavors. Franchised stores were able to offer between 16 and 45 flavors at any one time from recipes for 175 flavors. In contrast, operators for Baskin-Robbins can choose from at least 500 flavors and are in a better position to satisfy local demand. The attempt of Swensen's to achieve vertical integration by purchasing two ice cream manufacturing facilities failed, and these were later resold to Foremost Dairies. Foremost Dairies continued to manufacture the pints and half-gallons of ice cream sold under Swensen's brand name in the supermarkets.

Frozen Yogurt Competition: Competitive Victims

The frozen yogurt market is divided and does not have a dominating or leading company. Private labels, Kemps, Dreyer's/Edy's, Häagen-Dazs, Ben & Jerry's, Breyers, and Sealtest are all participants in this market. Top yogurt brands in the frozen market are Dannon, Yoplait, Kraft U.S.A., and the private labels.

Frozen-yogurt organizations such as TCBY Enterprises, Honey Hill Farms, Zachs, and others have not fared well because of diverse competitors. McDonald's, Ponderosa, Bonanza, and other restaurants serve yogurt. Ice cream organizations such as Ben & Jerry and Häagen-Dazs have also added yogurt to their offerings. One important problem of yogurt companies is that brands are not identifiable. Another obstacle is that ice cream shops have added frozen yogurt to their mix and therefore have broader appeal. Since more than 75 percent of yogurt is purchased by women, yogurt stores cater to a very narrow consumer segment. Ice cream stores, in contrast, have a good mix of male and female customers.

Yogurt sales grew primarily by taking customers away from ice cream shops. Now that ice cream organizations have diversified and many restaurant chains serve yogurt—and because yogurt lacks identifiable, strong brands—consumers can purchase yogurt any place. In general, the yogurt market is dependent upon location and convenience. TCBY, the largest yogurt chain, is experimenting with new products, including Mrs. Field's Cookies, but it is still too early to assess results. Menu diversification usually increases costs, and a great many independent yogurt stores and chains are experiencing failure. It is doubtful that stores selling only yogurt will be able to survive. The top ice cream and yogurt chains are Dairy Queen, Friendly's Restaurants, Baskin-Robbins, TCBY, and Carvel. An analysis of these chains, with the exception of TCBY, indicates that all have a strong presence in the ice cream market and have added yogurt to their mix.

A redeeming trend in the yogurt market is to broaden distribution sites. For example, nontraditional sites such as athletic stadiums, airports, employee and hospital cafeterias, and theaters have been targeted. Yogurt has also been served on airline flights in America. Another development has been to share operations with cookie or sub shops. There will be a shakeout of weak and independent yogurt chains, but the strong, with broadened menus and alternative location sites, will survive.

MARKETING STRATEGIES

The establishment of a definite target market for ice cream products can be quite elusive. Age, occupation, income, neighborhood residence, residence in metropolitan versus small-town geographical locations, ethnic background, and other demographic factors are all moderating variables that determine shopping patterns of behavior in purchasing various types of ice cream and certainly different flavors of ice cream. The use of a combination of demographic factors is much more feasible than the use of a single factor for developing strategies of market segmentation and product differentiation. There appears to be a positive correlation between the size of the family unit and the expenditures for ice cream purchased on an annual basis.

The decision process for buying ice cream varies depending upon the demographic characteristics of the population. Within the household unit, both the father and the children exert varying influences upon the purchasing decision. The father of the household influences the purchasing decision of ice cream most frequently in young-married-couple groups and high-income segments. On the other hand, children are highly influential when a father is not present and when the mother is the household head. The mother, who makes most of the purchases in the food store, seems to accede to the demands of various members of the household in purchasing ice cream. Flavor preference appears more decisive in many purchasing decisions. Since a premium brand of ice cream has the purpose of segmenting the market, it is presumed that brand preference would be greater in the purchase of premium brands. The low-calorie ice cream market may also have a higher degree of brand preference.

The ice cream industry has been moderately successful in extending the length of the buying season, and many families view ice cream as a year-round dessert. However, sales volume of ice cream products is still concentrated during the summer months. The ice cream industry has taken advantage of diet appeal by producing low-caloric types of products. On the other hand, anxieties about cholesterol have hurt industry sales.

The transition from the sale of ice cream in bulk to specific container sizes has focused efforts on packaging. Packaging in half-gallons, pints, and other sizes has proceeded in an orderly manner and permitted opportunity for further product differentiation. Ice cream is sold in bulk, gallons, half-gallons, quarts, pints, and novelty packages. Product differentiation is determined by a wide assortment of flavors, with some provision for market segments satisfied by sherbet, ice milk, and dietetic ice cream. As far as the consumer is concerned, it is very difficult for the manufacturer to make known that a particular brand of ice cream has superior ingredients or a better balance of ingredients if the price among brands is equal. Value would seem to be equated with price. Therefore, many consumers select the store brand as satisfactory for their desires. Other consumers may decide that the premium or superpremium brands have greater value and be willing to pay a little more for quality. Since there are unknown differences in the quality of ice cream, consumers have a propensity to select regular ice cream brands as well as national, regional, local, and store brands on the basis of price.

Physical distribution resources are critical to the ice cream industry. Years ago deliveries were made daily, but with improvements in technology, deliveries were gradually spaced from every other day to once a week and, in many cases, once every ten or twelve days. Deliveries can also now be made from further distances, allowing companies a wider radius of distribution. Ben & Jerry's, for example, has gained wider distribution with the cooperation and use of Dreyer's Grand Ice Cream facilities outside of the New England and Florida markets. It is frequently necessary for ice cream companies to operate their own trucks and to maintain their own facilities because of the perishable nature of the product.

Human resources are important, but no one individual in the ice cream industry has gained the stature of the late Sam Walton of Wal-Mart, Leslie Wexber of The Limited, or Bernard Marcus of Home Depot. Ben Cohen and Jerry Greenfield, of Ben & Jerry's, however, have earned public admiration for their publicity and promotional campaigns. Kraft, with Breyers, Sealtest, and Frusen Glädjé, is noted for its outstanding sales force. The sales force has helped Kraft to maintain the largest market share in the ice cream industry.

Image and brand identification are important. Ben & Jerry's has done well by emphasizing its "down-home Vermont" image and both Ben Cohen and Jerry Greenfield on its packaging. The Borden Company, with Lady Borden, also wins praise for high identification, or brand recognition. Häagen-Dazs wins high marks for innovation in the superpremium ice cream market, but loses ground due to conflicts with distributors. Baskin-Robbins has earned high grades for its 31 trademark recognition. Unilever's formidable array of brands, including Breyers, Sealtest, Good Humor, Klondike, and Popsicle, will increase the intensity of the ice cream wars. Giant firms such as Unilever and Grand Metropolitan are acquiring smaller rivals and increasing their market share. Therefore, equilibrium will not remain in the ice cream industry.

Success Does Not Guarantee Continued Success

Borden was once a major player in the ice cream industry. Unfortunately, Borden neglected its retailers and did not motivate them well enough. Borden operated too many diverse sales and distribution organizations, and this situation cried out for a more focused, integrated approach. Borden allowed the Lady Borden brand, which had high consumer recognition, to stumble, while Ben & Jerry's and Häagen-Dazs seized significant market share. Borden's sales force reflected a lack of direction and focus.

Sealtest, long Borden's chief rival, focused on market-segmentation strategies, while Borden stood still trying to serve a wide target market. Borden learned too late that it cannot be all things to all people. Strong market segmentation and product differentiation strategies emphasizing flavor assortment would have helped Borden to combat the competition. Moreover, unlike Sealtest, its competitor for many years, Borden lacked definite brand-positioning strategies. Borden remains a classic study of the use of market-driven rather than customer-driven strategies. Borden has tried to increase brand identification by reviving Elsie the Cow and has developed other marketing strategies, but these attempts have been for the most part unsuccessful. Unless Borden can develop stronger differential advantage strategies, the ice cream division will be ripe for potential acquisition.

Marketing Successes in the Ice Cream Industry

- The superpremium market has been successfully segmented by Häagen-Dazs, Ben & Jerry's, and Frusen Glädjé.
- Dreyer's, through improved technology, has increased territory coverage.
- Baskin-Robbins has successfully used product differentiation to offer a wide assortment of flavors.
- Kraft ice cream, acquired by Unilever, has maintained an exceedingly knowledgeable sales force.
- Ben & Jerry's has developed an outstanding image featuring an environmental orientation.
- Häagen-Dazs has been an innovator in the superpremium market.
- Brand positioning by Kraft with Breyers, Frusen Glädjé, Sealtest, and Light 'n Lively has been excellent.

Marketing Mistakes in the Ice Cream Industry

- Firms allowed private-labels to make significant inroads into the ice cream market.
- Firms reacted slowly to the demand for frozen yogurt.
- Firms responded slowly to changing consumer behavior preferences for superpremium ice cream.
- Firms were slow to innovate by improving refrigeration in truck distribution.

- Borden relied on past brand loyalties and subsequently lost significant market share to new competitors.
- Borden blurred its image by concentrating on a youth culture when the population was aging.

MANAGING CHANGE

Social and cultural patterns in the United States are changing rapidly, and many of these changes are reflected in eating habits. Although food eating habits are formulated early in life and difficult to change, social and cultural forces can be influential in later life. Therefore, ice cream marketers must adjust their marketing strategies to these social and cultural forces. Some firms have been very successful because they either made a shrewd appraisal of these changes or accidentally stumbled upon the correct marketing strategies.

An analysis of emerging lifestyle trends has produced three trends that have a bearing on marketing ice cream. The first trend has been called voluntary simplicity, which has its roots in material simplicity and the ecological ethic. The second trend has its roots in self-fulfillment and has been referred to as the "me generation." The third trend is reflected in the changing status of a mature population.

The values underlying voluntary simplicity are material simplicity, a more human scale in environments, self-determination, ecological awareness, and personal growth. Material simplicity does not necessarily mean adopting a lower consumption standard, but rather, valuing products that are handcrafted, durable, and aesthetically pleasing. Human scale implies a preference for smaller living environments and greater value associated with one's contribution to society. Self-determination refers to independence and self-sufficiency, which may well mean less interest in installment purchase plans and a growing distrust of large and complex social bureaucracies. Ecological awareness acknowledges the interconnection between people and resources. This new consciousness notes the need for the reduction of environmental pollution and is receptive to new products that preserve and maintain the natural environment. Personal growth refers to the ability of the individual to clear away external clutter in order to develop the inner life.

Ben & Jerry's has directed many of its appeals to a market segment that is keenly aware of environmental challenges. For example, the proceeds from its Rain Forest Crunch ice cream flavor went to save the Amazon. Recycling is an important environmental concern. At Ben & Jerry's, packing materials are recycled and approximately 60 percent of office paper is recycled. Ben & Jerry's constructed a water-treatment plant in 1989 and is also noted for its energy conservation within the manufacturing process.

The corporate structure is the antithesis of the large corporate bureaucracy, since fun and a laid-back atmosphere are promoted and encouraged. Ben & Jerry's is very successful in New England and focuses heavily on its small Vermont base, which is in accord with consumer preference for smaller living environments.

The lifestyle of self-fulfillment includes the psychological as well as the physical. This lifestyle suggests a self-indulgent, individualistic orientation. Consumers are anxious to spend money on themselves, seek nontraditional living arrangements, and try to "do their own thing." Those who subscribe to this philosophy want to purchase many diverse services, as they seek to enjoy life and find adventure. Self-expression is paramount. With little pressure to conform, followers of this lifestyle have been referred to as the "me generation." These consumers will have a tendency in the future to disassociate themselves from conspicuous consumption and will be more concerned with meaningful symbols that express who they are and what they would like to achieve.

Consumer enthusiasm for trying new flavors and ice cream creations often appears unlimited. Baskin-Robbins, with more than 500 flavors, seems to have benefited from the lifestyle trend of self-fulfillment. Consumer interest in superpremium ice cream products spurted dramatically in the 1980s and was a form of self-indulgence. Häagen-Dazs, Lady Godiva, and the Dove Bar responded successfully to this need for self-indulgence. During this time frame many consumers cut back on their expenditures by postponing the purchase of new cars or expensive gifts, but ice cream was considered an extra treat within their budgets. Although consumers were concerned about diet and physical fitness, consumers still purchased superpremium ice cream. Instant gratification with desserts was often the goal.

There is still another lifestyle trend that is reflected in the changing tastes of a mature population. The aging, or graying, of the population calls for greater attention to the needs and wants of an older generation and a corresponding reduced emphasis on the youth culture. About 25 million households are headed by someone aged 45 to 64, at the peak of his earning power, with the wife in the work force, grown children leaving the household, and the security of pension plans. Consequently, this market is in an excellent position to splurge after some years of self-denial. The aging of the baby-boom generation has resulted in a large adult population for whom ice cream seems to be a desirable snack or dessert. Adults consume three times as much ice cream as children. Older adults favor flavors with nuts or fruits. Adults are more prone to buy premium or superpremium brands, and the pint and single-serving containers are in demand by one- and two-person households.

MANAGERIAL INSIGHTS

There are a combination of factors and strategies that contribute to the success or failure of companies in the ice cream industry. These factors and strategies, consisting of innovation, target-market segmentation, image, physical environmental resources, and human resources, need to be utilized in varying degrees for success to occur. Since not one firm in the ice cream industry has a commanding market share, it can be assumed that performance is either very equal and that no one firm can surpass the others or that other considerations are present. The question must be raised as to the reasons for the huge success of private labels or store brands in the ice cream industry. One reason is that distribution is a major problem in the ice cream industry because of product perishability. Frequent deliveries to retail stores increase costs and cause high prices. Due to improvements in refrigeration, however, the number of deliveries have been reduced considerably, but distribution networks must still be in close proximity. Dreyer's is an exception to some extent, and has been able to overcome this limitation by its direct-store-distribution capability and the most advanced sales information in the industry. Another reason for the success of store brands has been the lack of consumer preference for specific products and brands. There are some exceptions, but generally national ice cream manufacturers have been unable to identify and differentiate their products.

Baskin-Robbins has been successful in the development of its 500-flavor concept. Baskin-Robbins has responded to the need of consumers to experiment with tasting new flavors. This strategy enabled Baskin-Robbins to differentiate its product line. Quality was also a factor, and Baskin-Robbins won many taste awards. Häagen-Dazs was very successful in segmenting the high end of the market for quality. Consumer self-indulgence played an important part in the Häagen-Dazs strategy. Although the Häagen-Dazs product conveyed an image as continental, costly, creamy, and cholesterol rich, sales soared. This product strategy was very successful in the 1980s.

Kraft, which is the most formidable player in the ice cream industry, has been successful because of the expertise of its sales force and the success of its other products in the frozen-food cabinets. The manufacturer with a great deal of glitter has been Ben and Jerry's. Ben & Jerry's has a strong image associated with environmental awareness. Pictures of Ben Cohen and Jerry Greenfield and New England scenes give the product high recognition. The employees and executives hired reflect the philosophy of the owners. An agreement with Dreyer's Grand/Edy's outside of Ben & Jerry's strong New England base has extended market penetration. Borden is attempting to reinforce a high-recognition trademark by reintroducing Elsie the Cow.

Whether or not a new generation will respond favorably to a trademark from the past remains to be seen.

In considering the successes and failures of ice-cream manufacturers, many mistakes have been made, and only those organizations that have been able to make constant adjustments to such changing variables as innovation, target markets, image, physical environmental resources, and human resources remained viable. Still, manufacturers have not been able to successfully compete with store brands.

Mistakes have been made in dealing with franchisees. Häagen-Dazs antagonized its retailers by selling to supermarkets and by improperly communicating this change in strategy. Carvel is situated on the East Coast, and in 1985 its operation had shrunk from nearly 800 stores to fewer than 500 stores. When Carvel moved into servicing supermarkets, it allowed franchises to solicit and service supermarket accounts. The franchisees made the products and delivered them to supermarkets. While some dealers claimed that sales then increased in the winter months, others maintained that profit margins to supermarkets were considerably less and that supermarkets were taking business away.

Borden did not coordinate its acquisitions of other dairy firms with its marketing objectives, and this meant that multiple representatives from Borden called on a supermarket chain selling different brands. Moreover, many of the ice cream manufacturers were very slow to react to the threat of frozen yogurt.

The nature of the product and its relatively low cost would appear to be important factors that limit manufacturers' strategies. Total consumer satisfaction escapes national manufacturers, as store brands continue to make dramatic inroads into the ice cream market.

CHAPTER 4

THE
SOUP
INDUSTRY

Customer-Driven Strategies
- Encouragement of outrageous objectives
- Focus on customer ethnic preferences
- Aggressive use of technology
- Regional market segmentation
- Ability to capitalize quickly on new opportunities
- Promotion of brand power
- Shift to non-price variables

Marketing Mistakes
- Use of market-driven rather than customer-driven strategies
- Slow to grasp importance of brand power
- Over reliance on price competition
- Reactive and not proactive to ethnic changes

A feature of the scenario of canned soup sales in the United States has been the dominance of Campbell's Soup, which sells more than half the soup to consumers. Private-labels, or store brands, make up only an insignificant part of canned soup sales. The driving force behind Campbell Soup is brand power, with the concomitant factor of brand loyalty and repeat patronage.

Campbell has marketed canned soup under its familiar red-and-white label for almost 100 years, and was one of the earliest companies to succeed in mass marketing. Although the firm first started in 1869 as a producer of jams and jellies, it was in 1897 that John T. Dorrance developed a process for canning soup in condensed form, and as a result Campbell became well known for its soups. Campbell does market brands in other food categories, including Pepperidge Farm, Prego, Swanson, and LeMenu product lines. However, the soup business remains Campbell's core, and the firm is best known for its soup globally. The Andy Warhol depiction of the Campbell Soup label has graced museums around the world and made the Campbell Soup label as familiar as any consumer package. Campbell has launched art contests among young people to update the work of Andy Warhol, and this contest remains an inspiration to young artists.

The mushrooming number of new soup products, the growth of soup mixes, and the increasing importance of Progresso and Lipton provide evidence of increased competition. The soup wars have intensified, and the strategy has been to use line extensions—product variations that retain an established brand name. New categories of soups have been created, but canned soup is still the business core. Dehydrated soup, microwaveable soup, and new frozen and refrigerated soups have grown in popularity. Among the soup-mix brands, Lipton has a dominant share, while Campbell is second, closely followed by Maruchan, Knorr, and the private labels. These new products and keener competition have caused Campbell's share of the soup market to diminish from about 80 percent in the early 1970s to about 60 percent today.

A renewed interest in the soup market has been ignited by changes in American lifestyles and other significant environmental alterations. The three most important trends affecting the soup market are the aging of population, its evolving ethnic composition, and its changing family structure. American food consumption patterns will be strongly influenced by an aging population. Since brand loyalty to Campbell is considered high, it is reasonable to expect that there is a splendid opportunity to retain repeat patronage. The elderly population is forecasted to increase significantly, and this presents another opportunity for Campbell to increase its market share. Tastes will change with age, and interests will be focused on health and fitness. Campbell is very adept at regional and demographic market segmentation.

The ethnic population is changing. The Hispanic population is the fastest-growing ethnic group in the United States. Goya Foods dominates the Hispanic market, and Campbell has been slow to learn how to compete effectively in this growing market. Campbell has developed a new entry brand, Casera, targeted to a younger, more affluent Hispanic segment, but inroads into existing market share have not been made as of yet.

The growth of the singles market, the double-income family, the entry of women into the work force, family members eating at different times, and changing, diverse lifestyles have all had an impact on the soup market. The soup market has responded to changing lifestyles by developing soups with less salt for those interested in reduced sodium, hearty soups for the ready-to-eat category, dehydrated soups, microwaveable soups, single serving soups, and upscale, creamy, condensed soups with no additives.

The soup war in the 1990s is a fierce struggle fought from pillar to post, from neighborhood to neighborhood. A homogeneous market is gone, and each soup company, whether it be Campbell, Lipton or Progresso, will find that its organization needs to do more stratifying, niche marketing, and lifestyle market segmentation. The soup firms, and in particular Campbell, have done a lot to withstand the assault of store private labels. Campbell has been the innovator, with its target-market strategy of regional market segmentation. Progresso has enhanced its image with its cultivation of consumers' Italian taste preferences. Lipton has been the innovator in the dry soup mix specialty. The physical colors of red and white and the art of Andy Warhol have made Campbell a legend in the soup industry. Finally, the sales representatives of Campbell have been outstanding in strengthening relationships with retailers.

Innovation, target-market segmentation and image, physical environmental resources, and human resources have been important variables that have spelled a basis for either success or mistakes in the soup industry. Campbell has effectively innovated with new production efficiency and cost control. Regional-market-segmentation strategies have been highly developed by Campbell and have earned the admiration of marketers even in other industries. Progresso's positive image in the ethnic Italian market and Lipton's in the dry soup market have countered challengers. Goya Foods, a small manufacturer, has achieved a breakthrough by establishing a positive image in the Hispanic market.

Both Campbell and Progresso have developed a sound distribution network and thereby have achieved, through strict inventory-control monitors, a minimum of out-of-stock situations. Campbell in the 1990s has encouraged its executives to try to accomplish what might be considered outrageous objectives or unattainable objectives. Sales representatives of Campbell are well trained and can rival the best of their counterparts in the entire food industry. On the other hand, mistakes have been made. For example, the soup industry developed single-size serving cans to serve the singles market, only to learn that families who do not eat together have more of a propensity to purchase this product than the singles target market.

MARKET STRUCTURE

The food-processing industry was composed of thousands of local and regional firms at the beginning of the 20th century. These firms were too small to take advantage of economies of scale in mass production and distribution. Consolidation through acquisition and merger began in the 1920s and gradually evolved, particularly in the 1960s and 1970s. Companies such as Campbell, Kraft, General Foods, Standard Brands, and Del Monte were established and soon became household words. Economies of scale were achieved with consolidation, and national market coverage became possible. Following World War II, more product differentiation developed, and some firms established subsidiaries in other countries. Emphasis from the 1960s to the 1980s was on brand diversification and product-line expansion.

Giant firms began to acquire other giant firms in the 1980s. In 1984 Nestlé acquired Carnation, and in 1985 R. J. Reynolds purchased Nabisco Brands and Philip Morris acquired General Foods. Subsequently, Philip Morris purchased Kraft. Along the acquisition trail, Swanson and Pepperidge Farms were purchased, but although Campbell is a diversified food organization, its core business is identified with soup by consumers. Soup remains Campbell's stronghold and has permitted the development of other brands, such as Prego, Franco-American, and Godiva. Progresso is a division of Pet, Inc., a division of Pillsbury, which was acquired by Grand Metropolitan in 1989.

The soup industry has been dominated by both Campbell and Lipton (a division of Unilever). In 1985, Campbell dominated the canned soup industry with competition from Van Camp (Ralston Purina), Libby (Nestlé), Crosse and Blackwell (Nestlé), and private labels (mostly made by Heinz). Campbell still dominated the canned soup industry a decade later, but competition now arose from Progresso (Pet, Inc.), Healthy Choice (ConAgra), Swanson (Campbell), College Inn (Nabisco), and private labels (made chiefly by Ralston Purina).

Lipton dominated soup mix brands in 1985, with competition from Campbell, Knorr Swiss (Beatrice), and Wyler (Borden). Lipton still dominated the soup mix brands in 1995, with competition from Campbell, Maruchan, Knorr, private labels, Oodles of Noodles and Top Ramen (Nissen), Mrs. Gross, and Soup Starter. A study of both canned and dry soup markets shows that while Campbell and Lipton, respectively, dominate these markets, the composition of competing brands has changed in a decade, and new threats, while not of a serious nature, are present.

The ethnic soup market targets mainly Hispanic, Italian, and Jewish consumers. Goya Foods dominates the Hispanic market, with competition mainly from Casera (Campbell); Progresso targets the Italian market; and Manischewitz dominates the Jewish market, with competition mainly from Rokeach. Manischewitz dates back to 1888.

The leadership of Campbell in the canned soup market, while challenged by Progresso as shown in Table 4.1, An Overview of the Soup Industry in 1996, is not that serious. Campbell is selling the concept of an established image that is associated with quality and reliability and a brand with a familiar red-and-white label used by generations. In contrast, Lipton is far ahead of Campbell in the soup mix market and has established itself internationally. The ethnic soup market has experienced fierce competition, and smaller firms such as Goya Foods, Manischewitz, and Nissen Foods are dominant in relatively small markets. The Italian ethnic market reflects wide consumer acceptance, and two giant firms—Progresso and Campbell with its Prego brand—are locked in combat. Progresso would seem to be dominant in a market with high sales volume. Table 4.1, An Overview of the Soup Industry in 1996, shows the healthy-soup market, where greater growth is anticipated. Both Progresso and Campbell are locked in a close struggle with other firms endeavoring to take advantage of this growth market.

Because Campbell's promotional campaigns stressed primarily demand appeals that focus on eating more soup, all soup companies benefited from these efforts. Generally, the company with the dominant market share benefits the most from primary demand advertising. However, in this case both Pet with Progresso and ConAgra with Healthy Choice have found Campbell's campaign profitable.

Campbell's marketing efforts have intensified in the soup industry. Competition has grown keener, with Pet, Progresso, Lipton, Goya, and Japanese

Table 4.1
An Overview of the Soup Industry in 1996

Company or Brand	Market
1. Campbell 2. Progresso	Canned Soup
1. Lipton 2. Campbell	Soup Mixes
1. Goya Foods 2. Campbell/Casera	Hispanic
1. Progresso 2. Campbell/Prego	Italian
1. Manischewitz 2. Rokeach	Jewish
1. Progresso/Healthy Choice 2. Campbell/Healthy Request	Healthy Soup
1. Nissen Foods 2. Campbell	Ramen Noodle

Source: Dominant brands for each market compiled from the literature in the field.

firms becoming major players. There are any number of opportunities for Campbell in the soup industry in international markets, but opportunity is doubtful in domestic markets. Increasing soup consumption will prove difficult, since soup consumption remains stable in the United States. Second, Campbell seems to have saturated the market and has achieved high levels of brand recognition and brand preference. The possibility does remain that market shares of domestic competitors can change, but profitability achieved through increased sales, cost cutting, and price competition seems limited.

MARKET CONDUCT

Regional differences are more distinct for some products than for others. To illustrate, Campbell sells Cajun Gumbo Soup in Louisiana and Mississippi and its spicy Ranchero Beans only in the South and Southwest. Consumers have also been demanding more fresh and refrigerated foods instead of canned or frozen products. These products, which include such items as soups, pastas, and sauces, have afforded new opportunities for food companies. Another trend in the food industry has been an increased preference for Hispanic food. Through acquisition, Campbell purchased Casera in 1986, a producer of a broad range of canned and frozen Spanish foods.

Progresso stirred up the healthy soup market in 1993 by offering five soups in lower-fat, lower-cholesterol versions with one-third less sodium. ConAgra launched its Healthy Choice soups. Campbell's Healthy Request 98 percent fat-free, ready-to-serve varieties provided keen competition for both Progresso and ConAgra's Healthy Choice. Moreover, Campbell's Home Cookin' ready-to-eat soups significantly increased market share. The soup industry previously had been complacent about satisfying consumer demands for more healthy soup, and this can be viewed as a mistake, since consumers may have eaten substitutes for soup instead.

Lipton has responded to competition by endeavoring to strengthen its soup mixes. In 1994, Lipton introduced Kettle Creations, a new line of hearty soup mixes. Lipton has received overwhelmingly favorable responses from consumers and has found this product line profitable. Recipe Secrets sales grew more than double the market in 1994 and was selected as one of five Unilever brands (Lipton is a division) worldwide to participate in an interactive marketing test program.

The *Market Share Reporter* in 1995 stated that the soups most frequently served were vegetable and chicken tied at 64 percent; broccoli, 57 percent; bean soup, 52 percent; seafood chowder, 51 percent; potato, 49 percent; beef, 47 percent; tomato, 45 percent; and minestrone, 43 percent.

The food-processing industry at the beginning of the 20th century was highly fragmented, with numerous regional and local firms too small to use economies of scale in mass production or distribution. During the 1920s, industry consolidation via acquisition and merger commenced. After World War II, the larger food organizations increased emphasis on market-segmentation and product-differentiation strategies. Some food companies became multi-international in scope, establishing subsidiaries globally. In the 1980s and 1990s, emphasis was on brand diversification and product line expansion. Acquisitions of smaller companies with products that had brand recognition and brand loyalty characteristics increased. In the soup industry, Campbell, Lipton, Nestlé, Ralston Purina, Pet, and Beatrice are food giants that have assumed leadership roles. Only in the ethnic soup market have smaller firms gained a foothold.

Strong brands in the soup industry have been the key to increased asset turnover and profitability. Strong brands were desired by wholesalers and retailers and gained ready acceptance. Strong brands facilitated product-line extensions, category expansions, and product reformations. Brand strength was the primary reason why manufacturers were able to compete with store-label brands. Soup manufacturers have focused upon serving customer needs and capitalizing quickly on new opportunities. The brand is the major link between soup marketers and consumers. If the consumer doesn't have a specific brand of a product in his memory bank, then that brand will not be purchased.

Brand awareness does not guarantee sales, but with repeated advertising, it is possible that brand awareness will become brand acceptance and brand preference when compared with brands that are in the nonrecognition stage. A firm's brand name, in this world of me-too products, is about the only thing a competitor cannot copy. To a large extent Campbell, Progresso, and Lipton enjoy a strong measure of brand loyalty in their specialty areas. However, this brand loyalty may not be that intense when such factors as price, size, color, or other characteristics are considered by consumers. Therefore, it would be a mistake for the companies in the soup industry to be caught in a price war.

CAMPBELL SOUP: KING OF THE SOUP INDUSTRY

Campbell Soup began making its first soup, ready-to-serve tomato, in 1892. The Campbell Preserve Company was renamed the Campbell Soup Company in 1922. John Dorrance, Sr., who joined the organization in 1897, was credited for the success of the firm. Campbell soon became a leader in the soup industry in the 1920s and by 1935 had more than twenty varieties of condensed soup with the red-and-white labels still used today. The objective was simply to provide the consumer with a high-quality, affordable soup.

Campbell tried to enter the baby soup market in 1945, and withdrew in 1949. A product line of six baby soups packaged in glass jars was introduced, but Campbell lacked a complete line of baby food and found it very difficult to compete with firms like Gerber, which specialized in a comprehensive baby food product line. Campbell also had difficulties with the containers, resulting in spoilage.

Campbell introduced frozen soups in 1954. The objective of this product line was to offer new soup varieties made with ingredients that had lost flavor and texture when heat processed. Campbell desired to offer new varieties of soup without compromising quality, and therefore marketed frozen soups.

Campbell introduced its Red Kettle brand of dry soups in 1961. The objective was to increase product offerings to include all soup types in the market. Unfortunately, the product line was not successful and was discontinued in 1966. The Red Kettle dry soup line captured only 6 percent of the dry-soup market. Campbell used the traditional red and white colors of the condensed soup line, and even though an aluminum can with a pull tab was used, consumers were confused over which variety they were purchasing. Although the colors were changed, a confused image remained in consumer minds, and sales still continued to decline.

A product line of institutional soups was introduced in 1965, and this proved successful. The product-line objective was to provide special soups, which were low in sodium for those on restricted diets, to institutions such as hospitals. Eventually, similar product lines were also made available to traditional soup consumers.

Campbell added the Chunky Soup line in 1970 to compete in the ready-to-serve soup market, and it proved successful. In 1976, Campbell began to use lifestyle market-segmentation strategies by introducing its Soup-for-One, which was a "semicondensed" soup because only half a can instead of a whole can of water needed to be added. Family structure was changing. Since family members operated on different schedules, more consumers ate separately. Moreover, the singles market was dramatically increasing.

The 1980s and 1990s presented a mixed picture of product successes and failures. The Gold Label and Soup-for-One lines were dropped, but the Home Cookin' and Creamy Natural lines added in 1986 and the Healthy Request line introduced in 1991 are still marketed. Campbell was late to enter the healthy soup market, and this can be viewed as an important error in judgment.

Although Campbell had dominated the soup market, new product lines were continuously introduced, product quality was always paramount, and market-segmentation strategies were carefully developed that successfully identified and satisfied consumer needs and wants. Success did not bring complacency. During the 1990s, Campbell was restructured. The soup product line still remained a stronghold. Campbell's strategy of target-market segmentation and its policies of quality and uniformity present strong differential advantages over competitors. Campbell is one of the most powerful brand names in the United States and over the years has earned the brand loyalty of scores of consumers. However, despite fierce consumer brand preference and in many instances brand insistence, Campbell will still be confronted with formidable challenges by the turn of the 21st century.

Campbell has demonstrated a willingness to break with the status quo and innovate. To illustrate, new soup products were introduced under some of Campbell's brand names in other food categories. A ready-to-serve soup under the Prego name was launched in order to compete with Progresso. Under the Pepperidge Farm label, a line of ultrafancy soups was marketed. Moreover, under the brand name Casera (which means "home cooked" in Spanish), Campbell now competes with Goya for the Hispanic market.

In 1990, CEO David Johnson was hired by Campbell, and under his tutelage earnings have multiplied at a five-year annual rate of nearly 18 percent. Johnson has been effective at mobilizing human resources behind a vision and communicating strategies to subordinates. Managers are encouraged to realize outrageous objectives. For example, when it was learned that low-fat cream soups were popular in Great Britain, corporate culture encouraged the risk of trying it in the United States, and this strategy proved successful.

Campbell's mission is to offer nutritional food products throughout the world. Growth strategy focuses on organizational strengths—soup and biscuits. Campbell's philosophy is to target-market locally and extend global penetration by using common technology. Campbell believes in brand power. Brands with strong consumer preference have been able to successfully compete with private-store labels. This power behind brand acceptance has been true not only of Campbell, but of Coca-Cola, Wrigley, and Nabisco as well. Well-known brands of the Campbell organization in the United States include Chunky, Delacre, Franco-American, Godiva, Goldfish, Healthy Request, Mrs. Paul's, Open Pit, Pepperidge Farm, Prego, Swanson, V8, and Vlasic. Campbell has extended its organization all over the world and acquired well-known brands in Great Britain, Japan, and other countries.

Campbell recognized that the United States was no longer a mass market for soup but a series of regional markets. Consequently, Campbell divided its sales force among twenty-one mostly autonomous regional operations, each responsible for local marketing planning and expenditures. Regional and local marketing is not just demographic segmentation. There was a change in corporate philosophy and a change in corporate structure. This means, in fact, that Campbell moved the marketing decision-making process from the corporate headquarters into the field, with an emphasis on bottom-up marketing rather than top-down marketing. Bottom-up marketing places the emphasis on the end user, or consumer, and makes it essential to analyze the difference between market segments.

Regional lifestyle market segmentation may reveal considerable variations in consumer buyer behavior. Marketers may have to modify their product, promotion, price, or distribution systems to accommodate these differences. For example, firms endeavoring to cultivate the Hispanic market may need to advertise in Spanish and use bilingual labeling to ensure that its products satisfy this market segment. Campbell sells a spicier nacho-flavored cheese soup in California and Texas and uses different campaigns to reach Caribbean and Mexican Americans. Despite its efforts Campbell was slow to enter the Hispanic market, and this has allowed Goya Foods, a small manufacturer, to penetrate this market.

MARKETING STRATEGIES

Entry barriers in the food industry are formidable, since this is a volume-driven industry. Economies of scale are paramount for production, marketing, and distribution efficiencies. Furthermore, there is a real contest among firms in the United States for supermarket and freezer shelf space. Price wars are a threat for organizations like Campbell, since unit profits are low and great volume is needed for a profitable operation. Most sensitive to price wars are shelf-stable items and frozen dinners. Although Campbell's market share of the soup industry has been approximately 80 percent, this market share has declined in some periods, but over time Campbell has proved resilient. Campbell's push for growth and diversification came in other product areas and globally came at the expense of the soup unit. In 1985, Heinz was second, with 10 percent of the market, but competition forced Heinz to withdraw from making its own soup brands and to shift its production to producing soups for supermarket chains. Even though the soup market is relatively mature, momentum has been generated for developing new types of soups in ethnic, dried, refrigerated, frozen, and microwavable areas.

Target-Market Strategies

In the 1990s, target marketing by Campbell from locality to locality and from region to region has significantly changed marketing in the soup industry. Marketers who understand regional and local differences that affect the values and lifestyles of consumers will find that this awareness can mean the difference between profits and losses. Geographical location is a good indication of what consumers desire to purchase. It is difficult to ascertain the reasons consumers purchase more popcorn in Dallas/Fort Worth, more ketchup in New Orleans, more iced tea in Philadelphia, and more coffee in Pittsburgh. However, the tasks for marketers are to mix this data with demographic profiles and develop regional strategies. Identifying market differences serves as a basis for segmenting consumer markets. The fundamental objective should be to focus upon market needs, the reasons for purchases, and changing lifestyles and consumer expenditure patterns.

Campbell's market share had declined from 80 percent in the early 1970s to about 65 percent by the beginning of the 1990s, but it regained its 80 percent market share by the mid-1990s as a result of regional lifestyle market segmentation. Consumers in the 1990s are more discriminating and demand products that closely adhere to their lifestyles and activities. Campbell's chicken noodle soup and variations demonstrates its reception in different parts of the United States, for chunky chicken noodle with mushrooms is the best seller in Detroit, red-and-white labeled chicken noodle is number one in Cincinnati, Home Cookin' chicken with broad egg noodles is the best seller in Seattle, microwave chicken noodle soup is number one in Milwaukee, Healthy Request Chicken Noodle Soup is the favorite in Baltimore, Family Size Chicken Noodle is number one in Salt Lake City, and Campbell's Chicken Flavor Ramen Noodle Soup is the best seller in Denver.

Americans enjoy Italian food on a regular basis and it is the most popular ethnic food category. Progresso has targeted the Italian food category and has continued to serve this market for more than 90 years. For example, Pasta Soups were introduced in 1993 and are a contemporary line of 10 flavors offering authentic, Italian flavor with the appeal of pasta. Progresso also provides quality ingredients for Italian and Italian-influenced cooking.

Lipton has targeted the dry soup market, marketing a comprehensive product line of Lipton Soup Secrets, Kettle Creations, Recipe Secrets, and Cup-a-Soups. In-store merchandising is an integral part of Lipton's marketing strategy. This technique of helping retailers display dry soup products in the correct sizes and varieties has helped Lipton to penetrate new merchandising markets. For example, in the mid-1990s Fleming, Super Valu, Kroger, American Stores, and Wal-Mart purchased approximately one-third of Lipton's dry grocery products. Campbell was incredibly slow in the 1980s to react to Lipton's penetration of the dry soup market. Campbell was not the innovator in this market segment and has found it difficult to gain significant market share.

In the early 1990s, Campbell segmented the children's market by introducing Souper Stars and Curley Noodles. Advertisements depicted the Campbell kids as astronauts for Souper Stars and fighter pilots for Curley Noodles. Moreover, Souper Stars was introduced as a dry soup mix. Campbell also expanded its offerings to include children's Cup of Noodles and Campbell's Double Noodle Soup. These efforts were successful, but limited in profitability.

In response to other competitors, Campbell introduced Healthy Request. As the baby boomers age, health and diet mania will continue. Nutritional awareness has altered the culture as consumers change their dietary practices and beliefs. Some supermarket chains are competing with health food stores in an effort to satisfy the gaining market for organic and natural foods. Low-sodium and fat-free soups that contain less than 150 calories have been launched. Progresso is a formidable competitor in this market segment, and the battle is on for supermarket shelf space. In the market segment of ramen noodle soups, Campbell's major competitor is Nissen Foods. Nissen Foods is engaged in niche marketing.

Product-Market Strategies

Campbell makes every effort to encourage risk taking on the part of product managers. The corporate culture reflects an entrepreneurial spirit. An effective use of family branding is called brand extension, a strategy by which an established brand name is applied to new products gaining relatively quick consumer acceptance. Brand extension decreases the manufacturer's high cost of promoting new brand names and generates instant brand recognition of the new product. However, if the new product fails, this might have an impact on the other products carrying the same brand name. Although product-line extension with the red-and-white-label soups has been successful for Campbell, brand extension could have cannibalized the primary customer base. Therefore, Campbell introduced a soup line under the Prego brand that was intended to compete with the Progresso Italian-style soups. Campbell has successfully used the strategy of brand extension with its Chunky Soup line.

Campbell introduced several line extensions, in 1986, with varying objectives. Golden Classics was launched to satisfy a premium market and consequently was in a higher-priced category than traditional red-and-white-label varieties but was unsuccessful. Special Request was a reduced-sodium product to appeal to the more health-conscious consumer. Creamy Natural was designed to satisfy consumers who did not desire additives in their products. In the 1990s, Home Cookin' was composed of both condensed and ready-to-serve varieties that were 98 percent fat-free, low in cholesterol, and lower than other soups in salt by one-third. The Home Cookin' brand appealed to health-conscious consumers.

Campbell had poor results with the Gold Label and Soup-for-One product lines, and both were withdrawn in 1990. Some line extensions cannibalized other existing lines. For example, the Healthy Request line took away sales not only from Chunky and Home Cookin', which are in the same ready-to-eat category, but also from the traditional red-and-white label condensed soups. Therefore, some product-line objectives to increase soup consumption merely shifted sales from one brand line to another.

The problem for the soup industry is that the consumer will eat only so much soup. Soup is in the maturity stage of the product life cycle. This means that there is a slowdown in sales growth, since the product has reached an acceptance consumption level by most potential buyers. Profits level off or may even decline as firms in the soup industry increase marketing outlays to defend their product line against competitors. Strategies in the market-maturity stage of the product life cycle emphasize and gradually intensify market segmentation. Retaining retail store distribution and making pricing competitive are other sound strategies. New channels of distribution such as Wal-Mart and Sam's Club have been added, but sales from these outlets affect supermarket store sales. Each firm endeavors to stress brand differences and benefits and to encourage brand switching. Cost reduction strategies are used to maximize profits.

Lipton's most well-known soup, its instant Cup-a-Soup, was introduced in 1972 and was successful. Campbell was slow to realize the potential of this market previously, but seriously reentered in 1985. Lipton countered this challenge by offering two new product lines: International Soup Classics and Hearty Soup Mixes. Although Campbell has gained market share in this market, Lipton is still dominant by a commanding margin.

The strongest competitor of Campbell is Progresso. Progresso began directly competing with Campbell in the 1970s. In 1974 Progresso introduced four new ready-to-serve soups that competed with Campbell's Chunky Soup line. Progresso by 1985 had a line of sixteen ready-to-serve soups that had a larger market share of the New York City and Boston markets than did Campbell's Chunky. Progresso's main thrust was to serve a market segment that desired an Italian flavor and influence. Although Campbell is the leader in most canned soup categories, Progresso leads the vegetable soup category, with a nearly 50 percent share.

PROMOTION STRATEGIES

A redefinition of mass marketing was developed by Campbell in 1987. Campaigns revolved around a new, regional marketing approach and a re-designed sales-force system. The regional marketing approach has diminished the use of national media and especially network television advertising. Campbell focused upon twenty regions that were demarcated along demographic and psychographic lines rather than geographic boundaries. Each region was administered by four sales brand managers handling products by category product lines. To illustrate, one regional brand sales manager is responsible for marketing soups, and another, canned foods. National brand managers allocate a part of their budget for regional promotional strategy to the regional managers. Regional managers may purchase media in their areas. Point-of-purchase store promotions are intensified.

By 1993, Campbell was trying to increase soup consumption in the summer months. Soup sales peaked in the winter and plunged in hot weather. Contraseasonal marketing is an important aspect of new promotional strategy. A dozen years ago supermarkets removed soup from store shelves in the summer to make space for best-sellers such as paper plates, charcoal, and other outdoor products. Campbell and other soup manufacturers have been successful in halting this extreme practice.

In the 1990s, Progresso launched its Healthy Choice soups and had the advantage of an innovator, but Campbell, with its huge promotional budget, followed rapidly with a Healthy Request soup line. Moreover, Campbell extended the Healthy Request brand from soup to spaghetti sauce in an attempt to use a new umbrella name for Campbell's healthy food. The response was to counter ConAgra's campaign in ten diverse products under the Healthy Choice name. Again, ConAgra was the innovator in the health food category.

Lipton, on the other hand, has been hurt in its Cup-a-Soup flagship products by its reduction in advertising. Ramen noodle marketers have been extremely aggressive. While Lipton has lost market share, Nissen Food's Oodles of Noodles has increased its sales volume significantly. Campbell has unsuccessfully fought back, and Lipton appears to be outmatched in this market. Lipton was very slow to realize the changes in ethnic food desires of consumers and thus has lost market share. This reactive rather than proactive strategy by Lipton can be viewed as an important mistake.

Campbell's sales force is an integral part of its promotion strategy and an important reason why Campbell has dominated the soup industry. The company has more than 1,000 salespeople involved in the marketing of its product lines in the United States. Approximately one-third of its sales force are account representatives who sell directly to supermarket chain head-quarters. The retail salespeople who visit individual stores have precise merchandising responsibilities that include convincing store managers to establish special displays, positioning new items, and maintaining inventory-control records. New product marketing is an important aspect of their jobs. Laptop computers used by the sales force are linked to the headquarter's mainframe. This increased productivity and efficiency of in-formation processing by reducing lead time from six to eight weeks to less than two days. Campbell was one of the first food manufacturers to dis-mantle its central marketing structure and change to a regional marketing approach. This approach advanced focused advertising of particular soups to specific audiences.

Campbell has had legal difficulties in the past and has earned a reputa-tion as an aggressive competitor. H. J. Heinz was pushed out of the soup market and resorted to making private labels for supermarket chains. H. J. Heinz filed a lawsuit under the Clayton Antitrust Act. Campbell was charged with using deceptive advertising and predatory tactics to lessen competition in the condensed soup market and geographic discrimination in promotion and advertising. Specifically, Campbell was charged with forcing retailers to extend more shelf space and holding down prices where there was competition and increasing prices where there was a lack of competition. The lawsuit was resolved out of court to avoid unfavorable publicity.

PRICE STRATEGIES

Campbell has reoriented its emphasis from growth to profit in the 1990s. Growth in the past frequently contributed to soaring costs. This change in policy has led to closing inefficient plants, downsizing operations, and pay-ing more attention to core-brand performance. A bottom-line culture has developed, measured by earnings, return on investment, increasing cash flow, and low costs. The emphasis on core brands was partially due to the fact that soup lines are the source of highest profit margins.

The bottom-line culture has extended to various cost-reduction strategies. For example, plans were underway to reduce the twenty-eight ingredients in the their vegetable soup to as few as eleven ingredients. This included eliminating okra, squash, and the pulverized beef that contributed to extra flavor. Consumer test groups were receptive, and similar adjustments were made to other soup lines. The resulting savings helped to save millions of dollars.

Campbell Soup and Progresso are competitively priced at retail levels. Generic brands and private labels offer considerable savings but without favorable brand images. Soup manufacturers have done a good job in developing brand power. Moreover, efficiency and low-cost business systems have given soup manufacturers an important advantage when competing with store brands. Campbell did attempt to sell a higher-priced soup line called Golden Classics, but encountered consumer resistance, and this product line was withdrawn. Price strategy has been increasingly used by the soup industry as an active rather than passive element of corporate and marketing strategies. Although private labels have not made significant inroads in market share, Campbell and Progresso would be making a serious mistake in using pricing strategy without considering costs. This strategy would not only reduce profitability, but would present an opportunity for store brands to increase market share.

Campbell Soup has lost condensed soup market share to foreign manufacturers such as Nissen, which markets inexpensive dry soups made from long, thin ramen noodles. Campbell has been slow to exploit this segment of the soup market. Lipton has also found it difficult to compete in the ramen soup market.

In an effort to decrease costs, soup manufacturers purchase ingredients of suitable quality in sufficient quantities only at certain seasons. Generally, ingredient inventories are at a peak during the late fall and decline during the winter and spring. The prices of ingredients do fluctuate significantly from time to time. Moreover, it would appear that the soup industry is not threatened by pending claims or litigation, which would impact pricing strategies. However, environmental-protection legislation is a constant source of concern, and soup manufacturers monitor pending environmental legislation closely.

DISTRIBUTION STRATEGIES

In the late 1980s, distribution strategy reflected the growing strength of the retailer, and consumer-product companies, including Campbell and ConAgra, Inc., reportedly reorganized their marketing departments around key retail accounts. Prior to the reorganization, Campbell had salespeople from each of its divisions, such as Pepperidge Farm and Swanson frozen prepared foods, servicing retailers. After the reorganization, a single sales representative handled all of the Campbell products. The advantage of this strategy was to increase sales across the board rather than emphasize individual brands. This strategy also allowed key account managers to negotiate with retailers on pricing, packaging, promotion, and delivery. Furthermore, sales representatives, with the aid of laptop computers, were able to perform overnight distribution analysis in order to better serve retailers. Moreover, Campbell has been able to lower costs by shipping truckloads of soup to large retailers, such as Kroger Company. Kroger, in turn, stores the soup in its warehouses and then transports and replenishes the supply as needed. Campbell does not sell direct to small retailers, but sells to wholesalers in large quantities, thereby diminishing handling costs.

In the 1990s, strategy changes reflected the regional market segmentation that was introduced by Campbell. In metropolitan areas, a personal selling force is used to directly service retailers. In rural areas, such as Iowa and South Dakota, for example, food brokers are responsible for distribution. Cost efficiency dictates the use of food brokers in rural areas, while in metropolitan areas as many as eight or nine retailers can be serviced within two or three city blocks. Sales promotion devices such as free samples, two for one purchases and in-store coupons are used to motivate consumers to try particular soup products. Regionalization means that a sales representative may service only a few stores. Closer monitoring of specific localities would allow for regional tastes to be satisfied, such as providing Brunswich Stew for the Southeast or Cajun Gumbo Soup for the Mississippi Delta area.

This approach allowed Campbell's Home Cookin' ready-to-serve soups to surge by 14 percent in 1993. The product line featured a redesigned label and new varieties of New England Clam Chowder and Chicken Vegetable. Campbell's Healthy Request 98 percent fat-free emerged to a leadership position in the "healthy soup" category. Such varieties as Italian Tomato and Golden Corn were added to the product line. Campbell's Double Noodle dry soup was introduced, and as a result its dry soup volume increased 11 percent. Regionalization fosters a partnership approach with retailers in which both manufacturers and retailers provide inputs, and has caused Campbell to regain its 80 percent market share of the soup market in 1990s.

Each soup manufacturer, Campbell, Lipton, Progresso (Pet, Inc.), and ConAgra (Healthy Choice), has enough size to maintain a select supplier program. A select supplier program establishes a partnership with suppliers of ingredients, packaging, equipment, and distribution services. The initial phase addresses such issues as technical capabilities, capacities, and compliance with regulatory agencies. The intermediate phase emphasizes database systems between the manufacturer and supplier and a just-in-time delivery program. The final stage involves continuous training of personnel and the refinements of productivity improvements and achievements. The long-term relationship between manufacturer and supplier should be beneficial in terms of product quality and cost containment.

Soup manufacturers have endeavored to design their distribution strategies around market geography, which deals with the physical location of markets and their distance from the manufacturer, and market size, which deals with the number of retailers in a given market. Regional market segmentation has permitted manufacturers to closely monitor market density, which deals with the number of retailers per unit of geographical area. Moreover, a breakdown of consumer behavior deals with local tastes and preferences and analyzes other demographic and behavioral characteristics of consumer segments. An understanding of these dimensions is essential to the success of marketing strategies.

The partnership approach represents a more sophisticated and comprehensive approach to retailer motivation. Essentially, the partnership approach is based on a careful delineation of the mutual roles of all institutions in the distribution process. It underscores the commitments expected by manufacturers and the support that retailers and wholesalers can anticipate from the manufacturer.

WHY CAMPBELL SOUP IS BLOOMING

Campbell Soup has altered its soup products to suit regional tastes, and this has been an important reason why Campbell is presently the leader in the soup industry. Campbell has far outdistanced the competition in the areas of regional market segmentation and the use of technology, particularly emphasizing inventory-control procedures with laptop computers and automated equipment in distribution centers. Campbell's strong emphasis on the professional development of personnel, especially sales representatives, is another feature that distinguishes Campbell from its competition. Image development is paramount, and Campbell has achieved a reputation for product quality. Brand power has been at the core of Campbell's success, and this strategy is wisely used. The red-and-white colors and the artwork by Andy Warhol have made Campbell a legend in the soup industry.

In summary, the ability to innovate with new soup products, a passion for product quality, and sales representatives who have strengthened relationships with retailers have all been ingredients that have spelled success. Moreover, top management has been effective at mobilizing human resources behind a vision and communicating strategies to subordinates. The successful use of innovation, image development, and market segmentation and the effective mobilization of human and physical resources is the reason why Campbell is still blooming. Moreover, Campbell plans to spin off businesses such as Swanson frozen foods and Vlasic pickles, and focus on its more profitable lines. This will allow Campbell to concentrate on its core soup business.

Campbell's sales representatives are well trained. Campbell makes it a practice to hire career-oriented individuals rather than job-oriented individuals.

Marketing Successes in the Soup Industry

- Industry participants, with Campbell Soup as the leader preventing store-brand entry, have implemented effective regional market segmentation.

- Industry participants have effectively cultivated ethnic preferences, with Progresso targeting the Italian market and Goya Foods targeting the Hispanic market. Campbell, with Casera, is going head-to-head with Goya Foods, a small manufacturer, for penetration of the Hispanic market. The ethnic population is increasing, and this market segmentation strategy is viewed as a forward step.
- Industry participants, particularly Campbell and Progresso, have made effective use of computer equipment for inventory-control purposes.
- Both large and small soup manufacturers, but especially Campbell and Progresso, have effectively used sales representatives.
- The major players, Campbell, Lipton, and Progresso, have all developed positive images with their customers.
- Distribution centers and distributors have been strategically situated and selected to insure maximum product availability and replacement.
- The soup industry, now in the maturity stage of the product life cycle, has focused on dealer incentives, thereby insuring retailer profitability and promoting cooperation.
- Campbell has effectively motivated top and middle managers, and this has served as a standard for the industry to follow.

Marketing Mistakes in the Soup Industry

- The soup industry has been slow to respond to consumer desires to consume more healthy soups with less sodium, lower fat, and lower cholesterol, thereby promoting market-driven rather than customer-driven strategies.
- There has been an overreliance on price competition without consideration of costs. This strategy has reduced profitability.
- The soup industry, in particular, Campbell and Lipton, has been reactive and not proactive to ethnic population changes. This slowness has allowed Goya Foods to dominate the Hispanic market and Nissen Foods to dominate the ramen noodle market.
- Campbell was slow to develop the Prego brand to compete with the Progresso Italian-style soups.

MANAGING CHANGE

The soup industry has responded to those consumers concerned with health and fitness. Campbell's Healthy Request is 98 percent fat-free. ConAgra has launched Healthy Choice. Progresso (Pet, Inc.) has been the real innovator in the healthy soup market by offering soups in lower-fat, lower-cholesterol versions and with one-third less sodium. Progresso was the first firm to really stir up the healthy soup market, and subsequently Campbell and ConAgra followed. The aging of the population, particularly the baby boomers, should make the healthy soup market more attractive in the future.

The ethnic composition of the U.S. population is also changing. Hispanics are the second-largest and fastest growing minority group in the United States. The Bureau of the Census projects that by 2010 Hispanics will account for 14 percent of the population and will outnumber African-American consumers. Hispanics already constitute a majority of the population in Miami, San Antonio, and El Paso. The Hispanic population is largely of Mexican (61 percent), Puerto Rican (15 percent), and Cuban (7 percent) origin. They have clustered in six cities: Miami for Cubans; Los Angeles, San Antonio, and Houston for Mexicans; New York for Puerto Ricans; and Chicago, which hosts a mix of all groups.

Hispanic Americans are more likely than the European American population to stress product quality, to value well-known brands, to be brand loyal, and seemingly to be receptive to new products. Thus the use of regional market segmentation strategies can be most useful in targeting precise segments of the Hispanic population, whether it be Mexican, Puerto Rican, Cuban, or Central or South American. The increasing interest of Americans in Hispanic food has contributed to change in the soup market. Goya Foods, Inc., a family-owned company, dominates the Hispanic soup market. Goya is well entrenched on the East Coast and in parts of the Midwest. Campbell, to increase its chances for success, targets Casera (which means home-cooked in Spanish) to the younger, more affluent Hispanic segment. This segment has yet to develop the brand loyalty of older generations. Many Hispanics purchase Goya and other food products in small neighborhood grocery stores, whereas Campbell and Progresso have ties with supermarket chains.

Soup marketing executives have responded to changes in technology with microwaveable soups. Consumers' time constraints have also promoted the sales of dehydrated soups. Since there has been a growth in the singles market and families with members on different schedules, the soup industry has changed its packaging to serve single portions of soup without leftovers. Even though mistakes have been made, the major players in the soup industry, Campbell, Progresso, and Lipton, have been able to prevent, to a large extent, the entry of store brands.

MANAGERIAL INSIGHTS

The competition between retailers' brands and manufacturers' brands has been called the battle of the brands. The battle is over shelf space, and in this battle, retailers have the advantage. Supermarkets have made many inroads into the market share of manufacturers' brands, but not in the soup industry. Large manufacturers like Campbell Soup and Lipton have considerable financial resources, which enables them to conduct superior product research and development and to satisfy changing consumer wants and needs with a constant stream of new products. Moreover, these large manufacturers are able to offer promotional support to middlemen and to retain control over the commodity components that make up the product, thereby underscoring cost efficiencies.

Soup manufacturers have dominated the soup industry through the strong development of brand preference. Campbell, Lipton, and Progresso have developed strong brand images to create consumer demand for their products. Consequently, retailers are assured of profits by stocking their soup brands, making it less likely that retailers will counter with their own store brands. Large retailers have an edge in gaining control by virtue of their close proximity to local markets, and generally are the winners with manufacturers of low-price consumer goods. However, in this case regional market segmentation by soup manufacturers, and in particular by Campbell Soup, has offset this inherent advantage by large supermarket chains.

In the absence of a strong consumer preference for manufacturers' brands, supermarket chains have been able to profitably sell their own brands. Soup manufacturers have gained power through strong brand identification, and this is especially important in the case of products sold through retail outlets such as supermarkets and other types of grocery stores. Only those manufacturers who enjoy extremely high levels of customer demand for their products, through entrenched brand acceptance, will be able to win the battle for shelf space in retail food stores.

In the past Heinz and currently Ralston Purina have produced the bulk of private-label or store brands in the soup industry. Market share of private-label soup brands is significantly under 7 or 8 percent, and therefore these brands have not been a large competitive threat to soup manufacturers. Large supermarket chains have made significant inroads with private brands in bakery, dairy, frozen fruit juices, and frozen vegetables. Canned fruit and vegetables are other areas that have lost market share to large supermarket chains.

The soup industry, specifically Campbell, has used several techniques to market soup to and through food stores. These techniques and strategies have focused on the use of advanced technology, the concentration on outrageous objectives rather than on continuous improvement, and the ability to capitalize quickly on unexpected new opportunities and to continually focus on satisfying the customer. Moreover, Campbell has been very creative at the tactical level. For example, all major storms moving across the United States are monitored during the winter months. This strategy allows

Campbell to advertise "hot soup for cold weather" on the radio before, during, and after a storm.

Laptop computers have been used aggressively by sales representatives of soup manufacturers to monitor retail inventory control. Campbell Soup has encouraged its managers to try to satisfy outrageous objectives rather than maintain the proven status quo. The soup industry has moved quickly in response to changing consumer demographic and behavioral purchasing patterns. The fulfillment of changing consumer health and fitness desires has been a goal quickly attained by the soup industry.

Mistakes have been made by soup manufacturers. Campbell entered the baby soup market and quickly withdrew, suffering heavy losses. Heinz lost its brand position through complacency and finally lost out to Ralston Purina in producing store brands. Campbell was slow to learn the value of brand power and lost considerable market share until it finally capitalized on brand promotion in the 1990s. The soup industry, with Campbell leading the way, has tried to lengthen the season for soup consumption, but consumers still have not responded well to these efforts.

CHAPTER 5

THE BREAKFAST CEREAL INDUSTRY

Successful Strategies
- Market segmentation and product differentiation
- Lifestyle market segmentation
- Benefit segmentation
- Branding and packaging strategies
- Promotion of brand power
- Monitoring environmental changes
- Good information systems
- Strength of product assortment

Marketing Mistakes
- Overestimating pricing strategies
- Overestimating sales promotion strategies (such as coupons)
- Reacting to trends rather than developing proactive strategies
- Slow to grasp changes in customer demographics
- High costs due to product failures

About a century ago Kellogg stressed the healthy, nutritious quality of cornflakes. Today, a century later, Kellogg, General Mills, General Foods, Nabisco, and others are still emphasizing the healthy, nutritious appeal of breakfast cereals. In the past, the Kellogg brothers were obsessed with substituting a product for the meat that lumberjacks ate for breakfast. Americans were living more sedate lives, and therefore their diets needed correction. Over a century later, such phrases as low in sodium, fat, and cholesterol have become buzzwords to guide dietary eating habits. Breakfast foods may have changed or been modified, but guidelines for healthy living are still present in the American culture.

Competition has been an important aspect of the breakfast cereal industry since the turn of the century. Twenty breakfast food companies were established by 1901, but Kellogg was still dominant. C. W. Post, as early as 1891, desired a partnership with Kellogg. When denied this partnership, Post developed his own brand of cornflakes. Kellogg accused Post of stealing its formula to develop Post Toasties, but this charge was never substantiated.

The breakfast cereal industry targets several diverse markets but focuses upon two large ones, namely the baby boomers and their children. Since a high proportion of the baby boomers are highly educated, health appeals are paramount. Thus the emphasis was placed on various types of oat-bran cereal. The other sizable market, targeted to children, has responded well to appeals from sports personalities and from trade characters such as Tony the Tiger. Marketing strategies have been developed and aimed at both of these sizable markets.

In the 1990s, the breakfast cereal industry raised prices so much that even members of Congress have wondered about and, indeed, investigated these pricing policies. Although there is some justification for the substantial increase in cereal prices, competition has forced openings. The door has been opened to private-store labels, and inroads have been made into the breakfast cereal industry. Competition from frozen waffles, pancakes, and French toast brands has been a concern in both the past and the present. New competition has arisen from the consumption of bagels and muffins for breakfast. Whether or not this trend reflects a change in dietary habits or cereal price increases remains uncertain.

One big problem confronted by the breakfast cereal industry has been the escalating promotional activity by all competitors in the U.S. ready-to-eat cereal market. This activity resulted in reduced profits and little change in market share in the 1990s. Inefficiencies were also generated by coupons and in-store promotions. For example, more than 95 percent of cereal coupons issued were thrown away and not redeemed, and approximately half of promotional expenditures do not reach consumers in the form of lower prices. The breakfast cereal industry has moved to lower prices due to these inefficiencies, congressional investigations, and competitive threats. Retailers devote significant shelf space to cereals because they are among the most profitable products in the store. Returns earned by cereal manufacturers exceed most other grocery products, promoting fierce competition among manufacturers.

Today, Kellogg's marketing strategies revolve around a combination of five attributes: nutrition and health, taste, convenience, price or value, and quality. Almost a century ago, the Kellogg Health Institute in Battle Creek, Michigan, appealed for better nutrition. Moreover, for the convenience of retailers and consumers alike, Kellogg was the first company to market cereal in boxes rather than barrels. It is amazing how similar values and appeals have withstood the test of time and are still present in today's market.

There are a combination of variables that contribute to the successes and failures of the breakfast cereal industry. These variables and strategies include innovation, target-market segmentation, image, physical environment resources, and human resources. Such factors must be combined in varying degrees in order to succeed. The breakfast cereal industry has shown innovation in product and packaging strategies. Breakfast cereal snack bars are a new product innovation. General Mills, with its Betty Crocker Dutch apple and cinnamon streusel flavors, makes clear the connection between the Betty Crocker brand and its appeals to dessert lovers. General Mills hopes to stimulate an industry suffering from the blahs of endless line extensions. New product introductions have not been winners, and consumers have looked to bagels and muffins for a convenient morning breakfast.

The breakfast cereal industry has been adept at target-market segmentation and promoting favorable brand images. The strategy of the cereal industry, and especially of the Kellogg Company, has been to provide a comprehensive assortment for retailers targeting specific market segments. Some of these efforts by Kellogg have been mistakes, such as Most, a high-fiber wheat cereal directed primarily to health-conscious adults, and Smart Start, a flaked corn and wheat cereal that was high in iron and directed toward working women. Graham Crackers and Crunchy Loggs, two pre-sweetened cereals directed to the children's market, were also mistakes. In contrast, Kellogg's Special K, directed at the low-cholesterol market segment, All-Bran, directed to the high-fiber segment and Product 19, for dieters, appear to have been successful brands. Quaker Oats has been successful in appealing to the children's market with Cap'n Crunch, and General Mills' Wheaties has stood the test of time.

The image of the breakfast cereal industry has been positive enough to withstand the assault of private-label brands. Family cereals, such as Kellogg's Corn Flakes and General Mills' Cheerios, have been around for years. Inroads have been made by store brands, and according to *Consumer Reports*, these brands are reasonably priced and good tasting. Cited among the raisin brans were Sam's American Choice Extra Raisin from Wal-Mart and Public, cereal from a supermarket chain in the southern states. Some years ago the taste of store brands was a negative factor, but this variable is changing.

Large cereal manufacturers with successful track records and huge advertising budgets, such as Kellogg and General Mills, don't have much difficulty in convincing retailers to give their new product introductions a chance. It is no secret, since it was revealed by Federal Trade Commission testimony in the 1970s, that Kellogg designed shelf-space allocation programs for supermarkets. Sophisticated computers and programs developed by members of the breakfast cereal industry now help to allocate shelf space according to turnover. The breakfast cereal industry has been successful in designing packaging for shipping and for display purposes.

MARKET STRUCTURE

Kellogg is the dominant firm in the breakfast cereal industry. General Mills is a close second, with Quaker Oats, Ralston, and Nabisco trailing far behind. Private labels have increased their market share in recent years, but hold less than 10 percent market share and are not considered a significant threat to cereal manufacturers.

Kellogg is well known for its Frosted Flakes, Corn Flakes, Raisin Bran, and Special K brands. General Mills, through the years, has developed best-selling brands such as Cheerios, Wheaties, Golden Grahams, and Corn and Wheat Total. Quaker Oats is well known for Cap'n Crunch and Life. Philip Morris has acquired Post and offers Post Grape-Nuts. Quaker Oats dominates the hot cereal market, while Nabisco, also acquired by Philip Morris, is a distant second, offering Cream of Wheat. The following brands have been mainstays over long periods of time: Kellogg's Corn Flakes, General Mills' Wheaties, Post Grape-Nuts, and Quaker Oats.

Table 5.1
A Market-Share Range for Cereal Manufacturers, 1996

Manufacturers	Selected Brands	Market Share
Kellogg	Corn Flakes, Rice Krispies, Frosted Flakes	34-37%
General Mills	Cheerios, Wheaties, Total	20-24%
Post	Grape Nuts, Raisin Bran	16-20%
Quaker	Hot Cereals, Cap'n Crunch, Life	6-7%
Ralston Purina	Private Labels, Chex	4-6%
Nabisco	SnackWell's, Hot Cereals	2-3%
Malt-O-Meal	clones of well-known brands	2-3%
Private Labels	N/A	8-10%

Note: Compiled from the literature in the field. Market-share figures are approximate, with constant fluctuations, and reflect recent price competition in 1996.

Table 5.1, A Market-Share Range for Cereal Manufacturers, 1996, reflects domestic figures only. Post, Kraft, General Foods, and Nabisco are all part of the Philip Morris organization. Post assumed a leadership role in the industry by implementing a price cut of about 20 percent on all of its cereals. Post was subsequently followed by General Mills, Kellogg, and Quaker. Private labels have also been making increasing inroads in the cereal market (because of low prices). Ralcorp, a spin-off of Ralston Purina, has become more aggressive by duplicating many of the major brands and placing the retailer's name on the boxes to make them store brands.

Malt-O-Meal has been marketing hot wheat cereal since 1919, and in the 1960s began making Puffed Rice and Puffed Wheat, ready-to-eat cereals. By the 1970s, Malt-O-Meal was producing low-cost, high-quality clones of the largest, most heavily advertised cold cereals. Malt-O-Meal offers retailers generous profit margins of 15 to 20 percent, compared with 12 percent from the largest well-known cereal brands. Store brands are produced for chains like Kroger, Safeway, and Super Value. Clones are offered of Golden Crisp, Fruit Loops, Cocoa Puffs, and Lucky Charms. Versions are offered of Crispy Rice, Puffed Wheat, Puffed Rice, Frosted Flakes, Corn Flakes, and Raisin Bran. Malt-O-Meal appears to be well positioned in a fast-growing category.

General Mills has acquired Ralcorp, a spin-off of Ralston Purina. Chex and the other brands have had no more than a 2 percent market share of the breakfast cereal industry. Ralcorp retained its interest in manufacturing private labels.

Technology has helped the breakfast cereal industry to improve its packaging, thereby maintaining a fresher product and protecting it for transportation. Kellogg was the innovator and, in 1914, was one of the first firms to use Waxtite, a plastic inside the cereal box that keeps the product fresh. Technology has also allowed cereal manufacturers to more accurately measure product contents so that each box receives the same amount of cereal.

The ready-to-eat cereal industry is composed of firms engaged in the manufacture and sale of prepackaged, processed foodstuffs made primarily from grain products. The consumer does not need to prepare the product prior to consumption, and it can be eaten in dry form or with milk and sugar. Cereal is used primarily at breakfast, but also can be consumed as between-meal snacks. The first products marketed were Wheat Flakes in 1894 and Corn Flakes in 1898, which were introduced by Kellogg. Although cereals constitute more than two-thirds of Kellogg's sales, cereals are estimated to represent no more than 15 percent of General Foods' sales and about 7 percent of General Mills' sales.

Competition is intense in the breakfast cereal industry. The research and development of new products are essential in order to successfully compete. Budgets for advertising and promotion have increased substantially in recent years in order to introduce new products and to maintain existing products.

The leading brands in the cold-cereal market are Kellogg's Corn Flakes, Frosted Flakes, Raisin Bran, and Rice Krispies; General Mills' Cheerios and Honey Nut Cheerios; Nabisco's Shredded Wheat; Ralston's Chex; General Foods' Raisin Bran; and Quaker's Cap'n Crunch.

MARKET CONDUCT

The market is composed of individuals and organizations with the purchasing power, the interest, and the desire to purchase a specified product. Therefore, the lifestyles of the people who comprise the market are an important consideration. Consumer markets are composed of individuals purchasing either for themselves or for their households. When markets are identified, marketers must analyze them to detect the opportunities and threats that may be present. To illustrate, Kellogg was slow to realize that consumer lifestyles in the 1980s were changing and consequently it lost market share to General Mills which was worth about $60 million in sales.

Consumers were changing their dietary habits to reflect more healthy eating habits. Consumers were, and still are, reading the labels and desiring something healthy like oats and bran. General Mills was quick to take advantage of consumers' shift in lifestyles and profited from these new opportunities. Kellogg eventually reacted to these changes.

Kellogg has used distribution strategy to gain control of the market. For example, providing assortment within the product category helps to dominate the market. Kellogg offers a variety of product choices, which lowers retailer's costs, since switching to another manufacturer increases the retailer's cost. The retailer, in order to displace Kellogg, would need to make agreements with many manufacturers that each cover only part of the product category.

Manufacturers, private-store labels, and generic brands repeatedly engage in a battle of the brands in which each endeavors to gain greater control over marketing strategy, product distinctiveness, maximum shelf space and favorable store locations, and a larger share of profits. Store-brand cereal comprises about 7 or 8 percent of all cereal sales and about 12 percent of cornflakes sold in the United States. This 12 percent market share is about double the market share captured in the 1980s. Kellogg sells its cornflakes for about double the price of store brands. Cornflakes has become generic, while Wheaties is still a brand that retains consumer loyalty. Kellogg's strategy has been to use coupons and other discounts, but this practice has been abandoned in favor of price reductions.

Eventually, Kellogg successfully targeted the health-conscious consumer market. All-Bran cereal was launched to appeal to the high-fiber market segment, and Special K to a low-cholesterol segment. Nutri-Grain cereals were targeted to fitness-oriented young adults, and Product 19 was positioned as a dieter's cereal. Finally, Nutrific, a combination of barley, bran, almonds, and raisins was aimed at consumers desiring a natural cereal. General Mills and Quaker also quickly reacted and developed more comprehensive product lines to satisfy consumer health needs.

The battle for the health-conscious consumer market segment has been fierce in the breakfast cereal industry. Kellogg was successful in establishing an image for its total product line of adult cereals. This image was linked to specific nutritional and health needs. The strategy of need segmentation was important for identifying target segments such as the high-fiber segment, the dieters, the nutrition oriented, and the natural-ingredients segment.

The leading companies in the breakfast cereal industry have developed a strategy that links the brand name to the company's name instead of identifying products by individual brand names. For example, Kellogg's Rice Krispies and Special K as well as General Mills' Total Raisin Bran and Total Corn Flakes are all cereals that have employed this strategy. This brand-identification decision by the leading firms in the breakfast cereal industry has helped them to successfully compete with retailers' brands. The battle is over shelf space and the consumer's dollar, and in this battle, retailers have an advantage. The breakfast cereal firms, however, have been able to fend off private-brand competition by offering product-line depth and high brand identification.

Another aspect of market conduct has been the development of snack cereal bars. Nabisco, with its SnackWell's brand, has entered the cereal aisle with fat-free breakfast bars. Granola bars, made with Nabisco best-sellers Oreo, Chips Ahoy, and Nutter Butter, are also available. Quaker Rice Cakes and Granola Bars are also competitors in this snack and break-fast market. It is important to consider this market as both a breakfast and a snack market. There are consumers who eat breakfast "on the run," and these snack cereal bars would satisfy their needs and also fortify them dur-ing the rest of the day. Kellogg's Nutri-Grain cereal bars appeals to people with these new lifestyles. Since these breakfast bars have appropriate stor-age capability and shelf life, retailers have readily accepted this new prod-uct. This product, aimed at the breakfast and snack market, has good potential for distribution in vending machines.

Quaker, in 1995, expanded its product line of value-priced cereals in bags, and this is considered a small but rapidly advancing product category. As long as technology and packaging make possible product innovation in the breakfast cereal industry, new product categories will be introduced and an otherwise flat sales market may be expanded. For example, Malt-O-Meal and Quaker Oats sell bagged, renamed versions of Cocoa Puffs, Lucky Charms, and Frosted Flakes for about one dollar less than the orig-inals. These firms have developed a cost-saving alternative and have made market-share inroads into the breakfast cereal market.

CASE STUDIES

Kellogg: An Effective Innovator

In 1894 Will Kellogg, a vegetarian from Battle Creek, Michigan, devel-oped a method to make nutritious wheat meal more appealing to patients in his brother's sanitarium. The process converted the unappetizing wheat meal into attractive, tasty, small cereal flakes. These crunchy flakes would change the breakfast meal in the United States so that it would never be the same again. Kellogg, a devoutly religious Seventh-Day Adventist, founded the Kellogg Company in 1906, launching a "cornflake crusade" to change the eating habits of the American population. Will Kellogg's innovation spawned the breakfast cereal industry, where a half dozen large competitors now battle for shares of a $6 billion market. Since the very beginning, the Kellogg Company has been the industry leader, with inno-vative technology and marketing strategies.

During the 1950s and 1960s, Kellogg and other cereal manufacturers prospered because of demographic trends and improved television tech-nology. The post–World War II baby boom appreciably expanded the mar-ket potential of the breakfast cereal industry. Kellogg launched new lines of presweetened cereals that included Sugar Frosted Flakes, Sugar Smacks, and Cocoa Crispies. Tony the Tiger and other cartoon figures sold the products on Saturday morning television.

Kellogg successfully implemented a product differentation and market segmentation strategy for the breakfast cereal industry. For example, Kellogg targeted the low-cholesterol segment with Special K, the nutrition-oriented segment with Müeslix, and the high-fiber segment with All-Bran.

The marketing environment changed in the 1980s as the aging baby boomers became weight conscious and concerned about their physical fitness. The baby boom had been replaced by zero population growth, and as a result, industry sales growth flattened. After decades of profiting from industry sales growth, breakfast cereal manufacturers were now battling in a stagnant market. In today's age of product diversification, Kellogg's decision to remain totally committed to the cereal industry is unusual. General Mills and Quaker Oats have diversified into other areas. However, neither has done well in areas outside of the food industry, and both have scaled back their efforts in favor of concentrating on food marketing.

Kellogg stumbled briefly in the early 1980s, when its market share declined from 43 percent in 1972 to 37 percent in 1983, but the leader regained its footing in the late 1980s. Kellogg launched a massive campaign to reposition its products and to satisfy desires spawned by changing lifestyles. For example, Kellogg attempted to capture the adult market with several high-fiber products, such as All-Bran, 40 Percent Bran Flakes, Bran Buds, Raisin Bran, and Cracklin' Oat Bran. Many of these brands proved unsuccessful, but consumers were given many choices about how they could eat their bran.

Kellogg has been confronted with fierce competition from General Mills. General Mills launched Triples Cereal, which is very similar to Rice Krispies. It also launched sugar-coated Wheaties Gold Cereal in order to compete with Kellogg's Frosted Flakes. General Mills has dominated the presweetened cereal market with Honey Nut Cheerios, Trix, Lucky Charms, and Golden Grahams. Kellogg has sought to overcome the advantage of General Mills in the presweetened market, but it is still behind. Through the years, Kellogg launched new product lines designed for specific market segments. This approach can be expensive, for example, when such brands as Common Sense Oat Bran, Kenner Rice Bran, and Heartwise proved unsuccessful. However, Kellogg's strategy of maintaining a comprehensive product line does satisfy retailers, and also helps to preclude competition. Offering retailers a comprehensive product assortment also has its weakness, inasmuch as a high product failure rate increases costs, which are then passed on to the consumers. This opens a window of opportunity for store brands to increase market share.

Another dimension of Kellogg's strategy continues to be aggressive marketing and advertising support for its products. Funds are also appropriated to expand and modernize production facilities and to maintain low production costs. The core of Kellogg's profits is generated by cereals, but the company has diversified somewhat along other food product lines. For instance, Mrs. Smith's pies and Kellogg's Eggo frozen waffles have been notable successes.

Kellogg's market share of the U.S. cold cereal market has declined from 40.5 percent in 1988 to 33.2 percent in 1997. Lower-priced private-label store brands are accountable for most of the erosion in market share. Another reason for this decrease in market share has been that consumers are substituting products such as bagels, muffins, and other on-the-go breakfast foods for ready-to-eat cereals. Kellogg has fought back by acquiring Lender's Bagels and marketing Nutri-Grain bars. Innovation seems focused on product-line extensions, such as the recent development of Honey Crunch Corn Flakes and Cocoa Frosted Flakes. Kellogg and other brand cereal manufacturers need to focus on cost control and profitability rather than engaging in price wars and concentrating solely on market share as a competitive weapon.

General Mills: Superior New-Product Management

The turbulent 1980s for the breakfast cereal industry caused the two leading cereal manufacturers to develop vastly different strategic plans. While Kellogg decided to concentrate its resources in the breakfast cereal industry, General Mills began an aggressive diversification program. The company, by the early 1980s, was operating in five major business areas: consumer foods, restaurants, toys, fashions and specialty retailing. However, by 1985 General Mills moved out of toys and fashions and began to concentrate instead on consumer foods and restaurants. Toys and fashions proved to be high in risk and capital-intensive, and required a specialized expertise not inherent within a food-oriented company. Obviously, such acquisitions as Parker Brothers, Izod Ltd., and Ship'n Shore were mistakes and were divested. Interestingly, Quaker Oats reached a different decision from that of either General Mills or Kellogg, deciding to expand its basic food businesses. Thus, the strategic choices about where the firm was going in the future—choices that consider company capabilities, resources, and opportunities—were different for General Mills, Kellogg, and Quaker.

General Mills' origins can be traced to 1866, when Cadwallader Washburn opened a flour mill in Minneapolis, Minnesota. From these beginnings grew General Mills, a prominent flour miller in the United States. In 1928, the network of grain and flour mills that became General Mills was to operate under a revised corporate mission.

Product planning and development resulted in 1931 in Bisquick, the first prepared mix. Cheerios, the first ready-to-eat oat cereal, was developed by 1941. Marketing efforts established such trade names as Wheaties (cereal), Gold Medal (flour), and Betty Crocker (mixes) into established brand names with national consumer recognition. Millions of young radio listeners were brought up with the long-running "Jack Armstrong, the All-American Boy" program sponsored by General Mills' Wheaties. The slogan "Wheaties, Breakfast of Champions," with modifications, has survived into the 1990s, as a series of athletes including Bruce Jenner and Mary Lou Retton have promoted the product.

Packaged foods accounted for 18 percent of General Mills sales in the 1950s as opposed to 9 percent in 1938. Flour declined from 74 percent of sales to only about half of sales. Eventually, in the 1960s, General Mills made the decision not to divest itself of flour entirely, but merely to maintain a presence, since flour was profitable but quite seasonal, and there were peaks and valleys of production and demand. This decision, made in the mid-1960s, struck at the very core of General Mills—it was no longer to be the largest flour miller in the United States.

By the mid-1980s, General Mills had learned some hard lessons about the difficulties of managing widely diversified businesses such as toys, food, and specialty retailing. Specialty-retailing businesses, such as Talbots and Eddie Bauer, were sold, and so were other divisions. General Mills had decided to engage in food marketing. Emphasis was placed on internal growth and joint ventures. General Mills signed a joint venture agreement with Nestlé in 1989. This strategic alliance aimed to develop a major breakfast cereal business in Europe to be called Cereal Partners Worldwide. In the United States, General Mills gained market share as a result of the oat-bran craze. Forty percent of General Mills cereals are made from oats. Kellogg was slow to react to this market change, and General Mills' market share increased from 21 percent in 1979 to 27 percent in 1989. Cheerios replaced Kellogg's Frosted Flakes as the most popular cereal in America. This uphill fight in the cereal industry was not without pitfalls. General Mills ran afoul of the Food and Drug Administration (FDA) in marketing Benefit cereal. Even though the cholesterol-reducing claim was dropped from the packaging and advertisement, Benefit was removed from the market in 1990 because of a lack of sales.

The early 1990s were profitable years for General Mills. Cheerios and Wheaties remained among the top cereals sold and were selected by McDonald's to be sold as part of their breakfast menu. The Cheerios and Total cereal brands accounted for nearly half of General Mills' cereal business. General Mills, with the acquisition of the Chex brand from Ralcorp in 1996, increased its brand power. General Mills has been aggressive in allocating its promotion budget, and this in part is responsible for its success. For example, more than $160 million is annually appropriated to promote just six cereal brands: Cheerios, Total, Oatmeal Raisin Crisp, Lucky Charms, Raisin Nut Bran, and Wheaties. Consequently, in recent years, inroads have been made into Kellogg's market share lead.

Marketing innovation and continuous product improvement has helped

General Mills to increase its market share of the breakfast cereal market in the 1990s. Effective promotion aimed at both parents and children for Kix cereal helped the more than fifty-year-old brand achieve a 7 percent volume gain. The tastes of Cheerios and Wheaties were both improved. The company's newest brands, Reese's Peanut Butter Puffs and Sun Crunchers cereal with sunflower seeds, represent distinctive new tastes in the cereal aisle. Fruit and nuts were added to other brands. Consumption in the breakfast cereal industry has increased in recent years, and General Mills has shared in this growth.

General Mills, like the rest of the breakfast cereal industry in the 1990s, has been caught in the middle of escalating grain prices. These increases in prices were passed on to consumers. It is uncertain about how much the impact of a congressional investigation influenced members of the breakfast cereal industry to lower prices. However, suddenly the prices for breakfast cereal were lowered on many brands. Post and General Mills decreased prices on their entire product line, whereas Kellogg was more selective. Moreover, General Mills views some of its cereal brands as possible snacks, and if promotion of this view is successful, will have the competitive advantage over both Kellogg and Post.

Post, the cereal division of Philip Morris, led the price cuts in 1995, and this in itself is significant, inasmuch as Post is the number three cereal manufacturer and trails Kellogg and General Mills. Post demonstrated an aggressive strategy, and Kellogg and General Mills may have much to fear in the way of future competition. Philip Morris owns both General Foods and Kraft, and there is little doubt that Post cereals will benefit from this strength.

Post: Effective Strategic Planning

Post is the third-largest cereal manufacturer behind Kellogg and General Mills. Kellogg has approximately three times the market share of Post, and General Mills has approximately two and one-half times the market share of Post in the breakfast cereal industry. Post's leading brand is Grape-Nuts, which is one of the ten best-selling cereal brands. Grape-Nuts was introduced in 1897 and has survived the test of time.

In 1891, Charles W. Post was a patient in the Kellogg brother's sanitarium in Battle Creek, Michigan, and it was here that he was first introduced to breakfast cereal. Post tried to purchase a partnership in the Kellogg organization, but his offer was refused. Post was a health fanatic who endeavored to lure coffee drinkers away from the caffeinated drink with a cereal beverage called Postum. The Postum Cereal Company was formed in 1896. Some years later, in 1929, this company acquired the General Foods Company owned by Clarence Birdseye. In 1985, Philip Morris purchased General Foods and acquired its Post Cereal Division, which had a declining sales problem. When Philip Morris purchased Kraft in 1988, the possible impact on the food industry became clearer. In 1989, Kraft and General Foods were merged into one giant entity.

Post became an innovator in 1996 by initiating the price cuts that were subsequently followed by Kellogg and General Mills. This is a case of a David in the breakfast cereal industry challenging two Goliaths, Kellogg and General Mills. It is interesting to note that this change in pricing structure was thrust forward in the breakfast cereal industry by a distant number three firm in market share. Innovation, which is related to market opportunity, may often be directly linked with product design, marketing, and manufacturing, so that it is integrated in product planning and strategy. Post, in this particular instance, evaluated this daring pricing strategy in the light of consumer buying patterns, especially income, rising prices of the product, and lifestyle habits. With the strength of Philip Morris behind Post, it can be expected that both Kellogg and General Mills will be confronted with other challenges for industry leadership in the future. Post brands such as Raisin Bran and Shredded Wheat are already making inroads into the market. Nabisco was once known for Shredded Wheat, but Post is now marketing this brand since Nabisco is now another division of Philip Morris.

Post Grape-Nuts and Post Raisin Bran are the two best-selling cereal brands. Kraft seems to have received more support and attention from Philip Morris. The cereal business has not been that significant as a component of total food sales. Post has the best opportunity of making inroads by developing cereal snacks that can be consumed throughout the day. Quaker and other cereal manufacturers have also targeted this market, and Post will be confronted by fierce competition in this market.

Quaker: King of the Hot Cereal Market

The Quaker trademark was registered in 1877, and Quaker was the first firm in the breakfast cereal industry to have high identification with consumers. American Cereal in 1901 became the Quaker Oats Company. By 1920, Quaker owned half of all milling operations east of the Rocky Mountains. Through the years Quaker's product line has been broadened to include a variety of food products, such as Cap'n Crunch and Life cereals, Aunt Jemima mixes, Ken-L Ration dog food, and Puss 'n Boots cat food. Quaker has also diversified into producing an extensive line of animal foods and chemicals for uses in various plastic industries.

Since population demographics indicated low birthrates, Quaker caught expansion fever and tried to broaden its product portfolio in the 1960s and 1970s. By the 1980s, Quaker decided that it was difficult to operate businesses in industries that it knew little about. Quaker, like a number of other food companies, has endeavored to narrow the company's market focus and return to the core businesses that it knows best. Quaker sold off its specialty retailing businesses, such as Jos. A. Banks (clothing), Brookstone (tools), and Eyelab (optical). The Fisher-Price toy operation has also been sold. Quaker used its new financial resources to strengthen current food brands by acquiring the Golden Grain Macaroni Company (Rice-a-Roni and Noodle-a-Roni) and Gaines Foods (pet foods), whose products strongly complement Quaker's.

Quaker has a commanding presence in the hot cereal market, with more than a 60 percent market share. Quaker's cereals business consists of several strong brands, such as Instant Quaker Oatmeal, Cap'n Crunch, Old-Fashioned and Quick Quaker Oats, and Life cereal. Sales over the past ten years have increased an average of 7 percent a year. Although hot cereals were Quaker's oldest, best-known, and most profitable products in 1994, volume was 5 percent below the previous year. Quaker has entered other markets, and Cap'n Crunch is the number two brand in the presweetened cereal segment. Life cereal is directed to parents who are concerned about nutrition.

The company successfully markets Quaker Rice Cakes and Granola Bars. While these products could be viewed as snacks, they also could be extensions to the breakfast cereal market. Consumers in a hurry can eat these snacks for breakfast and consider rice cakes and granola bars as a wholesome beginning to their day. Moreover, Quaker markets Aunt Jemima pancakes, mixes, and muffins. These products too can be considered a part of the breakfast market. Aunt Jemima pancakes, waffles, and French toast are strong entries in the breakfast market.

Quaker is in the fourth market position in the ready-to-eat cereals. The size of the ready-to-eat cereal market and the profitability of individual leading brands allow the company to generate attractive revenues from this market. However, Quaker is not in a growth position in this market. Aggressive competitors, Kellogg, General Mills, and Post, will soon erode Quaker's market share unless new products are successfully launched. The hot-cereal market is not a growth area, and while Quaker is the market leader in this segment, the size of this market will probably diminish in the future. It is interesting to note that Cream of Wheat is the number two brand in the hot cereal market, marketed by Nabisco. Nabisco is much stronger with SnackWell's Cereal Bars, which are the first fat-free breakfast bars. The wholesome variety market, which includes the Quaker Rice Cake and Granola brands, is a growth area where future development should be profitable. The Aunt Jemima brand is a market leader and should continue to do well. Quaker is a follower in regional marketing and targets the South for Quaker Instant Grits, but Quaker has not been an innovator in the past in the breakfast cereal market.

Quaker has done an outstanding job in brand strategy. Quaker has used its company name along with an individual brand name for each product.

The company name adds the firm's reputation to the product, while the individual name sets it apart from other company products. For example, Quaker Oats in Quaker Oats Cap'n Crunch demonstrates the company's stature for breakfast cereal, and Cap'n Crunch sets apart and dramatizes the product.

Quaker has also made an effort to increase its share of the ready-to-eat cereal market by marketing a product line of bag cereals favorably competing with Kellogg and General Mills at lower prices. The bag cereal product line is aimed at the children's target market. Prices are lower than competitors' box cereals. The product could be eaten as a cereal or a snack, and therefore Quaker hopes to increase its market share.

The Competitive Fringe Area

The competitive fringe area consists of frozen waffles, pancakes, French toast, bagels, muffins, pastry, eggs, and an assortment of other foods. All of these foods take sales away from the breakfast cereal industry. Some of the leading frozen breakfast brands are Swanson, Egg Beaters, Jimmy Dean, Second Nature, Morningstar Farms, and Weight Watchers. The leading frozen waffles, pancakes, and French toast brands, which take a lion share of the competitive fringe market, are Kellogg's Eggo and General Mills' Aunt Jemima. In this instance, both Kellogg and General Mills are still profiting from the competitive fringe area for the breakfast market.

A relatively recent development has been the growing popularity of the bagel and muffin market. Franchise bagel operations are growing at a rapid rate. These operations are relatively low in cost when compared to the franchising of hamburgers and pizza.

Another aspect to the competitive fringe area has been consumers choosing to eat breakfast in restaurants. Elaborate breakfast bars in restaurants and hotels certainly do include breakfast cereals, but pancakes, waffles, and French toast and ham or bacon with eggs seem more desired by consumers. McDonald's innovated the breakfast market by offering breakfast at a low cost. Other hamburger organizations such as Burger King and Hardee's have also joined the bandwagon to offer breakfast at a low cost. Dunkin' Donuts would also constitute another threat to the breakfast cereal industry.

The traditional breakfast meal for many consumers has been bacon or ham and eggs. Eating habits are difficult to change. However, the breakfast cereal industry did help to change eating habits of Americans as their lives became more sedate and work became less of an outdoor activity. The trend toward nutritious foods with low fat and low cholesterol contents will help the breakfast cereal industry as consumers become better educated. However, the competitive fringe area is a threat to the breakfast cereal industry. Moreover, it would seem that expansion in the breakfast cereal market has its limits in the United States. Therefore, in the future there is a high probability that market share will grow only at the expense of established cereal companies.

Another aspect of the competitive fringe area has been the growth of the breakfast snack bar industry. Snack bars such as Kellogg's Nutri-Grain and Low-Fat Granola Bars, Quaker Low-Fat Granola and Fat-Free Mini Rice Cakes, and General Mills' Nature Valley Granola Bars and Fruit Roll-Ups can be consumed for breakfast or during the day or evening. General Mills in 1996 introduced Betty Crocker brand cereals. The first two varieties were cinnamon streusel and Dutch apple.

The trademark, Betty Crocker, for seventy-five years has been synonymous with cakes and other desserts. General Mills hopes to link Betty Crocker to the cereal aisle and has segmented these new entries to dessert lovers. Few new cereals have been winners, and it is doubtful that even the $40 million marketing campaign Betty Crocker will launch will be successful. Another potential problem is that the Betty Crocker line may tend to cannibalize its snack products, such as Nature Valley, which may be consumed at breakfast by families who do not eat breakfast together. Whether General Mills' Betty Crocker cereals can successfully compete with the competitive fringe area of the breakfast cereal market is dubious. Kellogg, General Mills, and other members of the breakfast cereal industry have successfully penetrated the competitive fringe area and should find it profitable. But other entries, notably bagels and muffins, will encroach upon diversified cereal manufacturers. Kellogg already derives about 18 percent of its annual sales from its Eggo frozen waffle line, its Pop-Tarts toaster pastries, and its breakfast bars. The acquisition of Lender's bagel business will give Kellogg about a 45 percent share of prepackaged sales and diversify its breakfast offerings. This acquisition will give Kellogg a more dominant presence in alternative breakfast products and demonstrates that it is responding favorably to the trend of bagel growth. Through the years, Kellogg has adapted to market environmental changes, and this is an important factor explaining why Kellogg is still the champion in the breakfast cereal industry.

MARKETING STRATEGIES

Two strategies that have been used by the breakfast cereal industry with success have been product differentiation and market segmentation. The successful application of the strategy of product differentiation should result in an increased horizontal share of a generalized market. Product differentiation refers to the marketing efforts to distinguish a basically homogeneous product from competitors' products. Methods used to accomplish this are to alter the product's physical characteristics or to use branding, advertising, and packaging. The strategy of market segmentation increases the market share of specific, carefully defined submarkets. Market segmentation refers to marketing efforts to group potential buyers by demographic characteristics, geographical region, lifestyle, and usage patterns as well as the more modern approaches using both behavioral and quantitative factors. Thus submarkets are frequently established on the basis of income, age, sex, occupation, and complex behavioral and quantitative dimensions. A strategy of market segmentation can aid in developing particular market segments, in contrast to a strategy of product differentiation, which distinguishes a product among many similar products.

For example, the breakfast cereal industry has successfully targeted the health-conscious adult market and the children's market segment. General Mills has gone one step further by targeting the sports-minded with a picture of Michael Jordan on its Wheaties cereal box (and if purchasers satisfy certain requirements they can receive a basketball signed by their sports idol). Firms in the breakfast cereal industry have achieved outstanding expertise in the use of market-segmentation strategies. Alternate strategies of product differentiation and market segmentation are frequently complementary and used together by companies in the breakfast cereal industry.

Much of modern packaging is a development of the familiar Quaker Oats box. The Quaker Oats box was originally developed in the 1800s as an alternative to unsanitary open barrels. The paper container was the first package produced in four colors, the first to include cooking instructions, the first to appear in sample sizes, and the first to make possible attention-getting displays. Package graphics, whether it be colors, pictures, or lettering, are effective means for product differentiation. The breakfast cereal market has also added increments of sweetness, such as sugar, syrup, or fruit, to vary taste for consumers.

Branding is important so that product identification is eased, price comparisons are reduced, and the product is known for an established quality. The brand develops an image or a perception in the mind of the buyer. This image lessens customer risk, makes the product more acceptable to retailers and wholesalers, and increases the product's prestige. Kellogg uses the company trade name combined with individual product names such as Kellogg's Corn Flakes and Kellogg's Rice Krispies.

Kellogg has effectively used the strategy of market segmentation to target specific submarkets. Special K cereal is targeted to a low-cholesterol segment. The company also targets Product 19 for dieters, Müeslix for nutrition-oriented consumers, Just Right for the natural-ingredients segment, and finally, All-Bran for the high-fiber market segment. Kellogg has identified a broad segment of health-conscious consumers and defined specific market segments. Kellogg had successfully positioned some cereal brands as satisfying health and nutritional needs. The company had effectively changed the focus from an evolving children's product to an involving adult breakfast food by advertising nutritional benefits.

New product innovation has created a new market or new category known as breakfast cereal bars. Nabisco, a relative outsider in the breakfast cereal market, moved into this new category in 1995. SnackWell's cereal bars, Toastees toaster pastries, and a line of granola bars seized a respectable 12 percent market share from the established cereal manufacturers, Quaker, General Mills, Post, and Kellogg. Nabisco's Sun-Ups Cereal Bars in Canada became the number one breakfast bar in that country within its first year on the market. The wars in the breakfast aisle with a line of breakfast snack products has intensified, and with the trend for consumers to eat breakfast "on the run" and for them to eat healthier snacks, companies outside the breakfast cereal industry may enter this market.

WHY KELLOGG IS STILL CHAMPION

Kellogg since the early 1900s has developed an image for research in serving the health-conscious-consumer market segment. A health institute was established in Battle Creek, Michigan, for the purpose of conducting nutritional research. The Kellogg brand of cornflakes has turned into a generic, and through brand power, a patronage loyalty base has been established. Kellogg has successfully targeted the low-cholesterol, nutrition-oriented, and high-fiber market segments. The children's market has also been effectively targeted with Sugar Frosted Flakes and such cartoon figures as Tony the Tiger.

Kellogg has concentrated on effectively serving the entire breakfast market with Eggo frozen waffles and Nutri-Grain and Low Fat Granola Bars for consumers in a hurry; it has acquired Lender's Bagels in efforts to diversify in the breakfast market. Kellogg also has been an innovator in packaging by taking cereal out of barrels and into smaller packages and, in the early 1900s, using Waxtite, a plastic inside the cereal box that keeps the product fresher. Strength in product assortment has facilitated the introduction of new products and enhanced Kellogg's image with retailers. Retailers are pleased with the profitability of Kellogg brands.

Marketing Successes in the Breakfast Cereal Industry

- Kellogg, General Mills, and Quaker Oats have made effective use of market-segmentation and product-differentiation strategies.
- There has been effective use of lifestyle market segmentation by Kellogg with Special K, General Mills with Wheaties, and Quaker Oats with Instant Quaker Oatmeal.
- Companies have made effective use of benefit segmentation with Kellogg's Rice Krispies, General Mills' Cheerios, Post's Grape-Nuts, and Quaker's Cap'n Crunch and Life.

- General Mills has demonstrated superior product development strategies with Cheerios, Wheaties, and Total brands.
- Quaker Oats has been a leader in the use of trademarks and package coloring.
- The brand power of Kellogg, General Mills, Post, and Quaker has been at the forefront of developing profitability, which is among the highest in the food store.

Marketing Mistakes in the Breakfast Cereal Industry

- Companies have overestimated brand power and pricing strategies, allowing store brands to make inroads in the industry.
- Companies have incurred high costs due to repeated new product introductions. Firms need to be more careful in new product testing, and they need to delete marginal products.
- Overconfidence in consumer brand loyalty has permitted frequent price wars.
- Sales promotion strategies such as coupons have been relatively ineffective with consumers and have caused conflicts with dealers.
- Firms have been slow to grasp the impact from the competitive fringe area of muffins, bagels, waffles, and French toast.
- The industry reacts to trends and lifestyle changes slowly, for example, in offering snack granola bars, but it has the financial resources to recover.

MANAGING CHANGE

To counter slower growth, breakfast cereal manufacturers have made decisions in strategic planning that were sometimes similar and other times different. General Mills began an aggressive diversification program in the early 1970s, expanding from its food-processing business into restaurants, toys, fashions, and specialty retailing. Quaker Oats and Ralston Purina tried this strategy but soon retreated. Kellogg alone stayed the course in the breakfast cereal industry and adopted a focused strategy.

An important factor limiting growth in the breakfast cereal industry has been population trends. The birthrate has been declining since 1960, and as a result firms within the breakfast cereal industry expected a sales decline. The declining birthrate is not evenly distributed. The South has a slower rate of decline, while population in the East has remained virtually flat. The United States is still a country of urban dwellers, but many people are increasingly selecting smaller cities in which to reside.

Age distribution and projected shifts in the changing age mix are important to breakfast-cereal manufacturers because consumer preferences differ among age groups. Markets for some products contract in declining age groups. For example, this is an important reason why General Mills attempted to diversify its business interests into nonfood areas. Scatter-gun diversification floundered in the 1980s, and both General Mills and Quaker sold off many of their nonfood operations. General Mills and Quaker both returned to their core business, which was marketing food.

The most notable trend concerning age distribution and projections is the aging of the U.S. population. There will be a continuing increase of elderly citizens as the baby boomers age. The baby boomers, many of whom are now middle-aged, are concerned with health, nutrition, and physical fitness. To the credit of the breakfast cereal industry, a product formerly targeted to children is now targeted to adults. The adult market for cereal has opened up new horizons for breakfast cereal manufacturers. Kellogg has targeted Special K and All-Bran for those consumers concerned about nutrition and health. General Mills already had cereals with oatmeal as a base when scientific findings demonstrated its benefits, and the company has targeted Oatmeal Crisp, Multi-Grain Cheerios, and Total Whole Grain for the adult market. General Mills has designed Wheaties for both children and adults, and distributes Nestlé's Fibre One on a worldwide basis. However, it is Kellogg that is well known for continuing to conduct and sponsor extensive dietary research into the role grains and components of grain play in promoting a healthy diet.

The marketing strategy of benefit segmentation has been very useful for the breakfast cereal industry in enabling it to appeal to adults who value proper eating habits. Benefit segmentation divides buyers on the basis of need-satisfying benefits to be derived from product use, the rate of product usage, the degree of brand loyalty, and an understanding of consumer readiness to purchase the product. Benefit segmentation has been applied to food consumption, and the consumer segments profiled were child oriented, diet concerned, meat-and-potatoes sophisticated, and natural-foods oriented. Benefit segments are based on reasons why consumers buy, cause-and-effect relationships are emphasized, and relationships between motivations and purchasing patterns in specific situations are presented. For example, the diet-concerned food segment are more likely to be older and perhaps even retired people who prefer sugar substitutes, fresh fruit, skim milk, and diet margarine. The natural-food enthusiasts favor natural, ready-to-eat cereal, bran and high-fiber bread, granola bars, and rice. These consumers are more likely to be college graduates, younger, and in the upper-income bracket.

The breakfast cereal industry has responded well to changes in the dietary habits of many Americans. Kellogg's aggressive reactions to a changing marketing environment has been, in part, responsible for its continued success. The heart of Kellogg's push to capture the adult market was its expanded line of high-fiber bran cereals, such as Raisin Bran. Kellogg successfully tied high fiber to low-fat diets and healthy living. Moreover, Kellogg invested heavily in new brands aimed at adult taste buds and lifestyles, such as the Nutri-Grain product line, and Rice Krispies was repositioned by emphasizing that it has more vitamins and minerals than oatmeal brands.

Unless cereal consumption increases, a number of competitors in the industry may not survive. Snack breakfast foods such as granola products have attracted renewed consumer interest, but consumers in the past concluded that the products were too high in sugar and too low in nutrients, and this objection might surface again. The overseas market for cereal manufacturers appears much more attractive for expansion than the U.S. market. Consumption in the U.S. cereal market seems stagnant, and in the future firms will be simply reallocating the existing market share.

During the 1980s the breakfast cereal industry experienced a steady growth rate from 2 percent to 4 percent in contrast to the declining growth rate of between 1 and 2 percent in the 1990s. The result has been fierce price competition. During the 1990s, consumer real disposable personal income has slowed, and this has allowed private-label brands to increase their market share. Cereal manufacturers have made sizable price cuts, and operating margins are still about 15 to 20 percent, versus an average of about 7 to 10 percent for most other packaged foods. Increasing costs and more consumer choices, such as bagels, are cited as causes. Future price wars will only aid private labels in an environment that is cordial to price-conscious shoppers.

MANAGERIAL INSIGHTS

The Post and Nabisco divisions of Philip Morris cut domestic prices of Grape-Nuts and their other brands as much as 20 percent on April 15, 1996. Quaker Oats found that its sales volume declined 7 percent during the second quarter of 1996, partly because the company lagged behind Post, General Mills, and Kellogg in lowering retail prices. It is estimated that Kellogg's share of the U.S. cereal market decreased from an estimated 35 percent to an estimated 32 percent, while Post's increased from about 16 to 20 percent. Although cereal sales are falling by 3 to 4 percent a year, store-brand sales are increasing by about 10 percent a year. The sales of bulk "bagged" cereals are increasing even faster, and consumers are opting for alternative breakfasts, such as bagels and muffins. Consumers have demonstrated resistance to paying $4 to $5 for a box of branded cereal and have turned to store brands and other alternatives. A window of opportunity is present, and Ralcorp Holdings (General Mills), which makes 60 percent of the store brands in the United States, has announced that by decreasing costs, prices of private labels can be further lowered. Clearly, the cereal industry has overestimated brand power.

Kellogg, General Mills, and other members of the cereal industry have accomplished strategies of market segmentation and product differentiation very well. But there is a point when price considerations enter the decision-making process of consumers. Taste as a form of product differentiation can be misleading. The addition or subtraction of sugar or other ingredients may not be a powerful strategy when confronted with rising prices. The cereal industry has long withstood the impact of private labels or store brands and has thought itself above the inroads made by store brands in other segments of the food industry. Market segmentation strategies that target consumer segments that are nutrition oriented, desire a high-fiber cereal, are diet oriented, desire a natural-ingredients cereal, or are concerned about cholesterol are still important, but the strategy of product differentiation coupled with market segmentation has been overestimated. Product-differentiation strategies can be weak when confronted with price competition.

The best strategy for the cereal industry is to cut back on its many new product introductions, which frequently end in failure, and concentrate on the known brands while increasingly monitoring new product introductions. Kellogg's Corn Flakes and General Mills' Cheerios have withstood the test of time. New consumer market segments will continue to arise and must be satisfied. However, price competition is a strong factor in the cereal industry and must be acknowledged.

The state of brand management is continually changing. The strategy of cereal manufacturers has been to build powerful brands that generate consumer insistence. A characteristic of brand insistence is that purchasers are not willing to buy a substitute brand. Cereal manufacturers overestimated consumer loyalty. Brand preference has been developed, but price or other product differentiation characteristics such as packaging could change consumer purchasing patterns. Consumers may develop preferences toward several brands but not buy or insist upon one brand exclusively. For example, if Kellogg's Special K is priced much higher than General Mills' Total Wheat, then consumers may purchase Total even though if all factors were equal they would prefer to purchase Special K. For the children's market, General Mills' Honey Nut Cheerios might be purchased instead of Cap'n Crunch if a variable such as price is important and has been decreased. Each consumer family has its own threshold, so even a fifty-cent price differential might be perceived as greater for one family than for another.

Kellogg with Corn Flakes, General Mills with Cheerios and Wheaties, and Quaker Oats in the hot cereal market have established a strong foundation for brand preference. Elements such as a strong corporate name, a known corporate identity, or a well-known trademark and a good product have been interlinked with brand positioning strategy. Kellogg, for example, has linked the company trade name with individual product names, as in Kellogg's Rice Krispies and Kellogg's Raisin Bran.

Brand revitalization in the maturity phase of the product life cycle can be approached by market expansion. Market expansion can mean finding new uses for the brand or new users of the brand, or getting users to purchase more of the brand. For example, General Mills has attempted to attract new users for mature brands like Wheaties by advertising to adults. Brand repositioning requires changing the brand's appeal to attract new market segments. This might involve a new balance of ingredients.

Product positioning is a part of a natural progression when market segmentation is used. Segmentation allows the firm to aim a given brand at a portion of the total market. For example, Kellogg's Special K is positioned as a cereal that has a low-cholesterol appeal and whose characteristics are superior to other brands. Positioning a brand to avoid competition may be appropriate when that brand has unique characteristics that are important to buyers. Brand-extension strategy is an effort to use a successful brand name to launch new or modified products. General Mills has been successful by extending Cheerios with Multi-Grain Cheerios, Apple Cinnamon Cheerios, Honey Nut Cheerios, and Frosted Cheerios.

There is a positive relationship of reputation and credibility to brand success. For example, over the years Kellogg has promoted good nutrition, and that theme is still present in its marketing strategies. Key threats to long-term brand success are a lack of understanding of what the brand stands for, inadequate funding, and private labels. Many cereal manufacturers, in efforts to lower costs, have decreased advertising budgets. There is a temptation during turbulent times to view advertising as an expense rather than as an investment. This viewpoint lacks vision and will cause cereal manufacturers many regrets. For brands to be successful, continuous advertising is essential, and constant reinforcement of brand names and corporate identities with products must be interlinked. The weakness in the cereal industry's thinking seems to be a failure to consider the consumer's ability to interchange or purchase desirable substitutes if price becomes an important enough variable. Thus, even though many leading brands have withstood the test of time, they are still vulnerable.

CHAPTER 6

THE
BABY FOOD
INDUSTRY

Environmental Considerations
- The population boom
- Zero population growth
- Increased consumerism
- Increased nutritional concerns
- Changing economic environment
- Health and dietary changes

New Target Market Considerations
- Organic baby food
- Growth of submarkets
- International markets
- Diversification in other baby product lines

Marketing Mistakes
- Lack of strong consumer-oriented images
- Ignoring population forecasts
- Allowing corporate images to tarnish
- Inability to shift strategies
- Status quo mentality
- Reacting to trends rather than developing proactive strategies

Strategies in a Mature Market
- Image maintenance
- Improve relations with retailers
- Eliminate marginal items
- Encourage innovation

How many managers at Gerber, Beechnut, or Heinz envisioned the end of the baby boom? Business decisions have grown more complex as a result of a changing marketing environment. The macroenvironment is the larger societal force that affects the firm's strategy, its customer markets, its competitors, and, as a consequence, its product, price, promotion, and distribution policies. The macroenvironment consists of demographic, economic, technological, political, and cultural forces. Marketing managers at Gerber, Beechnut, and Heinz learned the hard way that the only way to insure profitability and survival is to provide an organizational environment that encourages strategic planning.

Throughout the 1960s, the marketing concept was a dominant guideline that became a pervasive force within entire organizations. Strategic planning, with its emphasis on the formulation of the business mission, the identification of strategic alternatives, and contingency planning, became the direction of the 1970s. The 1980s emphasized computerization, systems planning, and global strategies. The 1990s became a period for cost control and careful definition of the business mission. It is surprising to find, after all this emphasis on the identification and satisfaction of customer needs and the necessity for planning and strategy, that many firms plan only in the short run and do not really consider strategic planning.

The declining American birthrate, known as zero population growth or the "baby bust," caught many firms and industries off guard. However, Gerber saved itself by diversifying, and dropped the motto that reflected its business mission: "Babies are our business—our only business." A company that offers a comprehensive line of products has a better opportunity to win customer loyalty than a company that offers a limited line. Gerber has a competitive advantage in baby foods over Beechnut and Heinz, because it provides a full line of products that requires a great amount of space in supermarkets. Among the products provided by Gerber are branded food, apparel, and care items for children from birth through the age of three. These products include a bedding collection, nursers, pacifiers, bibs, diaper starter kits, and Gerber Graduate foods—a line of products designed to fill the needs of toddlers from 12 to 30 months old.

The declining birthrate had a devastating impact not only on the baby food industry but also on manufacturers of juvenile furniture, infants and children's clothing, and other industries related to supplying babies and infants. Marketing executives should note that environmental changes have vast implications for the marketing system, making it necessary to have a planned pattern of responses. Conditions that favor linking long-range planning—planning for more than a five-year period—with marketing planning and strategy formulated in the short range are directly related to the rate at which the environment of the firm changes. A strategic plan that considers long-range planning would permit an orderly pattern of responses to changes such as customer preferences, technology, competition, population, age patterns, income fluctuations, and legislation.

Developments in the marketing environment have shocked many business organizations in the food industry. New technology and competition have affected supermarkets and their relationships to suppliers. The fast-food industry has been influenced by consumers' preferences for ethnic food. The soup industry, with advanced computers, has been able to more closely penetrate diverse geographical regions. Change has been so fast that organizations in the supermarket and fast-food industries have experienced shakeouts, and some firms in the ice cream and soup industries have left the scene. Marketing executives should favor strategic planning in the following situations in order to consider new market opportunities and to avoid marketing myopia:

- When the uncontrollable environment is subject to accelerating rates of change
- When the firm is considering entering new geographical regions for a long period of time
- When the firm is establishing costly new facilities such as factory automation with computers and robots serving as the central nerve system
- When the firm is developing new products with a projected long product life cycle
- When the firm's basic business is so closely tied to a single factor, such as firms in the baby food industry, that a change in it could profoundly affect the firm's future

There are three scenarios associated with the development of the baby food industry. The first one relates that the son of the owner of a wholesale food company in the 1920s was left to baby-sit and had the task of mashing peas, carrots, and other vegetables for his infant. He fantasized how nice it would be if all this food was already provided in jars for the parents. The second scenario is less dramatic, but relates that the wife of this young father provided the idea during the course of infant feeding. A third scenario is that a physician suggested that peas should be mashed for the family's infant. Regardless of which scenario is accurate, the family in this situation was named Gerber, and a wholesale grocery company became the Gerber Baby Food Company in 1927. Thus the prepackaging of baby food in jars, directing itself to the convenience of parents, was to commence an industry that was to span not only the United States, but the entire world as well.

Two major problems have confronted the baby food industry, and in each instance, management executives have responded poorly. The baby food industry was not alert to changing demographic trends—namely, the slowing birthrate. Gerber executives denied the decline in birthrate trends throughout the 1970s. The expectation was that this slowing process was just a temporary phenomenon. The second problem involved social responsibility. The apple juice fraud scandal involved Beechnut and was finally settled in 1986 with Beechnut found guilty of over 200 felony counts. In 1986 Gerber experienced a problem due to bits of glass discovered in their peach jars while in transit. Gerber was not at fault, but did not exhibit much concern in explaining this situation to the public. Public relations was handled very poorly. In 1996, Gerber, after long ignoring concerns over good nutrition, managed to eliminate excess starch and sugar from its product line. Gerber's slowness to react to public concerns was to its detriment. None of the firms in the baby industry can be classified as innovators. Marketing myopia is much more characteristic. Variables of target market and image would reveal that in the United States, image has been tarnished, and with the exception of some efforts to develop the Hispanic market, strategies of market segmentation have not been well developed. Heinz, on the other hand, has successfully penetrated the baby food market in the international sector. With the acquisition of Earth's Best, perhaps Heinz will develop a more competitive stance. This has happened with Post in the breakfast cereal industry, and might occur in the baby food industry with Heinz.

The baby food industry has committed many mistakes and has lacked the flexibility to shift strategies. Both Gerber and Beechnut have reacted to trends rather than developing proactive strategies, and thereby have lacked innovative strategies. Gerber and Beechnut permitted their corporate images to tarnish. Beechnut and other firms were unable to capitalize on these mistakes. Baby food firms operate in a mature industry and need to eliminate marginal items, encourage innovation, improve relations with retailers, and maintain a positive image.

The leading baby food industry firms, namely, Gerber and Beechnut, would seem to be victims of their own success. Executives seem to lack the realization that with the food processor and other kitchen appliances, parents can serve their babies what they believe is better and higher-quality food. Unless high standards are maintained, more segments of the population will attempt to circumvent the purchase of baby food. Physical resources would seem adequate if not good in reaching supermarkets, and inventory-control measures would seem to please supermarket personnel. However, it is difficult to comprehend how Gerber and Beechnut, who are dominant in the baby food industry, have found it so difficult to become profitable organizations and how these firms could fail to gain a favorable image for conducting research on improving the nutrition of infants and toddlers. Marketing myopia has plagued executives in this industry.

MARKET STRUCTURE

Four firms, Gerber, Beechnut, Heinz, and Earth's Best, dominate the baby food industry. Gerber has a commanding, approximately 70 percent, market share of the baby food industry. About 500 salespeople are especially well trained and are equipped with laptop computers. Gerber chooses not to specialize in selling baby food, unlike Beechnut, Gerber's main competitor. Gerber not only carries a comprehensive product line of baby food but also provides products for toddlers up to the age of 3. Gerber's competitors do not offer a toddler product line. Gerber also has a life-insurance company, and parents insure their children very easily before this could become more difficult, for instance, when medical problems surface in later life.

Beechnut has had a history of firms acquiring it. For example, in 1973 Squibb sold Beechnut to lawyer-entrepreneur Frank Nicholas, and in turn Beechnut was sold to Nestlé in 1979. Beechnut was acquired by Ralston Purina in 1989, which in turn spun off Beechnut into a freestanding company called the Ralcorp firm. Finally, in 1996, Beechnut was acquired by General Mills. Throughout this history, Beechnut was always part of a firm that had other interests, and the marketing of baby food was not given a high priority.

Heinz sells more than 88 percent of its baby food products outside of the United States, but follows Gerber and Beechnut by a distant third in the United States. The company has major baby food operations in the United Kingdom, Italy, Canada, Australia, and New Zealand. Heinz has extended its baby food operations to Russia, Hungary, and the Czech Republic. Although Heinz has other interests that have had higher priorities, such as its division of Weight Watchers and its StarKist tuna, and is well known for its tomato ketchup and baked beans, Heinz has renewed its interest in baby food by acquiring Earth's Best Baby Food. Earth's Best

Table 6.1
A Market-Share Range for Baby Food Brands, 1996

Manufacturers	Brands	Market Share
Sandoz	Gerber	70-73%
General Mills	Beechnut	14-16%
Heinz	Heinz, Earth's Best*	11-13%

*The Earth's Best brand has about 2 percent market share.

holds a 2 percent market share of the baby food market and is the leading brand of organic baby foods. Since there is an increasing level of education and environmental concern, the market potential for organic baby food would appear promising. The Earth's Best brand will supplement the Heinz brand of infant cereals, juices, and strained junior foods.

Table 6.1, A Market-Share Range for Baby Food Brands, 1996, reveals that although market-share figures for the baby food market vary from period to period, it is estimated that Gerber has a lion's share of from 70 to 73 percent, Beechnut has from 14 to 16 percent, and Heinz has approximately 11 to 13 percent. The growth area would seem to favor Heinz, with organic baby food, but mitigating against this trend is the fact that retail prices are higher than for traditional baby food. Higher food-processing costs have increased retail prices for organic baby food. Table 6.1 depicts a moving market-share picture of the baby food market in the 1990s. Gerber's comprehensive line of baby food and infants' products has gained important shelf space. Gerber has experienced failures in its full product line for babies, but concurrently, this full product line has helped to establish a giant market share in the baby food business. Failures in marketing baby clothing and other products have affected the profit picture for Gerber. Finally, Gerber was acquired by Sandoz, a Swiss firm with distribution channels to expand the Gerber operation internationally. Gerber has not extended its product line to include organic baby food, which appears to be an important market segment in which Earth's Best is dominant.

MARKET CONDUCT

The changing demographics of the family structure in the 1970s was a surprise to many firms and in particular to the baby food industry. The population explosion faltered and was labeled zero population growth. Family mobility was evident as the sunbelt states grew beyond expectations. The growth of the elderly population startled many firms, and government seemed unprepared for this growth. Moreover, average household size diminished dramatically. In response to the growth of the elderly market, Gerber placed a picture of a senior citizen on their jars and managed to gain supermarket cooperation to establish a separate aisle for senior citizen food. The elderly market response was poor. This market did not desire to be singled out in such a way. The idea of special food in baby jars was abhorrent to this market. Gerber had made a major mistake.

In the 1980s, it was becoming apparent that the ideal American family, with the husband as the sole breadwinner and the wife as a full-time housewife taking care of the two (statistically, two and a half) children, was a fading illusion. Marriage at a later age, fewer children, a higher divorce rate, and more working wives have all helped to change our concept of the traditional American family. The question remains, what other surprises are there concerning the impact of demographics in the future?

Demographic market segmentation has been a popular base for segmentation studies because of its ease of measurement. Moreover, there is the belief that variables such as sex, age, marital status, and the number and ages of children are strong life-cycle factors associated with consumption habits. There is also accessibility to various media that are directed to these demographic segments, such as *Parents Magazine, American Baby*, and *Mothers Today*. Demographics have revealed a number of shifts in the changing age mix. Consequently, many firms have used these data to segment markets based upon age. For example, Johnson & Johnson broadened its promotional appeal to include adults as well as children. Gerber Products successfully diversified into life insurance. However, Gerber failed in marketing clothes and toys.

More than four million babies were born in 1990, and sales of baby food increased approximately by 11 percent. This baby-boom "echo" is expected to continue to the year 2000, but will gradually decline after 2000, as baby boomers pass out of the child-bearing years. There is a discernible trend that today's parents are less enthusiastic about traditional strained baby foods than parents of a generation ago. Consequently, the baby food manufacturers are concentrating more on products for toddlers. In the 1990s, consumption of baby food is between 53 and 54 dozen jars per year per family with a baby compared to 47 to 49 dozen jars per year in the mid-1980s and an average of about 66 dozen jars a year in 1972. Gerber's line of Gerber Graduates offers food for children aged 10 to 30 months. The twenty-three products include cereal snacks, apple-cherry juice, and microwaveable spaghetti with mini meatballs. Beechnut takes a more cautious approach to feeding the toddler market segment. Beechnut's Table Time meals are designed to allow busy parents the convenience of being able to serve their toddlers a complete meal—meat, vegetables, and a starch.

Gerber expanded distribution and marketing of its Tropical product line nationwide in the 1990s. Originally, this line of baby foods and juices was targeted to Hispanic populations in markets such as Miami, New York, Dallas, Arizona, and southern California. This product line has been accepted by non-Hispanics, and among the more popular baby food flavors are guava, papaya, peach, mango, and tropical fruit. Beechnut has also been responsive to environmental trends and has introduced Baby's First Spring Water, a drinking water that is also meant for use in preparing infants' cereals and formula.

In the age of no-fat desserts and bottled water, ultrahealthy baby food would seem like a winner, but parents have been slow to accept organic baby food. Beechnut dropped its organic product line, called Special Harvest, in 1993, only two years after introducing it. Since Americans have been feeding their babies Gerber for almost seventy years, buying habits have worked against purchasing the new organic product line. Earth's Best, the leading brand of organic baby food, has been purchased by Heinz and will probably gain strength from renewed marketing momentum. Part of the problem for baby health-food makers is high prices. Organic food is more expensive to grow, and some products leave out inexpensive fillers such as starch. However, there is hope on the horizon. Better-educated families with fewer children and double incomes are spending more money on their children's clothes and toys, and this eventually should also happen in the baby food grocery aisles.

The low birthrate of the 1970s has been attributed to a number of causes, including the rising cost of raising a family, greater access to effective birth control procedures, and the changing role of women. It would seem reasonable to believe that couples will have smaller families, that child-rearing costs will continue to increase, and that women will in even greater numbers seek careers and not just jobs.

The baby-boom years did not conclude until 1965, and a rising birthrate is evident in the fact that great numbers of young women are in their early thirties. Thus, a rise in elementary school enrollment will eventually ease some pressures on manufacturers of goods earmarked for elementary schools, such as publishers of school materials and manufacturers of school equipment designated for this age level. Already there has been an unexpected rapid rise in births in the Pacific, south central, and mountain states. Therefore, there should be increased activity among manufacturers of baby food, children's apparel, and toys. The decline in the birthrate should begin by the year 2000 and continue for the next decade. The Hispanic market segment, which will be the fastest growing group, has already responded well to ethnic marketing campaigns, and baby food manufacturers would do well to continue to cultivate this market. African-American consumers have not responded well to separate ethnic campaigns by the baby food industry. It is estimated that the white birthrate from 2000 to 2010 will be the slowest growing market segment. The demographic picture for the baby food industry for the first decade of the 21st century is contraction.

Gerber, in 1996, developed for its core line of baby foods new formulations made without added starch and sugar. Reflecting a growing consumer awareness of good nutrition, this move was reactive rather than proactive and pinpoints a weakness in Gerber and the entire baby food industry. Leadership for new marketing innovations is essential and has been lacking.

CASE STUDIES

Gerber: King of the Baby Food Industry

Although Gerber remains the champion of the baby food industry, consumer loyalty has wavered due to a number of incidents that have led to a tarnished image. In 1996, Gerber announced that it was taking the sugar and starch out of forty-two kinds of baby food in response to consumer demand for healthier fare for babies and toddlers. Gerber had not been alert to this consumer sentiment, and as a result market share had declined from approximately 71 percent in 1993 to about 67 percent in 1996. In 1994, Gerber was acquired by Sandoz, a Swiss drug, chemical, and nutrition giant. Gerber previously had been unsuccessful in many overseas ventures because it lacked financing resources and an established distribution network. This situation is in contrast to the successful overseas ventures of both Campbell Soup and Kellogg, champions in the United States in their respective industries. Gerber lost significant financial resources in the past by venturing into such businesses as furniture, day-care centers, trucking, and even humidifiers. In 1993, Beechnut and Heinz offered deep promotion allowances to retailers, and Beechnut also slashed prices after Gerber announced a 5.5 percent price increase. Gerber reacted very slowly, and profits declined as a result. To make matters worse, Gerber, Heinz, and Beechnut were served with a half-dozen class-action lawsuits alleging a price-fixing conspiracy. Gerber was most notably affected by all of the ensuing news media attention since it had not responded well to competitors' discounts. In some areas, the difference in price between Gerber and Beechnut was as much as $.28 a jar. Gerber's baby food orders plunged. In 1986, bits of glass were found in Gerber's peach jars in numerous states. The company declined to recall the peaches and reacted by not even responding to the publicity. After a similar incident in 1984, Gerber had recalled some 700,000 baby food jars and advertised heavily to reassure consumers. This turned out to be an isolated incident resulting from breakage during shipment, but as a result of the product recall Gerber incurred millions of dollars in expenses and lost profits. The company concluded that it had overreacted in its desire to be socially responsible. Eventually, the Food and Drug Administration cleared Gerber in the 1986 incident of any wrongdoing, but Gerber's market share declined from 72 percent to 52 percent. It was not until the following year that Gerber increased advertising spending by 50 percent to counteract the negative publicity from the glass scare. Johnson & Johnson commanded the respect of consumers during the Tylenol scare in 1982, but Gerber did not handle its situation as well. The question remains that with all of these adverse incidents, what has Gerber done to remain the king of the baby food industry?

Gerber has many strengths. The company has successfully segmented not only the infant baby food market but the toddler market, to the age of 3 years, as well. The product line has been expanded to the growing Hispanic market. This market niche of a product line designed to satisfy the infant and toddler market has not been successfully challenged by either Beechnut or Heinz. Moreover, Gerber is marketing an assortment of products, such as bibs, that can be distributed through supermarkets. This gives retailers an opportunity to offer a more comprehensive product line if warranted. Gerber has stressed product innovation by offering the Grow-Up Plan for new babies and a new vegetable and snack line for toddlers. Gerber Life Insurance is sold to parents who desire coverage for their infants, and this insurance increases in coverage as the infant becomes an adult.

The use of human resources has helped to revitalize a company that was plunging into stagnation. Alfred Piergallini and Jim Smith correctly decided to focus on the infant and toddler markets and divest the firm of other unprofitable product lines such as furniture. Gerber also merged its sales force, and now regards its sales employees as associates, thereby providing faster and more efficient service for retailers. Gerber has invested in modern technology that allows its headquarters and sales associates to focus better on inventory control and to satisfy retailer needs in diverse locations. Future opportunities for Gerber include marketing abroad and monitoring different ethnic groups in the United States.

Private-label marketing, which has made inroads into general food manufacturers' market share, has not been a factor in the baby food industry. Supermarkets do not want their personnel to handle glass jars, which are subject to breakage. Whereas some union contracts may preclude food manufacturer sales representatives from setting up displays on store shelves, baby food products are excluded from this contractual clause. Consequently, even the adverse publicity that in the past was directed to Gerber has had only a temporary impact. Gerber has successfully sold an image of a company that knows how to satisfy baby requirements and how to develop new products that satisfy additional needs.

Promotion has changed over the past few decades. Gerber originally advertised on network television and radio and increased advertising to accompany new product offerings. This situation gradually began to change in the late 1980s, and now much of its promotional budget is appropriated for direct mailings and coupons. Gerber has also included a toll-free number to handle parents' questions. Thus Gerber has gone direct to the consumer, and this would seem to be an advantageous strategy.

Gerber, in 1994, was acquired by Sandoz AG of Switzerland, a drug, chemical, and nutrition giant firm without a presence in baby food. Gerber had failed in its quest to go global. Appropriate distribution channels proved elusive. In the past, Gerber made many mistakes that had an impact on profits. Gerber tried to extend its marketing operations to day-care centers, furniture, clothes, and toys. All of these efforts failed. Marketing efforts in food had mixed results. For example, Gerber's Chunky line of baby food failed, but Gerber Graduates, a line of juices, cereals, bakery products, meat snacks, microwaveable meals, and hot dogs for toddlers, has had mixed results. Consumers resisted Gerber's high prices, and the line has fallen short of expectations. In 1993, Gerber stumbled in a shrinking market, but Beechnut posted an increase in sales and Heinz sales remained flat. Gerber has great strength in the baby food industry, but legal difficulties and marketing mistakes have been costly in the past.

Beechnut: Lacking in Marketing Muscle

Ralston Purina acquired Beechnut in the late 1980s and spun it off to the Ralcorp firm. Deep discounts were given to retailers, and sales volume increased but profits lagged. This price war upset the equilibrium of the baby food industry in the 1990s. Ralcorp, a few years later, decided it really did not want to be in the baby food business. Finally, in the mid-1990s, Beechnut was sold to General Mills. None of the previous owners of Beechnut, including Squibb, Frank Nicholas, Nestlé, and Ralston Purina, had given the marketing of baby food a high priority.

Beechnut had never really recovered from the adulterated apple juice scandal of the 1980s. At that time Beechnut was a division of Nestlé; however, it was suspected that the deceitful practice started before Nestlé acquired Beechnut. Finally, in 1986, Beechnut pleaded guilty to 215 felony counts and admitted violations of the food and drug laws by marketing adulterated apple juice from 1981 to 1983. Beechnut's admission of guilt of selling millions of jars of phony apple juice shocked industry executives. Beechnut, founded in 1891, had been known for its high standards, purity, and natural ingredients. This focus on quality was the foundation of its corporate culture and its marketing campaigns. It is suggested that as early as 1977, Beechnut executives had knowledge of its deceptive practices. The rationale of these executives was that many firms were selling fake juice and that Beechnut had to remain competitive by doing the same. Second, Beechnut executives were convinced that the adulterated apple juice was perfectly safe. These rationalizations were flawed. At least 95 percent of the apple juice marketed during this period was legitimate. Beechnut was able to sell its fake apple juice at lower prices than the competition. The real motivation would seem to have been greed. Moreover, it was never conclusively proven that the fake apple juice was not a health hazard. After paying $25 million in fines and legal costs and experiencing negative publicity, in 1987 near-record losses staggered Beechnut. Consumer trust had been destroyed.

In 1991, Beechnut became the first major baby food manufacturer to introduce a product line, called Special Harvest, made with organic ingredients. Again, Beechnut was plunged into controversy, for Earth's Best Baby Food, a firm that had introduced a line of organic baby food three years previously, accused Beechnut of adhering to lower standards. The Earth's Best line contained twenty-one products, including cereals, juices, and prepared fruits and vegetables. None of the products contained salt, sugar, preservatives, or fillers. Beechnut was operating within the law, but its standards regarding synthetic chemicals was not as high as Earth's Best. Finally, Beechnut discontinued its Special Harvest product line after poor sales performance.

Beechnut has been tainted by the past. General Mills, its new owner, is a sophisticated marketer and may be able to overcome past mistakes. General Mills, with its cereal product line and other product lines, is firmly established in supermarkets and other stores that sell baby food. General Mills has had lots of marketing muscle in the past, but if Beechnut is to be placed in a corrective position, the marketing of baby food must be given a high priority.

H. J. Heinz: King of the International Baby Food Industry

The H. J. Heinz Company markets more than 4,000 varieties of food globally, which is a far cry from the original 57 varieties made famous through advertising at the turn of the century. The current product mix encompasses soup, sauces, pet food, frozen potatoes, tuna, tomato ketchup, snacks, pasta, and baby food, among the many varieties. In the United States, Heinz has 52 percent of the retail ketchup market share, 49 percent of the retail frozen potato market share, 45 percent of the tuna market share, and 32 percent of the canned cat food market share. Globally, it has 90 percent of the Italian baby food market, and 34 percent of the U.K. baby food market, but it is a sleeping giant in the United States.

In 1869, Henry J. Heinz and L. Clarence Noble launched Heinz and Noble. The business prospered until 1875, when an overabundance of crops brought bankruptcy. Heinz started again, but without Noble, and by 1896, at the age of 52, he was a millionaire. In 1893, pickle pins were introduced at the Chicago World's Fair, to become one of the most popular promotions in the history of American business. By 1896, the magic number of "57 Varieties" was world renowned. The Depression became a period to launch new products and take new chances for Heinz, unlike many other companies, and soups and baby food were added to the product line. Both were to become top sellers during this period. Corporate culture emphasized product quality.

Although Heinz is the world's leading baby food producer, and in the 1990s expanded further in Europe, India, and Latin America, the company has only about 10 or 11 percent market share of the baby food industry in the United States. Heinz has bolstered its image and market share at least another 2 percent in the U.S. baby food industry by acquiring Earth's Best. Earth's Best was founded in 1987 and is the leading processor of organic baby foods. The company sells its product not only through supermarkets, but through natural-health-food stores, which constitute approximately one-quarter of its sales. Earth's Best does not use any fillers, salt, sugar, or preservatives, and it also manufactures a junior product line. Since many consumers are double-income families and have small families, there is a market niche for a premium baby food category that can return profitability to the supermarket baby aisle. Unfortunately, supermarkets, in the past, have used baby food as loss leaders to increase store traffic. Three major California supermarket chains—Vons, Safeway, and Lucky—have added the Earth's Best product line, which is priced roughly $.25 cents per jar more than Gerber or Beechnut jars. While baby food sales have decreased about 14 percent in the 1990s, Earth's Best sales have increased by 27 percent. By 1996, Earth's Best products were distributed in nearly 45 percent of U.S. supermarkets. Earth's Best was so successful that Beechnut withdrew its Special Harvest organic product line, a direct competitor. A pesticide scare has frightened parents, and they seek other alternatives to traditional baby food. The medical industry has found that baby food contains more pesticides than is considered healthy.

Heinz, in an attempt to serve a market niche for parents who are concerned about potential health hazards, has developed bottled water for infants. Heinz Pure Spring Water for Babies was introduced first to health professionals, and then a consumer panel was invited to test the product. The product is marketed on the basis of the convenience factor of not having to boil water. Heinz is therefore moving in the direction of expanding further into the baby food industry in the United States.

Heinz, in 1995, announced a change in overall company advertising strategy that might bolster its presence in the baby food industry. Company executives maintained that it was too expensive to advertise Heinz brands individually and that abandoning product-specific advertising in favor of brand building and direct-marketing efforts would be more profitable. The rationale behind this strategy change was that due to competitive pressures, Heinz had to find new techniques to promote brand loyalty. However, in the baby food industry, both Gerber and Beechnut have established brand preference, and the strategy may prove unsatisfactory. Heinz might strengthen brand loyalty more by widening its presence in marketing to the segment of parents who are very concerned about their babies' future health.

MARKETING STRATEGIES

Firms within the baby food industry have operated on a set of assumptions about their own situation. For example, Gerber may see itself as the industry leader and as having the best sales force, while Beechnut may see itself as a low-cost producer and Heinz may see itself as a socially conscious firm. Such assumptions about its own situation will guide the development of the firm's strategies and the way it reacts to change. These assumptions about the firm's situation, however, may or may not be accurate. If the assumptions are inaccurate, strategies may have an intriguing impact. For example, the baby food industry has believed that it could increase prices and that since there was great consumer brand acceptance, these price increases would have little impact. Instead, consumers have tried for various reasons to use substitute juices and other products. One reason may be high prices and another may have been the tarnished image of baby food manufacturers over a period of time. It was not just the "baby bust" that decreased sales.

Timing is a paramount variable in determining marketing strategy. Sometimes a firm may gain an important advantage from being among the first to take a specific action. The first major brand in the market may have lower costs for establishing and maintaining a brand presence, since there is a lack of competition. Gerber, for example, exploited this advantage in the baby food industry. However, those firms that enter a market later may be able to avoid the high product- or market-development costs borne by the first major firm to establish itself in the industry. Learning from mistakes of competitors can also be profitable, so that companies that enter the market at a later stage may be in an advantageous position.

Competition in the baby food industry has had both desirable and detrimental effects on the entire industry. Gerber over a period of time emphasized product quality and service to retailers. Gerber also advertised heavily and helped to evolve the industry into one with a few strong brands and high entry barriers. Suddenly, Gerber's image became tarnished through glass breakage in transit, a situation that Gerber's public relations department handled poorly, and the entire industry lost the confidence of the public. Beechnut, historically, reinforced positive dimensions of the industry through its high advertising volume, frequent product introductions, and stable prices. Suddenly, Beechnut was acquired by other firms, and the infamous apple juice fraud scandal undermined the entire industry. The public became very concerned over ingredients in baby food, and this led to a lack of confidence and mistrust. Although Heinz had an enviable reputation in marketing numerous food products, Heinz has repeatedly upset the equilibrium of the baby food industry with a low-price strategy in a futile effort to overtake Gerber and Beechnut. The acquisition of firms in the baby food industry may well modify goals and objectives so that environmental turbulence becomes a dominant force.

The classic mistake in developing strategy was Gerber's contention that the birthrate would continue to increase beyond the 1950s. This assumption proved false, as the birthrate declined steadily until about 1979. Gerber was to suffer the consequences of this erroneous assumption. Moreover, Gerber's lack of vision in overseas markets allowed Heinz to gain a strong foothold abroad.

In spite of the mistakes of the baby food industry, brand acceptance is a reality. Consumers have a high level of brand familiarity and are aware of both positive and negative aspects of company performance. The level of brand familiarity may affect the development of marketing strategy. For example, Gerber believed that there was high brand familiarity and proceeded to enter the clothing, toy, furniture, and life insurance business. Entry into the furniture, toy, and clothing business sectors turned out to be mistakes. Gerber, Beechnut, and Heinz have achieved high levels of brand recognition, which means that consumers have heard of and remember these brands. Earth's Best, owned by Heinz, does not have such high recognition. However, those consumers with special interests in health food may have seen the brand in health-food stores, so recognition may be present. Devices at the point of purchase or direct marketing may be needed to sell this brand. Gerber, Beechnut, and Heinz have achieved different degrees of brand preference, which means that customers will generally select one of these brands over other brands. Brand preference can help a firm achieve a favorable position in a monopolistic competition situation. However, consumers will purchase another brand at times if there is a special sale or if the preferred brand of baby peas, to illustrate, is temporarily out of stock.

Gerber was the innovator in the baby food industry and demonstrated during the market-development stage that demand existed, but armies of imitators marched in to capitalize on and help create the market-growth stage. The baby food industry could do no wrong during the baby-boom years from 1945 to 1964. Competition increased many costs, including those for promotion and distribution. Unfortunately, baby food manufacturers, notably, Gerber and Beechnut, made mistakes, and their image became tarnished. As the industry moves through the 1990s, Gerber has been acquired by Sandoz and Beechnut by General Mills. Heinz has accelerated its interest in baby food by acquiring Earth's Best. Marketing strategies and campaigns should grow more sophisticated as these giant firms with larger financial budgets and greater marketing expertise intensify efforts to increase market share.

Success Does Not Guarantee Continued Success

Gerber and Beechnut made mistakes but were able to survive because they maintained a respectable batting average. Gerber and Beechnut were notably successful and dominated the baby food industry, but at the very pinnacle of their success, they made mistakes that considerably slowed their momentum. For these firms, success promoted vulnerability and complacency.

There is a need for growth, but not reckless growth. Gerber plunged into the furniture business, the toy business, and the clothing business like a swimmer who cannot swim plunges into the water without a life jacket. Gerber expanded its target market without adequately researching the competitive environment and without controlling its physical resources. Abilities of its personnel were exceeded in unfamiliar business sectors. Gerber also tried to develop trade channels in overseas markets, but did not realize it lacked expertise and financial resources.

Image development of a firm or brand is paramount. Gerber tarnished its image by handling public relations poorly when glass jar breakage occurred in transit. Beechnut tarnished its image when it admitted to selling adulterated and mislabeled apple juice intended for babies. The product contained little if any apple juice and was composed of mostly beet sugar, cane sugar, corn syrup, and other ingredients. Beechnut entered a guilty plea and paid $2 million in fines. Two Beechnut executives were fined and imprisoned. To change or upgrade an image is usually a long process. Many consumers equipped with modern kitchen appliances were able to prepare their own baby food. The baby bust was another factor that caused both Beechnut and Gerber problems. Both firms were slow to grasp the importance of demographic trends, and both firms lacked strong financial resources to escape quickly from a negative or fuzzy image. Neither Gerber nor Beechnut was characterized by the development of adaptive and innovative strategies by management.

Marketing Successes in the Baby Food Industry

- Penetration of international markets by Heinz
- Targeting the organic baby food market
- A strong sales-representative staff by Gerber
- Strong brand recognition

Marketing Mistakes in the Baby Food Industry

- Failure to recognize environmental considerations such as the baby bust
- Slow response to consumers' nutritional concerns, allowing Earth's Best to gain market entry
- Complacency with success
- Allowing corporate images to tarnish without strong corrective action
- Lack of adaptive strategies
- Reacting to trends rather than developing proactive strategies

MANAGING CHANGE

The baby food industry has earned low grades for managing change. Even after the baby-boom years were over, Gerber maintained that the baby birthrate would increase substantially. A reversal of the baby-bust years, from about 1965 to 1978, did not occur until 1979. During a pronounced period of contraction, Gerber and other firms in the baby food industry continued to develop strategies that ignored trends. Principally, Gerber expanded into other product lines such as furniture, toys, and clothing, believing that population trends warranted diversified expansion. These assumptions proved to be mistaken. Population-growth trends can be more accurately forecasted, and a number of other industries did profit from correct predictions. The baby food industry did not manage change well even when it became certain that baby birth rates were decreasing. Forecasting figures from the Census Bureau were available and largely correct, but the baby food industry operated under delusions.

Heinz did realize that opportunities existed internationally. Gerber and Beechnut, for whatever reasons, allowed Heinz to become entrenched overseas and then tried to penetrate these markets, without success. In this area Heinz has achieved success, becoming the largest producer of baby food in world markets. Heinz has a commanding market share in Italy, Great Britain, Hungary, and the Czech Republic, and is strengthening itself in the Middle East and Russia. In Canada, Australia, and New Zealand, Heinz enjoys about 90 percent of the jarred baby food business. Heinz is currently endeavoring to penetrate the market in India and in parts of Africa. Heinz has envisioned correctly that ample opportunities exist in baby food markets overseas and has tried to position itself accordingly.

Failure to anticipate environmental change is potentially disastrous for the business organization. Yet firms in the baby food industry were unable to incorporate monitoring techniques into their planning. The need to envision the future greatly broadens the firm's environment. This search enables the business organization to move away from its immediate environment by perceiving future trends that will modify and alter corporate strategies. Plans for the future can then be developed from scanning and monitoring demographic, economic, social and cultural, political and legal, technological, ecological, and competitive forces.

Both Beechnut and Gerber have failed to understand greater consumer awareness of the ingredients in the composition of baby food. Beechnut underestimated the fallout from the apple juice fraud perpetrated on consumers. Gerber needed to withdraw starch and other ingredients used in its products because of consumer concern. Consumers are better educated than ever before and are closely monitoring the ingredients within products. There has been heavy pressure by consumer advocates to fortify labeling legislation, and this vigilance will probably continue in the future.

MANAGERIAL INSIGHTS

The baby food industry does not have the reputation or the public image of the breakfast cereal industry in promoting research to improve health and nutrition. Finally, in 1996, Gerber yielded to consumer concerns and developed a new formula that eliminated added starch and sugar in its product line. This strategy was implemented not so much in the interest of improved nutrition for babies but as a competitive response to inroads made by the Earth's Best brand of organic baby foods. In 1986, bits of glass were found in Gerber's peach jars due to breakage in transit. The public relations department chose to ignore the incident until lagging sales caused it to react. Again, the image of Gerber was tarnished. Beechnut, after some years of unfavorable press coverage, in 1986 finally pleaded guilty to 215 felony counts and violations of food and drug legislation in selling adulterated apple juice from 1981 to 1983. The public's perception of the baby food industry was changed appreciably because of the phony apple juice scandal, and it undermined consumers' image of baby food standards and purity. While not proven conclusively, it was intimated that Beechnut executives knew of this abhorrent situation as early as 1977.

Previous to these incidents, both Gerber and Beechnut had reputations for high standards and quality. Neither firm really considered that the resulting bad publicity and negative public reactions would linger long in consumers' memories. But the product involved infants, and thus these incidents were more inflammatory than expected. The Beechnut debacle should be sobering for many firms in the food industry. It should raise some anxieties about possible damage to the firm's image, which can be difficult to repair. To ignore such adverse incidents can be viewed as apathy. These challenges, if ignored, can turn into problems that will not readily go away.

Even though Gerber was not really at fault in the glass incident, an adversarial stand may only heighten public concerns. The old adage, "Where there's smoke, there's fire," can only fuel public qualms. A social problem should be addressed with a spirit of cooperation. After all, Johnson & Johnson was not at fault in the 1982 Tylenol affair, but it handled the situation delicately and earned the respect of the public and the admiration of other business organizations. Both Gerber and Beechnut needed greater sensitivity in areas involving corporate social performance. Otherwise, these firms and perhaps the entire industry can be confronted with a deteriorating image problem. Babies are precious, and those firms appealing to this market need to be keenly aware of their social responsibilities. The health of babies and toddlers will not be compromised, and if the baby food industry places that health in jeopardy in any way, it will not be readily forgiven.

Gerber did not remove added starch and sugar from its product line until 1996, demonstrating a lethargy that can only be described as marketing myopia. There are some major points to be learned from the baby food industry's painful procrastination in responding to public pressures:

- Public relation deficiencies are costly. Even if the company is not at fault, response should be quick, before potential problems escalate. The public relations efforts of Beechnut, in particular, and also of Gerber seemed impotent. Not even the social-performance model developed by Johnson & Johnson in the Tylenol affair served as an example. As a matter of fact, this incident, which earned Johnson & Johnson praise, has often been ignored.

- Corporate images are vulnerable. Beechnut had a reputable image before the apple juice fraud scandal, but learned that a corporate image can quickly be besmirched. The power of social awareness and activist groups should not be underestimated. This power of social awareness has grown in the past decade. Firms such as Beechnut and Gerber are prominent in the baby food industry and therefore have greater visibility and public recognition than lesser-known firms. In addition, infants are viewed as helpless and precious, and any act that detrimentally affects their health will be viewed with greater public anger than acts that take place in other business sectors.

- Companies must be responsible corporate citizens. Beechnut and Gerber are doing business in a sensitive area and need to prove that they are responsible corporate citizens. Heinz and other firms serving the infant market do not have the prominence of either Gerber or Beechnut. The longevity of a besmirched reputation is difficult to estimate.

Beechnut's troubles have continued for a number of years. Other firms have acquired Beechnut, but they had other interests that deserved higher priorities. Beechnut has never really bounced back, for one reason or another, from the apple juice fraud scandal that was finally settled in 1986. Gerber, on the other hand, was not really at fault in the glass fragment incident, though it handled the situation poorly. The starch-and-sugar controversy was resolved, but reveals that management had a reactive rather than a proactive perspective. It is difficult to conceive that in an industry where two firms dominate, there is not high profitability for both firms. Unfortunately, in 1996 the Federal Trade Commission requested that Gerber desist from making false and misleading advertising claims about its baby food. Specifically, the campaign boasted that four out of five pediatricians recommend Gerber baby food to parents, when actually only 12 percent of those surveyed made such a statement. Gerber just doesn't seem to realize the value of good public relations and the impact of negative criticism relating to infants.

The baby food industry ignores marketing techniques, at least until great damage has been done to company image and market share. It demonstrates the consequences of marketing myopia. The problem was that the industry expected the status quo in regard to accelerating births to continue. A firm needs to be adaptable and prepared to adjust to a changing environment. Poor demographic forecasting and poor public-relations strategies have been characteristics of the baby food industry in the past. The baby food industry should accurately forecast market potential first and untapped potential second. To some extent this was done in serving the toddler market and in Gerber's establishment of a life insurance company. A potential market should be carefully selected and solid marketing strategies developed. This was not done in the past. Placing pictures of the elderly on baby jars in attempting to serve the senior citizen market was a fiasco. In any event, if other markets are selected for possible penetration, the public image of the firm must be scrupulously protected.

CHAPTER 7

THE ETHNIC FOOD INDUSTRY

Environmental Changes
- Ethnic population increases
- Popularity of ethnic food
- Health and dietary changes
- New upscale markets
- Fierce competition
- The graying of America
- Increased multiculturalism

Responses to Environmental Changes
- Promote take-out food
- Emphasize healthy offerings
- Mainstream ethnic products to non-ethnic groups
- Attempt food store distribution
- Neighborhood segmentation
- Geographic cluster segmentation
- Bilingual human resources

The first immigrants were predominately white Protestants from a Western-European culture perpetuated by an upper class. Subsequent waves of Germans and Irish had to assimilate in a culture basically influenced by British aristocracy. As the Germans and Irish moved upward in social class standing, other immigrants from southern and eastern Europe immigrated. A great wave of immigrants arrived in the United States during the years from 1890 to 1910. These immigrants were by and large uneducated and unskilled. As generation succeeded generation, these groups also assimilated and moved up in social class standing. Consequently, there tends to be an ethnic variable in social class hierarchies. Although ethnic communities may be voluntary, this did not prevent the development of subclasses in communities of Italian, Polish, Scandinavian, or other ethnic extraction.

A similar process appears to be operating within Hispanic and Asian groups. Although recent immigrants tend to hold on to their culture and language, their offspring in turn tend to adopt the social and economic ways of thinking of mainstream America. Subgroups within the immigrant group, such as Hispanics from Cuba and Mexico, may behave differently and might find the assimilation process more difficult. African-American groups were in the United States well before the Civil War, but assimilation was delayed because of slavery until the middle part of the 20th century. A common factor in the assimilation of all ethnic groups, with the exception of African Americans, has been language barriers.

When assimilation has taken place, there are generally feelings of status anxiety. This may take the form of conspicuous consumption in consumer behavior. Thorstein Veblen coined the term "conspicuous consumption," and it was meant to characterize individuals who obtain products simply to visibly display them. But certain items can express social class status and might be quite important to an individual who desires, or has achieved, social class mobility. As a result of culture contact, people tend to resist change in whatever was learned early in life and more readily change whatever was learned late in life. Consequently, food eating habits tend to be retained in later life. Hispanics are known to be heavy consumers of beans. For example, the children of successful Cuban Americans may retain their preference for black beans, the children of successful Puerto Rican Americans may retain their preference for red beans, and the children of successful Mexican Americans may retain their preference for refried beans in adult life. Even though these immigrants and their children may have become successful professional people, food preferences may be handed down from one generation to another. Food eating habits are hard to overcome and may be the last to change in the assimilation process.

There are numerous factors that enter into the selection of a particular subcultural group as a target market. While size is a significant variable, there are other determinants in marketing strategies aimed at subcultural groups. For example, the number of Jews in the United States who insist on kosher products is relatively small. Yet, they appear to be considered a significant ethnic market segment. For example, marketers have extended the preferences of this subcultural group to the total population with marketing campaigns, for example, that state, "You don't have to be Jewish to like Levy's rye bread." This strategy has been used by other firms to sell kosher hot dogs and other meat products. Marketing campaigns tried to persuade consumers to perceive the word "kosher" as indicating high quality.

Although the Chinese population is relatively small in the United States, Chinese restaurants are ample in metropolitan areas, and generous shelf space is given in supermarkets for the sale of Chinese food. The United States is characterized by both cultural assimilation and structural pluralism. Cultural assimilation means that the major ethnic groups in the United States tend to share a common culture, but structural pluralism means that each of these groups retains a sense of identity.

The power of subcultures and their impact on potential marketing strategies is evident when it is considered that some of the largest cities in the United States, including Baltimore, Chicago, Los Angeles, Miami, San Antonio, and Washington, D.C., have majority populations of Asians, African Americans, Hispanics, and other minorities. Ethnic groups can be referred to as subcultures because they have values, customs and traditions, and activities that are peculiar to a particular group within a culture.

Consumer eating habits have changed noticeably in the past decade. Consumers have not only embraced ethnic foods but have become more health conscious and concerned about the fat and sodium content of foods. Moreover, adults are monitoring their weight. Consumption of poultry products such as chicken and turkey has increased, while the consumption of red meats has declined. Lean meats with lower cholesterol content are a significant consumer preference. The method of food preparation—whether food is broiled or fried—has become another concern.

In considering the successes and mistakes of food marketers, mistakes have been made, but these organizations have survived by making constant adjustments of such variables as innovation, target market and image, physical environmental resources, and human resources. These food organizations did not necessarily earn high grades in the use of all variables, but some of the variables were implemented in an exceedingly capable manner. Americans have been able to sample ethnic food by eating in ethnic restaurants, and as a result, innovation has focused upon mainstreaming ethnic products to and through food stores. Hunt-Wesson brands such as La Choy, Chun King, Rosarita, and Gebhardt products represent attempts to penetrate the Asian and Hispanic markets and to mainstream ethnic products to and through food stores. Mainstreaming ethnic products is the key to the future. Although Hunt-Wesson is innovating in growing ethnic markets, many firms are not this future oriented. Companies like Goya Foods are going head to head with Fortune 500 firms such as Sara Lee, but many of these giant firms still only allocate 5 to 10 percent of their marketing budget to ethnic marketing. Progresso and other firms are successfully targeting ethnic markets. Campbell Soup has acquired Casera and has successfully developed a favorable image in targeting the Hispanic market. Empire Kosher Poultry has not only successfully targeted the Jewish ethnic market but has broadened its appeal to serve the non-Jewish population as well. Favorable images have been developed by many firms serving ethnic markets, but future marketing should involve not only the targeting of ethnic markets but the inclusion of the nonethnic population.

A company's physical resources, such as distribution centers and warehousing, are extremely important in reaching diverse ethnic markets. Although many ethnic markets are situated in California, Texas, and New York, these populations, in succeeding generations, will relocate to other states. The hiring of bilingual personnel by large Fortune 500 companies has been effective but not necessarily outstanding. However, many ethnic food manufacturers are relatively small in size and resources and therefore have penetrated either local or regional markets.

Some ethnic food marketers have made mistakes because their executives were not bilingual and lacked both the depth and breadth of knowledge concerning the ethnic culture to be targeted. Many firms approached ethnic markets by simply using general materials and dropping in a few foreign phrases, believing that this was all that was needed. This monolithic approach ignored cultural and geographical realities. Many ethnic groups like to buy products that remind them of home. Colgate-Palmolive and Nestlé have realized these sentiments and in response have imported products from Latin America to sell to Hispanics in the United States.

Cultural sensitivity and language capability would seem to be the keys to success in marketing to ethnic food markets. For example, in an advertisement placed in Miami, an orange juice manufacturer used the word "china," which is the Cuban word for orange, but to Puerto Ricans, the word "china" had sexual connotations associated with the male reproductive organ, and they were offended. Another classic mistake was when "Schweppes Tonic Water" was changed to "Schweppes Tonic" in Italy, where "il water" indicates a bathroom. Buying habits also differ among ethnic markets. Hispanics of Mexican origin use dried herbs extensively, but Puerto Ricans generally prefer capsules.

MARKET STRUCTURE

The United States has several important subcultures that have some distinctive values, norms, and behavior, which in turn identify them as market segments for food marketers. These segments include ethnic markets such as Hispanics and Asians, religious groups such as Jews and Catholics, and geographic groups such as Californians and New Yorkers. The values and norms of geographic groups may reflect the influences of religion, nationality, and even climatic conditions. Thus race, nationality, religion, and geography can be useful in defining subcultures. Age and social class can be other variables. Food marketers must consider subcultures within the United States in formulating appropriate marketing strategies.

The 1990 census reported that between 1980 and 1990, the Asian population grew by 65 percent and the Hispanic population increased by 44 percent. The Asian population comprised only about 3 percent, while the Hispanic population increased from 6 to 8 percent from 1980 to 1990. African Americans have maintained a steady 12 percent share, while the European-American share has decreased slightly from 86 percent to 84 percent. Immigration is increasing, with the largest number of newcomers coming from Mexico, Central America, and South America. A significant number of immigrants still come from Europe, but Mexico accounted for 15 percent of all immigrants and was the leading country of origin.

Table 7.1 shows the food preferences of ethnic groups. Although Italian, Hispanic, Asian, Jewish, Cajun, Greek, and French populations may be small in the United States, the food preferences of these segments have become more widespread and constitute a relatively important part of the consumption patterns of nonethnic group members. There are certainly other ethnic groups, such as Polish and African Americans, but the food preferences of these groups are becoming more widespread in mainstream America.

Italian food is the leading favorite among consumers. Although the Italian population is relatively small in the United States, non-Italian Americans have embraced Italian food. The restaurant penetration of Italian entrees in order of preference is as follows: lasagna, spaghetti with sauce,

Table 7.1
Food Preferences of Ethnic Groups, 1996

Ethnic Groups	Subcultural Segments
Italian	
Hispanic	Mexican, Puerto Rican, Cuban
Asian	Chinese, Filipino, Korean, Vietnamese, Asian Indian, Japanese
Jewish	Orthodox, Conservative, Reform
Cajun	
Greek	
French	

Source: Adapted from U.S. census classifications.

pizza, veal or chicken parmigiana, and ravioli. There has been, in the 1990s, a remarkable increase of Italian cheese production, including Parmesan, provolone, mozzarella, and ricotta cheese. The consumption of Italian food far outpaces the consumption of any other ethnic food.

Hispanics are the second-largest and fastest growing minority market in the United States. The Bureau of the Census projects that by 2010, Hispanics will account for 14 percent of the population and will outnumber African-American consumers. The Hispanic population is largely of Mexican (61 percent), Puerto Rican (15 percent), and Cuban (7 percent) origin. They have clustered in six cities: Miami for Cubans; Los Angeles, San Antonio, and Houston for Mexicans; New York for Puerto Ricans; and Chicago for all groups. Hispanics are growing increasingly affluent and thus becoming an important market. Since Hispanics have distinctive food purchasing patterns, marketers are trying to learn more about food preferences and to satisfy a much greater potential demand in the future. Other Hispanics have immigrated from Central and South America, and like groups from Mexico, Puerto Rico, and Cuba, have their own distinctive food preferences and purchasing patterns. Cuban immigrants have obtained more formal education before coming to the United States than either Mexican or Puerto Rican immigrants. Twice as many Cubans have university degrees as do other Hispanics, and more than 60 percent have graduated from high school, compared to a little more than 50 percent for other Hispanic groups. Cuban Americans have a relatively higher median age, and this may account for differences in education and income levels.

African-American consumers represent the largest minority group, with 12 percent of the population. Their numbers are expected to increase to 35 million by 2000. African-American females represent a potent force in the African-American family since almost half of the African-American families with children are headed by a female. Dual-career African-American couples are narrowing the traditional income gap. African-American consumers are more likely than European-American consumers to live in the crowded, poorer neighborhoods of large urban cities. Although the African-American population in the South decreased slowly until 1980, the South still accounts for about half of the African-American population in the United States. A reverse migration pattern has taken place from the Northeast to the South, but this pattern has not been significant.

African-American and European-American consumer expenditure patterns reveal more similarities than differences when considering spending behavior. Spending patterns, however, differ significantly within certain broad expenditure categories. These differences may be linked to African Americans' lower incomes and their concentration in large metropolitan centers. In some cases, African Americans and European Americans may constitute a single market, but for other products and services they constitute two distinct markets. African-American food preferences have not become widespread in mainstream America.

Asian consumers, like Hispanic consumers, are composed of many different nationality groups. Filipinos, Chinese, Koreans, Vietnamese, Asian Indians, and Japanese, in that order, will be the largest groups in that population mix by 2010. Asian consumers have settled in primarily five states: California, Hawaii, New York, Illinois, and Washington. Projections are that the Asian population in the United States will increase from approximately four million in 1980 to about ten million by 2010. Education is highly prized by Asian Americans. They are more likely to obtain a college education than the average American. They also aspire to managerial and professional status. It is likely that in the future, this market segment will integrate like immigrants in previous generations. Marketers would do well to position luxury goods to this market in the future. Eating habits are generally the last to change in the assimilation process, and this potential market should continue to be attractive for marketers. It is also likely that European-American consumers will increase their preferences for Asian food.

In summary, with growth rates that exceed 2 percent until 2030, the racial and ethnic groups with the highest rate of growth will be the Hispanic-origin and the Asian and Pacific Islander populations. The total U.S. population, even during the baby-boomer years, never had such a high growth rate. The Hispanic-origin population may become the second-largest ethnic group by 2010. By 2050, it is projected that the Hispanic group will comprise about 25 percent and the African-American group about 15 percent of the population. Since accelerating growth rates characterize Hispanic and Asian groups, marketers would do well not only to satisfy the food preferences of these groups, but to realize that many food tastes of these Hispanic and Asian groups may be adopted by the remainder of the population.

Whereas these ethnic population figures are important, food marketers still need to understand food preferences not only for ethnic group segments but for the broad spectrum of consumers. Although food preferences may change from time to time, the preference for tasting different ethnic foods would seem to be a basic consumer behavior characteristic in the United States for a variety of reasons. Although Jewish, Greek, and French populations are relatively small in the United States, the food preferences of these groups have become mainstream food preferences.

MARKET CONDUCT

Food marketers should be aware that the Hispanic market is highly individualistic in its product and brand preferences, which are frequently reflective of cultural distinctions. This market is very significant for food purchases. Hispanics, partly because of their larger-than-average families, spend more per week on food purchases than do other groups. Hispanic families also visit fast-food restaurants more often than non-Hispanic consumers. Hispanic Americans tend to be highly brand loyal, trusting well-known, high-quality, and familiar brands. Many Hispanics view shopping as a social event. They want to spend hours browsing and chatting with friends. While shopping, they also like to eat food and listen to music that reminds them of home. Stores with festive colors and designs make them feel more comfortable.

Hispanics have not integrated as quickly as earlier immigrant groups. Because of their frequent contact with their homelands and their local concentrations, Hispanics are clinging to their language and culture. Although the average Hispanic has resided in the United States for nearly 13 years, only about half are fluent in English. More than 60 percent of Hispanics speak Spanish at home, and about half speak Spanish at social functions. However, younger Hispanics are most fluent in English and are better able to communicate in English than older Hispanics. Those Hispanics who have either recently immigrated or have difficulty mastering English feel lost in giant supermarkets and are inhibited about asking questions. Therefore, they do much of their shopping in bodegas, which are small neighborhood stores where only Spanish may be spoken. For example, in New York City, bodegas account for 30 percent of the grocery volume among Spanish-speaking residents.

Television and radio are both important media for communicating with the Hispanic market. There are a number of Spanish television stations in the United States that feature Spanish-speaking advertising. Spanish television generally costs advertisers much less than general-market television advertising. Since Mexican stations have been added to cable networks, the marketer is increasingly able to reach the Hispanic market by using this medium. Moreover, there are at least 150 U.S. radio stations that present Spanish language programming on a full- or part-time basis. Radio ownership is high, and so is frequent listening—higher than the general population. Spanish-language television and radio audiences are both composed of less acculturated Hispanics, who generally have fewer resources.

African Americans have been slow to adopt generic and private brands. Brand loyalty is a distinguishing characteristic. African Americans tend to spend more on baby products and breakfast food than European Americans. Brand preference and purchasing expenditures demonstrate that for some types of products, marketers would do well to segment the African-American market. Food preferences, in particular, are learned early in life and seem to continue in later life. Education and income, however, may well modify many early influences and preferences. There are fewer differences between middle-class European Americans and middle-class African Americans than between middle-class African Americans and poorer, less-educated African Americans. Since it is possible to segment the European-American market, it is also possible to divide the African-American market into a variety of submarkets.

African-American consumers tend not to shop by telephone or by mail order as much as European-American consumers of comparable social classes. African-American upper-middle-class women are more fashion conscious than their European-American counterparts. Lower-class African-American consumers tend to make frequent trips to neighborhood grocery stores. Moreover, African-American consumers have more of a propensity to shop at discount stores compared to department stores than their European-American counterparts.

The most important African-American medium is radio. Approximately one-half of all African Americans listen to African-American radio stations. However, African-American magazines such as *Ebony* and *Jet* are widely read by African-American men and women. African-American magazines have a higher African-American readership than general-market magazines. African Americans strongly relate to African-American media since African-American achievements in government, business, sports, and the arts are emphasized.

Asian consumers, like Hispanics, place an emphasis on family shopping. Traditional Asian culture demonstrates deep respect for family elders. Shopping decisions may therefore be considerably influenced by older family members. The Asian market segment has the most similar consumer behavior patterns to the predominant ethnic majority in the United States. While food preferences may seem to be pronounced for this consumer segment, assimilation will modify these preferences.

Subcultural analysis enables marketers to segment their markets to satisfy the needs, attitudes, activities, interests, and values that are shared by members of a specific subcultural group. There is not any single ethnic market segment any more than there is a single European-American market segment. Rather, a heterogeneous group of segments within ethnic groups exists just as in the European-American market segment. These patterns can be described in terms of environmental influences on consumer behavior. The important distinction between a lifestyle and a subculture is the latter's capacity to endure.

Ethnicity, religion, and race represent market-segmentation variables. For example, Campbell Soup sells a product line of Hispanic foods and uses different campaigns to reach Caribbean Hispanics and Mexican Americans. Burger King uses Spanish-language advertising campaigns.

In a survey conducted by the Food Marketing Institute, the percentage of consumers eating each type of ethnic food at least once a week was reported as follows: Italian, 39 percent; Mexican, 21 percent; Chinese, 18 percent; Cajun, 5 percent; Middle Eastern, 3 percent; French, 3 percent; Indian, 1 percent. Sales of Islamic Halal food products, similar to Jewish Kosher foods, have increased as much as 70 percent since 1993, as the numbers of U.S. muslims grow.

There is a strong location factor behind all of these ethnic food preferences. For example, a preference for Cajun food would be evident in New Orleans and the state of Louisiana. This preference would be much stronger in larger metropolitan centers rather than in small rural areas of Montana or Arizona. Mexican food, while it is very popular, would witness stronger sales in California, Texas, Arizona, New Mexico, and Nevada and proportionately weaker sales volume in Maine and New Hampshire. There has been a relatively large influx of Greek immigrants to the Baltimore, Maryland, area and this accounts not only for a disproportionate number of Greek food courts but also for a growing preference for Greek food by the non-Greek population.

The marketing task in the future for food marketers is to transcend local and regional ethnic food preferences and to make these food preferences more widespread. For example, Italian food preferences are not so much regional in nature, but are present nationally. The penetration of Italian entrees, such as lasagna, spaghetti with sauce, and ravioli, in restaurants serving primarily American food is quite pronounced. Even the food store sales of spaghetti sauces, such as those by Ragu, Prego, Hunt's Classico, and Healthy Choice, have grown appreciably. To some extent, the producers of Jewish ethnic food have already tried and will continue to try to make their products more national in scope. Some years ago, a slogan was expressed: "You don't have to be Jewish to eat Levy's rye bread." This slogan should serve as a suggestion for producers of ethnic food to market their products to a broad spectrum of consumers. Consumers would seem to have a propensity to try or to experiment by eating different ethnic foods.

Italian, Hispanic, Asian, and Jewish subcultures, and their food preferences represent definable target groups for specific products and logical units for segmentation. Sales of Italian and Asian food, for example, penetrate beyond the relatively small Italian and Asian population numbers in the United States. Therefore, it is obvious that the specific food preferences of these ethnic groups have spread, as non-Italian and non-Asian Americans adapt their eating preferences for the enjoyment of Italian and Asian foods. With the influx of new immigrant groups into the United States, sophisticated consumers appear more inclined to sample new ethnic foods. Throughout the United States, small, independent ethnic restaurants are springing up to satisfy consumer demand for different ethnic foods. For those Americans who travel, there are eight Italian schools that offer cooking vacations, such as the International Cooking School of Italian Food and Wine, and Venetian Cooking in a Venetian Palace. In the long run, ethnic food preferences will become even more popular, and ethnic food will mainstream into restaurants, food stores, and homes.

Cultivating Italian Food Market Preferences

Well-known companies and brand names attempt to cultivate Italian food market preferences of consumers in the United States. The Italian ethnic food market ranks first, followed by the market for Mexican and oriental food. Hershey Foods, Borden, and CPC International are the three largest pasta producers, according to supermarket sales. Such brands and firms as Stouffer, Lean Cuisine, Weight Watchers, Michelina, and Healthy Choice dominate Italian frozen entrees. Italian sauces are dominated by Classico, Ragu Today's Recipe, Ragu Fino Italian, Progresso, and Francesco Rivaldi. The Ragu brand of pasta sauces, made by the international corporation Unilever, is an example of the importance of the Italian ethnic market in the United States. Classico, the industry leader among Italian sauces, is made by Borden. The most popular new products introduced in the 1990s are Italian and Mexican.

One of the most notable aspects of the growing preference for Italian food is in America's heartland. The largest markets are in New York City and Philadelphia, but the fastest growing markets are in Cincinnati/Dayton, Kansas City, Wichita, Peoria, Columbus, Toledo, and Green Bay. Anyone who has traveled across the United States realizes that there are many regional differences in consumption behavior. For example, in the South and Midwest white bread is preferred, while on the East Coast rye, whole-wheat, French, and Italian bread are preferred. Although these geographical preferences still remain, there is a growing preference for Italian food that is spreading to other regions of the country not previously viewed as lucrative markets. The increasing demand for Italian food has contributed to the growth of restaurant chains such as Olive Garden, owned by General Mills, which has more than 100 units, and Sbarro, which has more than 500 outlets in forty-eight states. The acceptance of Italian food is not a fad. This ethnic food preference has staying power. Italian restaurant distribution is strongest in the mid-Atlantic, Pacific Coast, south Atlantic, and eastern and north central states. The Spaghetti Warehouse, a restaurant chain based in Garland, Texas, is now selling franchises and stepping up expansion. The Italian meals most often served are lasagna, spaghetti with sauce, pasta with red sauce, fettuccine, and pizza. Brands that dominate their market segments for Italian food are Chef Boy-Ar-Dee and Franco-American for canned pasta, Progresso for canned soup, Ragu and Prego for spaghetti sauces, and Stouffer Lean Cuisine and Michelina for frozen Italian entrees.

The popularity of pizza need scarcely be mentioned. Pizza Hut has more than 8,000 units in the United States, and Domino's Pizza has more than 4,000 units. By comparison, Pizza Hut has at least 2,000 more units than Burger King. There has also been an increase in Italian restaurants catering to both casual and fine dining. Obviously, America's enthusiasm for Italian food has transcended ethnic background.

The bulk of Italian immigrants migrated to the United States during the period from 1890 to 1910. Many of these immigrants settled in New York City, Philadelphia, and Chicago. The older generation tended to preserve the customs and language from Italy. As generation succeeded generation, fluency in the Italian language diminished. However, food habits were passed from one generation to another. While these food preferences are not as strong in younger generations, to some extent they still exist. The melting-pot phenomenon of non-Italian Americans with the willingness to try different ethnic foods would seem to be as strong as ever. Italian foods and sauces are clear-cut favorites and continue to dominate the ethnic food market.

The Hershey Pasta Group is the number one company in its category and has reported record sales in the 1990s. The branded category composed of San Giorgio, American Beauty, Ronzoni, Skinner, and Light'N Fluffy provided the largest of sales volume growth. The profile of a typical pasta user is a female, married, most likely between the ages of 18 and 44, with an annual household income between $25,000 and $50,000, with at least one child living at home, with three or more packages of pasta and at least three different shapes of pasta in the cupboard but who consumes spaghetti more than any other shape. This consumer eats pasta one-third of the time when dining out and believes that pasta is a good source of complex carbohydrates and is economical, convenient, and filling.

Pasta has had positive press. Since 1975, the volume of pasta consumed

in pounds has more than doubled. Pasta is a food high in complex carbohydrates, and for those consumers concerned with proper eating habits,
this is a factor that constitutes significant patronage motivation. Moreover,
pasta has a long shelf life and is convenient to store and prepare. Another
reason pasta is popular is that consumers have grown up using Hershey
Pasta products, resulting in a loyalty element. Also, pasta is viewed as relatively inexpensive.

As Americans become more health conscious, various research organizations have conducted research studies on food. Italian food has been
ranked healthy and beneficial. This has been true of pasta but not necessarily of pizza and some types of cheeses that are used. However, there are
other cheese alternatives that are more beneficial for good health. On the
other hand, consumers have learned that there are various types of Chinese
food and Mexican food that are very high in fat content, sodium, and
cholesterol.

Italian food, to some extent, has been mainstreamed into restaurants,
food stores, and homes. This accomplishment should serve as an example
for marketers of other ethnic foods, such as Asian and Mexican. Marketers
have only superficially been alert to the potential of marketing Greek, Polish, Russian, and other types of ethnic food. Although not significant in
numbers, there is a new wave of immigration from Russia, India, and some
of the Arab countries that has profitable possibilities for food marketers.

Cultivating Hispanic Food Market Preferences

The task for food marketers is not only to identify food preferences of
the Hispanic market but to learn whether a broad spectrum of Americans
would also enjoy consuming the same types of food. Hispanics have been
a good market for food, beverage, and household-care products. Hispanic
consumers tend to be brand conscious and believe in the price-quality relationship. Generic products have not sold well to this market segment.
This market segment exhibits a high degree of brand loyalty, and therefore
it is important for firms to cultivate this market before competitors do.

Marketers use diverse approaches to segment the Hispanic market. One
approach is to offer one product or campaign as if it were a homogeneous
market. Another approach is to segment according to country or region of
origin. Other firms use lifestyle and psychographic variables. A fourth approach is to use Hispanic music and celebrities in advertisements. Although
language may be a common base, this subcultural group is not a single
market, but rather a number of subcultural markets indigenous to their
countries of origin. Therefore, marketers should be aware that what might
work in New York might not succeed in either Miami or California.

According to the available studies, Hispanics and European-American
consumers differ in terms of a variety of key buyer behavior variables.

Hispanic consumers generally exhibit high brand loyalty and have a preference for well-known or familiar brands. Brands that are perceived to have an image of status are viewed favorably. There is a high propensity to shop at smaller stores and to purchase brands that are promoted by the stores catering to their particular ethnic group. New product adoption may be inhibited by language difficulties. Hispanics are less confident shoppers than Anglo consumers and tend not to be impulse buyers. Moreover, Hispanic consumers tend to be more careful shoppers and more price oriented.

There would appear to be considerable differences in brand preferences, as reflected in brand share, between Hispanic and non-Hispanic consumers for some types of food products. For example, Hispanics have a higher preference for Libby's canned fruit, fruit-flavored Hawaiian Punch, Breyers ice cream, Oscar Mayer hot dogs, and Parkay margarine. Moreover, multiculturalism is creating new tastes. The increase in Mexican food in restaurants may just be the tip of the iceberg. To illustrate, from 1993 to 1994 the sales of shelf-stable Mexican food have increased more than 6 percent. The sales of frozen Mexican food increased by more than 5 percent. Furthermore, the sales of salsa (Mexican sauce) soared more than 12 percent. Tortilla sales have been steadily growing by about 12 percent every year for the last fifteen years. Supermarkets account for this increase as due to immigration factors and the changing consumer perception of ethnic foods. Mexican food restaurant chains are also growing appreciably, and Taco Bell has purchased Chevy's Mexican Restaurants, which experienced sales gains of 30 percent from 1991 to 1992. Taco Cabana and Azteca Mexican Restaurants are also experiencing phenomenal growth rates.

For some product categories, the differences in brand preferences between Hispanic and non-Hispanic consumers will have little or no impact on consumption patterns. Since the growth of interracial marriages, the deemphasis of religion by some, and the adoption of English language usage, the assimilation process has operated well. These forces have helped to blend the "melting pot" and to minimize differences among people.

Some marketers have believed that reaching the Hispanic consumer requires targeting separate Hispanic markets. For example, Anheuser-Busch targeted advertising to the Puerto Rican community by using scenes set in a disco and by featuring salsa rhythms. Commercials for Mexican-origin consumers were set in a rodeo to mariachi music. Advertisements to the Cuban market segment were set on a private ship because Cubans are the most affluent Hispanic group. Other manufacturers may use the same advertisement for the entire Hispanic market, believing that country of origin would not be that significant in determining purchasing behavior for their products. Still another dimension of segmenting the Hispanic market may be in terms of Hispanics' degree of acculturation to the dominant American cultural values and customs. This acculturation may well reflect comfortableness with the English language and the length of residence in the United

States. The extent of higher education may yet be another determinant of how marketers may approach and communicate effectively with the Hispanic market segment.

The Hispanic market is the fastest growing ethnic market. Its profitability in the long term should be considered attractive. A bilingual approach by marketing executives is essential for breadth and depth of market penetration. A new generation of consumers will be even more receptive to new types of ethnic food.

Cultivating Oriental-Food Market Preferences

The Asian market is the market segment that may have the most similar consumer behavior patterns to the population majority in the United States. Asian consumers, like Hispanic consumers, are composed of many different nationality groups. Filipinos, Chinese, Koreans, Vietnamese, Asian Indians, and Japanese, in that order, will be the largest groups in that population by 2010. Asian consumers have settled primarily in five states: California, Hawaii, New York, Illinois, and Washington. Projections are that the Asian population in the United States will increase from approximately four million in 1980 to about ten million by 2010.

Education is highly prized by Asian Americans. They are more likely to obtain a college education than the average American. They also aspire to managerial and professional status. It is likely that in the future this market segment will integrate, like immigrants in previous generations. Marketers would do well to position luxury goods to this market in the future. Emphasis, as for Hispanics, is on family shopping. Traditional Asian culture demonstrates deep respect for family elders. Shopping decisions may therefore be considerably influenced by older family members.

Hunt-Wesson is a subsidiary of ConAgra, a diversified food company that is a leading food organization in the United States. Although Hunt-Wesson is well known for its Peter Pan peanut butter, its Wesson cooking oils, and its Healthy Choice soups, Hunt-Wesson is also an important manufacturer of Chinese food. Hunt-Wesson produces and distributes La Choy products such as chow mein noodles and Bi Pack Dinners and Chun King products such as vegetables, sauces, and dinners. The Chun King and La Choy brands have a decisive distribution advantage in supermarkets over competing brands. Once Americans ate oriental food only outside the home, and it usually was Chinese, but now they want to duplicate the items eaten in restaurants in their own kitchens. Asian items placed on supermarket shelves include the familiar soy sauce, fried noodles, and fresh ginger, as well as the more unfamiliar wonton wrappers, oyster sauce, and Vietnamese fish sauce. Hunt-Wesson under its La Choy label distributes frozen egg-roll entrees that have been successful sellers in supermarkets.

Oriental food has invaded the supermarket shelves with significant penetration and has become a food in the mainstream.

Americans have become increasingly health conscious, and this has been reflected in their eating habits. Beef consumption declined by almost 5 percent during the 1980s, as the public became more aware of health risks. When a *60 Minutes* episode in 1991 suggested that red wine helps prevent heart disease, sales increased by 28 percent. The American public was surprised by a 1993 study that showed that some types of oriental food have more calories and a higher fat content than a Big Mac with fries. To illustrate, a Big Mac with fries has approximately 900 calories and 68 grams of fat compared to a serving of sweet and sour pork, which has approximately 1,600 calories and 71 grams of fat, and kung pao chicken which has 1,600 calories and 76 grams of fat. It is still too early to predict whether or not this study by the Center for Science in the Public Interest will be ominous for oriental restaurants such as the General Mills' China Coast restaurant chain and for oriental brands distributed in food stores. There are instances when consumers "do one thing and say another," and this Center for Science in the Public Interest report may not be taken seriously. For that matter, consumers may switch to steamed dishes and more healthy entrees such as chicken chow mein, hunan tofu, and shrimp and garlic sauce. Designating a portion of the menu for low-caloric, low-fat entrees would do much to ease the minds of those who are health conscious. Moreover, the labeling of oriental sauces and other oriental food sold in supermarkets should also improve the situation. As long as consumers have options between healthy and perhaps not-too-healthy entrees, it is doubtful that there will be much impact on sales.

Nearly a third of the Asian restaurant market is located on the West Coast. Another third of the restaurant market is located in the mid-Atlantic and southern Atlantic states. Oriental units comprise more than 6 percent of total U.S. restaurants. Although oriental food has grown increasingly popular with the emergence of Thai food and Vietnamese cuisine, a national oriental food chain that would be a counterpart to Domino's Pizza has not been successful, and significant time may elapse before a Taco Bell or Pizza Hut of the Asian market emerges. Health and dietary concerns can be turned into an advantage for Asian food, and national oriental restaurant chains with take-out food have interesting profitable possibilities.

Cultivating Jewish Food Market Preferences

Social and cultural patterns in the United States are changing rapidly, and marketers consequently must adjust their marketing strategies to these forces. Many firms have been very successful because they were able to make a shrewd appraisal of changes occurring in consumer markets. An effective method is to isolate future market opportunities by analyzing structural and behavioral dimensions of consumer markets.

Culture refers to the values, ideas, attitudes, and meaningful symbols created by a society to shape human behavior. Culture is transmitted from one generation to the next. The roles, goals, perceptions, consumption patterns, and consumption aspirations of a society reflect, to some extent and in varying degrees, the impact of culture on individuals and groups and, subsequently, on their purchasing behavior.

Many traditional values have been changing over the years. Kosher-food companies have been long associated with matzo and gefilte fish, but are now endeavoring to cultivate the mass marketplace. Kosher linguine, kosher frozen pizzas, kosher frozen yogurt and kosher baby cereal are among the results. Hebrew National, owned by ConAgra, Inc., increased its sales more than 4 percent from 1992 to 1993, and Empire Kosher Poultry increased its sales by more than 6 percent. About 60 percent of Hebrew National's frankfurter customers are not Jewish. However, some old-line kosher companies have been slow to adapt to these environmental trends; Manischewitz and Rokeach Foods each experienced sales declines of approximately 3 percent.

The general public appears to believe that kosher certification is a quality check on government food inspections. The term kosher would seem to be the equivalent of a Good Housekeeping seal of approval in the 1990s. For health-conscious consumers, a kosher designation has become important.

Although American Jews number only approximately six million in population, their higher-than-average incomes and concentration in key major markets make this group sought after targets for national brands. For example, Gerber Products Company acquired the kosher designation for its dry baby cereals. The Dannon Yogurt Company found that the Circle U label placed on a number of its products in late 1990 added $2 million in annual sales. This strategic plan helped Dannon gain shelf space in smaller stores and generated free publicity in Jewish media. The number of kosher-certified products has increased from about 18,000 in 1989 to about 23,600 in 1993. Growth is estimated at over 5 percent annually.

The kosher designation means that sources of ingredients and cleansers are checked to insure that no food is processed with derivatives of animal fat, such as gelatin. Beef and fowl animals must be slaughtered humanely and then completely drained of blood before processing. Periodic inspections are scheduled once kosher standards are certified. The control over the use of animal fats is perhaps the main reassurance that consumers find in a kosher endorsement.

Companies that have had kosher endorsement over the years include H. J. Heinz; Best Foods, the makers of Hellmann's mayonnaise; and Kraft, for such products as Breakstone dairy products and Post cereals. Maxwell House Coffee has segmented this niche for generations. Both *Food & Wine* magazine and *Rolling Stone* declared the kosher designation as one of the leading trends of the 1990s. Such brands as Coors Beer, Pepperidge Farm cookies, Nabisco's Grey Poupon mustard and Ben & Jerry's ice cream have been certified in the 1990s. This is added proof that the kosher designation has moved into the mainstream.

As an older generation disappears for one reason or another, kosher food companies like Hebrew National must reach out to a new generation. For example, a small company has been marketing kosher oriental pot pie and a kosher Mexican pie. Both cultural integration and a high rate of intermarriage has changed the traditional population base. The traditional Hebrew companies must change or risk the entry of small companies into marketplace as the window of opportunity opens. Empire Kosher Poultry sells its chicken for more than its competitors. One reason is that the observance of Kosher standards costs more. Therefore, Empire has tried to prove that its brand can compete on the basis of taste. In a blind test performed in a study by Pennsylvania State University, Empire was chosen the tastiest and most tender chicken over four leading consumer brands. Marketing efforts have targeted a market that desires a premium brand, and this strategy appears successful, since non-Jewish consumers have become more quality conscious. Brands such as Goodman have been slow to realize the profitable possibilities for mainstreaming their brands.

MARKETING SUCCESSES AND MISTAKES

Social and cultural patterns in the United States are changing rapidly, and therefore marketers must adjust their marketing strategies to these forces. Each culture includes various subcultures, which provide a more precise identification of individual consumers. Ethnic subcultures offer food marketers an opportunity to identify more exactly behavioristic purchasing patterns of Hispanic, Italian, Jewish, oriental, and other market segments. Special marketing strategies fail when marketers believe that, for example, all Hispanics make up one homogeneous subculture with common needs, motives, and attitudes. To illustrate, Hispanics include Mexican Americans, Puerto Ricans, Cubans, Latin Americans, and Central Americans. There are significant differences between these market segments that relate to language, values, lifestyles, and customs, and it would be a mistake not to acknowledge these differences.

Another important aspect of subcultures for food marketers is that products sometimes flow from a specific subculture into the more general population. Tacos, pizza, bagels, and sukiyaki are examples of ethnic food that have been accepted in mainstream America. Marketers are making a mistake if they do not try to mainstream ethnic food.

Marketers should also recognize that members of ethnic groups have a tendency to move toward homogeneity. Although many Hispanic, Italian, and Jewish consumers may hold on to some of their food preferences for many generations, their purchasing behavior will broaden, and new foods will be accepted as members of these ethnic groups strive for middle-class status. Much of consumer behavior is influenced by social pressure, and consequently, if ethnic group members desire to identify with middle-class culture, they will behave in ways acceptable to mainstream Americans. If integration is desired, then members of ethnic groups will be assimilated, and this will be reflected in their purchasing patterns.

The risk of a tarnished image is especially deadly for ethnic food marketers. In 1991, Manischewitz pleaded no contest to federal price-gouging charges. The company paid $1 million in fines and contributed an additional $1.8 million in food for charity. In 1996, it was found that a 5-pound box of Manischewitz matzo retailed for $3.99 in Century City, California; $4.98 in Brooklyn, New York; $8.95 in Atlanta, Georgia; and $11.99 in Boca Raton, Florida. An investigation of Manischewitz and its distributors is still pending. Older consumers who are affluent and perhaps some who are not so affluent may be willing to pay almost any price for ethnic food for appropriate occasions, but this will be less true of younger consumers. Any suggestion of price gouging will alienate younger consumers, and companies will stand to lose future potential markets. Younger consumers, for whatever the reasons, are anxious to declare their independence, and negative company images will accelerate this trend.

Marketers have been successful inasmuch as they are satisfying some ethnic group preferences. However, there has been little attempt to mainstream Greek, Polish, or other types of ethnic food. The main criticism directed against marketers is that they have moved slowly in cultivating preferences for ethnic foods. For example, Campbell Soup targeted Italian and Hispanic food preferences only after competitors first penetrated these markets. Baby food manufacturers were also late in cultivating ethnic food preferences. By the year 2030, it is conceivable that half the population in the United States will not be of European-American backgrounds and that more ethnic foods will be desired. What has saved large food manufacturers in the past has been the ability to buy out small firms that satisfied specific ethnic markets. In the future, ethnic food preferences may accelerate, and it would be a mistake not to innovate in these markets. Hunt-Wesson, with such brands as La Choy, Chun King, and Rosarita, has penetrated the Asian and Hispanic markets by developing a mainstream image and locating physical resources strategically to insure product availability.

MANAGING CHANGE

As the immigrant returned from work in an alien America, the smell of familiar cooking greeted him and were links to his past. Food has served to link individuals to groups, family, and friends. Ethnic food patterns, in the past, helped to establish and strengthen ethnic communities. For Italians, Eastern European Jews, and Chinese, conventional American cuisine was not an important staple in the immigrants' diets, and therefore ritually prepared food was essential. Ethnic food stores in ethnic neighborhoods functioned like ethnic churches or community centers. Credit was extended and neighbors shared gossip, recipes, and advice. Women shopped every day, and ethnic food was linked to religion, which helped strengthen the ties of communal identity. For Italians and Jews, it is not really possible to understand family structure until one understands the role of the mother and food preparation.

The connection with mainstream America was established by the ethnic restaurant. Originally, these ethnic restaurants were places for men who had come to the United States to earn enough money to send for their families who had remained abroad. Later, these restaurants were patronized by ethnic-group members on special occasions—anniversaries, birthdays, or marriages. Finally, these restaurants served mainstream Americans looking for their roots, for the exotic, or simply for something different. Today, the customers of Italian and oriental restaurants are rarely Italian or oriental. The descendants of the immigrants declared their independence by eating different types of foods and adopting new ways of food preparation.

The challenge remains to attempt to explain how Italian, Mexican, oriental, and other ethnic foods have become accepted into the culture of mainstream America. The past two decades have witnessed an acceleration of open housing patterns, increased travel and education, and an increase in interethnic marriages, among other factors. Therefore, no single factor is responsible for consumers' greater interest in ethnic foods, but rather a combination of factors. These factors are environmentally based upon more rigid enforcement of antidiscriminatory housing laws, more interest in travel not only within the United States but abroad, more students stimulating their curiosity about cultures other than their own through college education, and a trend toward a higher rate of intermarriage.

The disappearance of traditional housing patterns, where individuals of similar ethnic groups clustered in neighborhoods, has opened up new horizons. Schools have integrated, allowing children to sample one another's lunches and become familiar with a variety of different foods. Neighbors of different ethnic backgrounds have exchanged recipes and have been dinner guests. Since more women have entered the workplace, there is more desire to eat dinner out, and perhaps to try the ethnic food of one's neighbors.

Educational attainment is one of the factors that explains the maturity and sophistication of the American consumer. More education on the part of consumers should create additional demand for such products as books, art, and travel as well as the curiosity and willingness to try different foods. Food manufacturers are already responding to pressure to specify the balance of ingredients in their products. As of 1960, only about 8 percent of all adults 25 years and older had graduated from college, compared to almost 19 percent of all adults by 1990. Traditionally, cultural organizations such as museums, operas, ballets, and theaters, which have targeted upper-income groups, will need to broaden their appeals to include these new market segments. Moreover, as education increases, consumer tastes are likely to reflect this trend, possibly heightening the current interest in ethnic and health foods.

Travel is another variable associated with education and high-income families. Travel both within the United States and abroad has introduced consumers to a host of ethnic foods. Luxury cruises have allowed passengers to briefly see different ports and to try different foods. Customers try out these different foods both through travel and ethnic restaurants and then try to serve these foods in their own homes. Wendy's envisioned the increased interest in ethnic food by adding Mexican food to its salad bar. Travel and education both result in a desire to try and enjoy different ethnic foods. Among some consumer market segments, a developed taste for different ethnic foods is the mark of the attainment of a higher level of sophistication.

Interethnic and interfaith marriages have also increased consumer awareness of different types of food. The extended family is another dimension to the enjoyment of new foods. Christmas and Chanukah will be observed in new kinds of family structures, and the exchange of favorite foods will be at the center of these celebrations. As these new types of family structures emerge, there is a willingness not only to enjoy the favorite foods of loved ones but also to try the exotic and to become more venturesome in the selection of ethnic restaurants.

The newer immigrants to the United States include Mexicans, Puerto Ricans, Cubans, Chinese, Filipinos, Japanese, and Asian Indians. These groups have clustered in metropolitan areas and established ethnic restaurants and food stores. Although French influence is centered in New Orleans and some southern states, there are some expensively priced restaurants in other sections of the United States that have added this ethnic food to their menu. Taco Bell, which is owned by Pepsi-Cola, serves Mexican food and operates more than 5,000 units throughout the United States. Chinese restaurants are situated not only in metropolitan areas but in small towns as well. The Japanese steak house is viewed by many consumers as a restaurant to visit for either a special occasion or as an introduction to the exotic. Many of the ethnic foods of the new immigrants will become accepted into mainstream America and will be served, as Chinese food is now, in the privacy of their homes.

MANAGERIAL INSIGHTS

Good nutrition and physical fitness have impacted all consumer groups that are concerned about their health. This market is estimated to be a $30 billion–plus opportunity. As the baby boomers age, spending for physical fitness may contract. However, the health and diet mania will continue. Nutritional awareness has changed the culture as consumers have changed their dietary practices and beliefs. Some supermarket chains are competing with health-food stores in an effort to satisfy the growing market for organic and natural foods.

The consumer engages in internal memory scanning for relevant information on the product and on store alternatives, and in external seeking of information from a variety of sources. It is possible that a search will not commence if the product is accessible. The consumer can derive information from several sources, such as personal, commercial, public, and experiential sources. Overt search by the consumer tends to reduce risk of uncertainty and, thereby, risk in purchasing situations.

Ethnic food marketers would do well to use a strategy known as benefit segmentation. Benefit segmentation is a powerful form of market segmentation that classifies buyers according to the different benefits they seek from the product. Benefit segmentation usually implies that the marketer should focus on satisfying one benefit group. Benefit segmentation is closely allied to psychographic and product-usage bases. A consumer's attitudes, values, lifestyle, and past purchasing habits have a great impact on the benefits sought in specific purchasing situations.

One study identified profiles of five segments of food consumption as child oriented, diet concerned, meat-and-potatoes, sophisticated, and natural food oriented. These food preferences can be used for the strategic positioning of a product. There are many health-conscious consumers who desire to avoid preservatives, additives, salt, fat, cholesterol, sugar, and caffeine. Ethnic food appeals could be directed to those consumers who wish to maintain good dietary habits. For example, authentic Mexican food focuses on fresh vegetables, grilled fish and chicken, and whole beans. Instead, Mexican restaurants in the United States add a lot of sour cream, cheeses, guacamole, and refried beans made with lard. Chinese restaurants generally serve health food, but those consumers concerned about health would need to avoid fried egg rolls, fried rice, anything "crispy," kung pao dishes, Peking duck, and nut dishes such as cashew chicken. Moreover, soy sauce is loaded with sodium. Some Italian foods, especially pasta dishes, are beneficial, but other dishes, such as meat or cheese antipasto and fried calamari, are not.

On restaurant menus, ethnic food marketers could direct consumers to those specialties that are especially healthy. Moreover, strict labeling and dietary information at the point of purchase in food stores could also motivate those consumers concerned with good dietary habits to purchase many items that they had eaten in restaurants. In this way, consumers would be able to make many ethnic specialties and enjoy eating them at home. Sophisticated food consumers are generally located in larger cities, are upper income, and have attained higher educations. These consumers are generally more widely traveled than the norm and like to try food from different countries and different cultures. Appeals to the exotic should stimulate purchase motivation in food stores.

Ethnic food marketers are only beginning to realize the potential in targeting members of nonethnic groups or different market segments. For example, kosher food manufacturers have taken years to try to mainstream their products, despite the fact that the number of kosher-certified products increased from about 18,000 in 1989 to over 24,000 in 1994. To illustrate, Manischewitz is just beginning to broaden its appeal to the non-Jewish population. Already, Hunt-Wesson, a division of ConAgra, is marketing Rosarita products with refried beans, salsas, picante sauces, and taco and tostado shells. Either these relatively small ethnic food companies will broaden their appeals or giant food firms will soon realize the growth potential in ethnic markets and will proceed to serve them. By the year 2010, ethnic groups will comprise about one-third of the population in the United States, and ethnic group market segments will be much more important for food marketers to penetrate. The future belongs to those firms that have the vision and expertise to market ethnic food to the nonethnic population.

New upscale markets for ethnic food have developed as an outgrowth of multiculturalism. This is evident in the acceptance of Thai food. A trickle-down effect should permeate these markets. As an older population is replaced with baby boomers, ethnic food should increase in popularity. Larger firms will realize the profit possibilities and enter the market. Smaller firms should establish their marketing niches now, before competition intensifies.

CHAPTER 8

THE
SNACK FOOD
INDUSTRY

Customer Driven Strategies
- Highly developed marketing systems
- Use of category management teams
- Excellent use of niche strategy
- Innovation in servicing customer needs
- Successful brand extension strategies
- Acquisitions to service customer logistical needs
- Product differentiation

Marketing Mistakes
- Slow responses to consumer health concerns
- Inadequate budgets for marketing research
- Reliance on past patronage loyalties
- Slow to shift strategies
- Brand images not distinct

The scenario of the snack food industry in the United States is best characterized by the dominance of Frito-Lay, a division of Pepsi-Cola. The driving force behind Frito-Lay is brand power and a marketing system that is well known for its excellence. Frito-Lay has conceived a brilliant marketing plan and has excelled at implementation, or day-to-day execution. A number of positive aspects of the marketing-system design exist, especially regarding how this system impacts the sales force. Systematization of the sales function was possible with Frito-Lay because of predictable retailer and end-user buying patterns. Moreover, interrelationships between training, compensation, and call patterns show a sensitivity to the needs of customers and sales representatives. Frito-Lay has developed policies with a clear marketing theme and a vision that makes strategic marketing planning operational.

Frito-Lay is one of the masters of geographic segmentation. Frito-Lay identifies the traditional demographic characteristics of consumers through a computerized data base and determines brand consumption purchasing habits of consumers. Next, Frito-Lay does the necessary task of identifying retailers in neighborhoods with appropriate resident characteristics, in order to properly stock and provide promotional support for designated products. To illustrate, Frito-Lay has been able to segment neighborhoods and match consumer demographics with the Lite-Line of Chee-tos, Doritos, and Ruffles. The mission of the Frito-Lay sales force is then to educate and emphasize to dealers the match between the store's shopper profile and the product line's demographics. An important reason for the success of Frito-Lay is the dedication and enthusiasm of its sales force. The sales force believes in Frito-Lay as a company, as a marketer of high-quality snack products, and as a good place to work. The effective motivation of human resources is a key reason why Frito-Lay has been able to dominate the snack food industry.

There are other companies in the snack food industry that also deserve much praise for their systems. For example, Mrs. Field's Cookies uses a sophisticated marketing information system to develop marketing strategies, communicate with individual stores in 15-minute intervals, and monitor weak performance. Although the chain has fallen upon hard times in recent years, its marketing information system has been instrumental in instructing store managers about changes in cookie assortments, thus ensuring consistent operations throughout the chain. Lance is a small company that has followed a niche strategy. Lance was the first major snack food manufacturer to provide consumers with a large assortment of cholesterol-free, low-cholesterol, fat-free, and low-fat products. Innovation has helped Lance to compete with larger firms such as Frito-Lay, Borden, and Nabisco.

Accelerating distribution has been a driving force in the snack food industry and is an important aspect of a successful organization. Mrs. Field's, Mister Donut, and others bake their goods as needed in their stores. Frito-Lay has pledged to replenish store shelves on a 24-hour basis in order to avoid costly stock-out conditions. If a few companies in the snack food industry find a way to serve customers faster and better, the competition is forced to reexamine its performance in innovation and distribution and to improve strategies, or face losing market share.

The key ingredients for either success or failure in the snack food industry have been innovation, target-market segmentation, image, and the effective utilization of human and physical resources. Frito-Lay has been an innovator, with a highly developed selling and distribution system that has made the company an outstanding model of success in the snack food industry. Lance, a relatively small firm, has been able to compete with industry giant firms by using a successful niche strategy and by cultivating a favorable image through targeting health concerns of consumers. Nabisco was able to effectively deploy human resources by establishing category management teams. Frito-Lay was able to utilize physical resources by implementing a distribution system that made direct delivery from manufacturer to retailer more efficient. Eagle made mistakes due to an inefficient logistical system. Keebler lacked the innovative spirit even though distribution resources were available. Mrs. Field's Cookies, although originally an early innovator, did not monitor the changing needs of consumers closely and ignored competitive pressures. A false step in the snack food industry cannot be taken lightly, since large Fortune 500 firms have the resources to compete effectively.

MARKET STRUCTURE

The snack food industry consists of snacks, cookies, nonchocolate bars, gums, filled crackers, nuts, mints, granola bars, and crackers. Chapter 9

Table 8.1
Leading Snack Food Organizations, 1996

Company or Brand	Market-Share Range
Frito-Lay	35 to 40%
Eagle (Anheuser-Busch)	4 to 7%
Borden	4 to 6%
Keebler (Sunshine)	3 to 5%
General Mills	3 to 5%
Beatrice	3 to 5%
Nabisco	3 to 5%
Procter & Gamble	2 to 4%

Note: Market share is estimated from literature in the field.

is devoted to the candy industry, and consequently chocolate bars and other products considered candy will not be discussed in this chapter. Frito-Lay, Eagle, Borden, Keebler, General Mills, Beatrice, Nabisco, and Procter & Gamble are the largest companies competing in the snack food industry. Potato chips, snacks, and cookies are important categories for store brands. A comparison of the importance of snack food store brands could be made to cold cereals.

Frito-Lay, owned by Pepsi-Cola, dominated the snack food industry in 1996, with a market share of 35 to 40 percent, as represented in Table 8.1, Leading Snack Food Organizations, 1996. Eagle, Borden, and Keebler, which are ranked three, four, and five respectively in market share, are a considerable distance behind Frito-Lay, the market leader. Eagle, owned by Anheuser-Busch, has been selling chips, nuts, and pretzels for fifteen years but has yet to make a profit. It is important to consider another aspect of the competitive framework: the snack food industry competes not only with the candy industry but with such breakfast cereal products as granola bars, General Mills Bugles, and Kellogg's Nutri-Grain Bars.

Borden has intensified its marketing efforts in the snack food sector and will probably increase its market share in the future. For many years, Nabisco has controlled most of the shelf space for cookies in supermarkets, but competition from Mrs. Fields, David's, and Famous Amos plus established firms like Keebler, Sunshine, and Pepperidge Farm has weakened Nabisco's dominance. A breakdown of the tortilla chip market demonstrates the dominance of Frito-Lay and the position of private labels. To illustrate, Doritos and Tostitos have more than a 50 percent share of this market. Private labels have only approximately 6 percent, and Eagle and Eagle El Grande have no more than 5 percent market share. Supermarket shelves are crowded, and it is going to be very difficult for competitors to gain entry and seize market share away from Frito-Lay.

American Brands with Sunshine, Anheuser-Busch with Eagle Snacks, Borden with Wise and Cheez-Doodles, and Procter & Gamble with Pringles and Fisher Nuts distribute their products throughout the United States and are competitors of the market leader, Frito-Lay. The Keebler Company, with Krunch Twists and Tato Skins, also distributes throughout the United States and is a company that Frito-Lay needs to monitor continuously. Nabisco, with Planters, has successfully segmented the peanut and cookie markets, which do not compete directly with Frito-Lay since Nabisco is not in the chips market. Lance distributes its products in most of the United States, but has segmented the low-fat, low-cholesterol market and does not compete fully in the chips market.

Sales of salted snack foods have steadily increased over the past decade. Approximately half of the snack food market is comprised of potato, corn, and tortilla chips. The remainder of the market consists of snack nuts, popcorn, pretzels, cheese curls, and pork rinds. While some manufacturers are touting their low-salt or salt-free products, salted snack foods are still in high demand. The low-salt market is growing, but much of the snack food market is composed of consumers under the age of 45, who are not prone to disregard taste. Consequently, salted snack foods have a commanding presence in the snack food industry. The salty-snack food market is an example of fierce direct competition. For some years, the industry leaders were Frito-Lay and Borden, but with over $10 billion in annual revenue at stake, new and formidable competitors such as Procter & Gamble, Anheuser-Busch, and Keebler have entered the salty-snack market. One percent of market share in salty snacks is worth over $100 million, and consequently, it is not surprising that competition has intensified. Borden, in combating the competitive challenge, rolled back its prices and increased promotional expenditures by as much as 25 percent.

New product development has centered on, for the most part, line extensions of existing brands, new flavors of existing products, and new formulations such as less salt, fat, oil, or use of the fake-fat olestra. Consolidation was emphasized in order to reduce physical distribution costs, and industry giants such as Borden and Frito-Lay continued to acquire regional producers. Shorter distribution routes have been an important factor in the success of regional snack manufacturers, and therefore the industry giants were eager to make these buyouts. Competitors used a store-to-door delivery system whereby trucks owned by the snack food company made deliveries. Snack food firms stocked products according to individual store needs. Food retailers did not want to stock shelves since snack foods are subject to breakage and damage.

The majority of snack food products seemed to have reached the market maturity stage of the product life cycle. Growth in sales volume is not anticipated to exceed population growth. Increasing numbers of consumers are becoming concerned about consuming unhealthy foods, and health-conscious consumers are tending to eat more fresh fruits and avoid traditional snack foods.

A competitive or differential advantage can be achieved through product innovation and change. When Procter & Gamble developed Pringle's Potato Chips, it had to create a new product shape, a new package, using a different formula from existing potato chips, and a new brand name.

MARKET CONDUCT

Behavioristic segmentation divides buyers on the basis of need-satisfying benefits to be derived from product use, the rate of product usage, and the degree of brand loyalty, and on consumer readiness to purchase the product.

Groups of purchasers traditionally have been identified on the basis of common demographic characteristics. However, behavioristic segmentation uses causal factors, on the supposition that buyers are really differentiated by the benefits they seek. In behavioral segmentation, consumers are grouped by their purchases. As such, product classifications are directed by consumer actions. To illustrate, the snack food market might be segmented by those consumers who are nutritional snackers, weight watchers, guilty snackers, party snackers, indiscriminate snackers, and economical snackers. Marketers would then determine the demographic and lifestyle characteristics of each behavioral segment.

Benefit segmentation is closely allied to psychographic and product-usage bases. A consumer's attitudes, values, lifestyle, and past purchase habits have a great impact on the benefits sought in specific purchasing situations. For example, indiscriminate snackers may be comprised of a high proportion of teens. Their lifestyle and personality characteristics tend to be hedonistic, and their consumption level of snacks tends to be heavy. Teens who are indiscriminate snackers tend to eat candy, ice cream, cookies, potato chips, pretzels, and popcorn. The major benefit sought is that the snack should be good tasting and satisfy hunger. In contrast, nutritional snackers have a tendency to be better educated and have younger children; their lifestyle and personality characteristics reflect self-assurance, while their consumption level is light. The nutritional snacker segment tends to eat fruits, vegetables, and cheese. The major benefit sought is nutrition without artificial ingredients. Between these two polar extremes are the economical snackers. Economical snackers tend to be better educated and come from larger families. Economical snackers tend to be self-assured and price-oriented; their consumption level of snacks is average. The major benefits sought would be low price and value for the price, and no specific snack products can be designated since the purchasing situation is paramount.

There are many advantages of benefit segmentation. First, benefit segments are based on specific reasons why consumers choose to buy a given product, with emphasis placed on cause-and-effect relationships. Second, relationships between motivations and purchasing patterns in specific situations are presented, and explanatory segment names can be used, such as Hedonists, Elitists, Worriers, and a host of other segment classifications. Third, a variety of methods such as focus groups, mail, and telephone and personal interviews can be used to generate the data. Finally, benefit segmentation can be related to purchase occasions, purchase intentions, and psychographics. The limitations of benefit segmentation would be that benefits must be identifiable and not abstract, and market segments must be recognizable and accessible to a firm's marketing strategies. Moreover, costs can be exceedingly high for the services of trained specialists to conduct the analysis.

Psychographic segmentation is a technique that can be used either separately or in combination with benefit segmentation to analyze the snack food market. Market segmentation and lifestyle are two related concepts that are potent strategies for satisfying consumer preferences and maximizing profitability. Lifestyle analysis is composed of consumers' activities, interests, and opinions. Activities are classified as sports, work, entertainment, and hobbies. Interests include job, home, family, fashion, and food. Opinions are classified as social issues, political issues, education, business, and the future. Demographic factors, such as age, occupation, geography, and stage in the family life cycle, are used along with the factors of activities, interests, and opinions as a potential basis for identifying market segments.

Many studies have reported links between diets high in cholesterol and sodium and increases in the incidence of heart disease. Although these causes lead to a high incidence of heart attacks, snack food organizations continue to provide high-fat and high-salt products. Though a small health-conscious segment exists, the overriding majority of consumers indulge themselves. To illustrate, potato chip consumption is an important part of the snack food market. To satisfy various consumer segments, products must be differentiated. Some product differentiation methods include potato chip flavors: sour cream and onion, salt and vinegar, and white corn. Consciously, consumers may desire to eat properly, but when choosing a snack, potato chips seem to be viewed as a "deserved binge" because of the anxieties of life. This has resulted in an expanding potato chip market.

CASE STUDIES

Frito-Lay: An Outstanding Marketing System

The Frito Company, founded in the early 1930s, developed a new product known as Fritos brand corn chips. At about the same time, the Lay Company was founded. The Frito Company distributed its products from Dallas, and the Lay Company, from Atlanta. The two companies worked together in expanding their geographical-distribution market, and eventually merged in 1961 to form Frito-Lay, Inc. In 1965, Pepsi-Cola merged with Frito-Lay to form PepsiCo. The company operates under three business groups: World Wide Beverages (Pepsi-Cola), World Wide Foods (Frito-Lay and PepsiCo Foods International), and PepsiCo Food Service International.

The success stories about Frito-Lay have become legend, having been presented in such major business books as *In Search of Excellence* (1982) and *A Passion for Excellence* (1985), by Tom Peters. There is usually a combination of reasons for the success of a company rather than a single reason. However, if any two reasons can be singled out, they would be selling and distribution, which have been refined to such heights that they serve as a competitive model for all organizations participating in the food industry. Frito-Lay has developed a ten-book programmed-learning course that covers everything from likely consumer behavior to how to pack the delivery truck for maximum efficiency. Despite the rigidity of the Frito-Lay system, the enthusiasm of its salespeople is exceedingly high. Salespeople earnestly believe that Frito-Lay is a quality employer and a manufacturer of high-quality snack products.

Company policy requires that all stock purchased by the store must be opened and inventoried in the presence of the store manager. Frito-Lay salespersons are authorized to merchandise store shelves by arranging displays and arranging the goods. Each detail is specified for the salesperson. For example, Doritos go to the left of Fritos, and each product is stocked in a precise pattern that is universal in all stores. Frito-Lay products are marketed to and through existing channels of distribution. Since Frito-Lay has a large number of items in its product line, economies of scale are achieved. Lower costs associated with economies of scale are an important source of competitive advantage.

Frito-Lay is an exceedingly successful company inasmuch as it has strongly defined markets, an in-depth understanding of its customers, and the ability to motivate its employees to attain high quality and value for its customers. Frito-Lay has a state-of-the-art information system, and because there is strict attention to detail, the company has an excellent implementation record for strategic planning strategies. For example,

Frito-Lay boosted operating profits by 26 percent when the company took advantage of a special corn oil and a reduced-oil cooking process to create new light snacks as extensions of such existing lines as Doritos, Ruffles, and Chee-tos Cheese Puffs.

Frito-Lay reacts to a consumer-driven market rather than a market-driven consumer. At Frito-Lay, this approach is almost an obsession. Snack food and development costs have about doubled in the past decade. No detail is left neglected. Frito-Lay researchers use a $40,000 simulated human mouth made of aluminum to measure the jaw power it takes to crunch single chips. The thickness of chips is measured to 36/1000 inch for flat chips and 91/1000 inch for Ruffles. Other researchers conduct tests on flavor preferences. The goal at Frito-Lay is to know more about consumers than they know about themselves. Consumer profiles are developed that reflect distinct personality differences among eaters of various snacks. For example, consumers of Lay's Potato Chips are envisioned as affectionate, casual, and fun members of the family, while consumers of Ruffles Potato Chips are envisioned as expressive and highly self-confident.

The marketing system of Frito-Lay is the envy of other food manufacturing organizations. Frito-Lay demonstrates how strategic conceptual planning can be implemented in day-to-day functions. Its marketing system emphasizes control and consistency. Fundamental to the success of Frito-Lay is strong leadership, which has defined the scope of the business and the interrelationship of functional operating parts. This depth and breadth of the Frito-Lay business environment increases coordination and detailed implementation of strategic planning. There is a culture within Frito-Lay that encourages executives to be "great." This spirit of healthy competition, excitement, and innovation has been transmitted to the sales staff and support employees. Frito-Lay succeeds because it has not only an excellent understanding of its customers but the ability to motivate employees as well. The heart of Frito-Lay is a marketing system that makes strategies work.

Nabisco: The Cookie and Cracker King

Nabisco, the cookie and cracker king, was under attack in the 1980s by Frito-Lay, Procter & Gamble, and Keebler. Consumer preferences for softer, chewy cookies versus the traditional harder cookies led to new product introductions. Nabisco, with more than one-third market share, had been virtually unchallenged for a number of years.

Frito-Lay introduced Grandma's Cookies and Procter & Gamble introduced Duncan Hines Chocolate Chip Cookies in efforts to seize market share with softer, chewy cookies. Nabisco retaliated by introducing a fifteen-variety line called Almost Home, and the cookie wars intensified. Moreover, Nabisco reorganized its brand-management system. A category-management system was adopted whereby brand managers reported to a category manager who had total responsibility for an entire product line. This system was further refined by Nabisco. Instead of having several cookie brand managers, Nabisco established three cookie category management teams. There was one team for adult rich cookies, a second team for nutritional cookies, and a third for children's cookies. Each team included brand managers, a sales-planning manager, and a marketing-information specialist. Specialists from other departments within the company, such as finance and research and development, also assisted. The traditional brand-management system had been product driven, versus customer driven. Brand managers often concentrated so heavily on a single brand that emphasis on product position within the marketplace was lost. Category management focuses on groups of products, for example, "cookies" as opposed to "Oreos." However, proper emphasis must be placed on the needs of consumers and retailers. The old standby products of Nabisco, such as Chips Ahoy, Oreos, Ritz Crackers, Planters Peanuts, and Fig Newtons with line extensions, helped to fight off competitors. New products such as SnackWell's cookies and crackers, Chunky Chips Ahoy, Fat-Free Fig Newtons, and Planters Heat Spicy Peanuts were newer product introductions in the battle of the brands.

Not only has Nabisco used new-product innovations to remain king of the cookie and cracker sector, but also it has been a leader in using a technique known as market aggregation and product differentiation. Market aggregation, also referred to as undifferentiated marketing, results in a single offering aimed at the total market. Market aggregation does not use market-segmentation strategies. To illustrate, Nabisco, with its Premium Saltine Crackers, would aim the product at a total market that would include consumers of all ages, races, personality types, income groups, social classes, and geographical areas. Product differentiation is a strategy used to distinguish Premium Saltine Crackers from the field of competing products. Therefore, Premium Saltine Crackers have been promoted as "the cracker with CRUNCH." This characteristic is an intangible, and it is difficult for consumers to assess the degree of crunch or if crunch is an exclusive attribute of Premium. This strategy of using a special characteristic is supposed to differentiate Premium from other crackers. Premium is also packaged in "4 Keep Fresh Recloseable Bags," which is stated on the box and is another product differentiation strategy.

Nabisco, the cookie and cracker king, has been foremost in the industry for more than a century. The National Biscuit Company (forerunner of Nabisco) started to distribute Premium Soda Crackers (now known as Premium Saltine Crackers) in 1876. Premium Crackers achieved fame because of their unique texture. This was to be an early application of product-differentiation strategy. In 1891 Fig Newtons were distributed, and in 1898 Nabisco Graham Crackers were sold. In 1934 Ritz Crackers were launched, and Chips Ahoy Cookies were introduced in 1963. These brands were very successful and contributed to Nabisco's becoming the cookie and cracker king of the industry.

A much larger issue now confronts Nabisco. Are brand loyalists a dying breed? Are consumers faithful or fickle? One argument for vanishing brand loyalty is that some firms have reallocated promotional dollars from advertising to sales promotion, which includes such strategies as coupons and in-store displays. Advertising may promote brand loyalty, but sales promotion stimulates brand-switching behavior. Sales promotion has an impact on short-term behavior. Second, there is greater consumer awareness of price levels. More educated consumers are aware that less expensive alternatives are available. Consequently, consumers may select either the store brand or, for example, the least expensive brand of chocolate-chip cookies. Third, as more brands are launched in the market, product differentiation becomes less distinct, and thus brand loyalty diminishes. Finally, more specialty niches develop, such as potato chips dipped in sour cream or regular potato chips. Thus, consumers may buy multiple brands to satisfy different needs at different times, further reducing brand loyalty.

Consumers can be divided into four groups according to their loyalty status: the hard core, the soft core, the shifting, and the switches. The hard core purchase one brand all the time. The soft core are those consumers who are loyal to two or three brands. Those with shifting loyalties change their allegiance from one brand to another for various reasons. Switches are consumers who favor one brand over another perhaps based on price or on some other brand offered, or consumers who are simply variety prone.

Hard-core consumers can be deceptive inasmuch as what might appear to be brand-loyal purchases may actually reflect habit, indifference, a low price or the nonavailability of other brands. When Nabisco first launched a new bite-sized graham cracker snack product, it was called Honey Maid Honeycomb Graham Snacks and packaged in a subdued blue box. Sales were sluggish, and the product was renamed Honey Maid Graham Bites and repackaged in a bright yellow box. Sales soared. This anecdote would suggest that brand loyalty is less than hard core for at least some Nabisco snacks. Product differentiation refers to marketing efforts to distinguish a basically homogeneous product from competitors' products. Methods used to accomplish this would be to alter the products' physical characteristics or to use branding, advertising, or packaging. These methods can be especially successful in an affluent society. Nabisco is the cookie and cracker king, but its loyal core is not hard core.

Lance: A Master of Niche Strategy

Lance was founded in 1913 and was a traditional, conservative company until 1988. The corporate mission of Lance reflects a company receptive to change inasmuch as Lance desires to be consumer driven, providing quality food and related products in ever-changing domestic and international markets. In 1988, Lance became the first in the snack food industry to respond to the changing environment that emphasized consumer health concerns. Lance changed over to produce cholesterol-free, low-saturated-fat, low-salt, and low-sugar snacks. The company found that while consumers were interested in nutrition, taste is also an important concern. Sales lagged, but Lance reformulated, and by 1989 revenues increased.

Since 1988 Lance has been a master of niche strategic planning. Lance decided that instead of pursuing the whole market or even large segments of the market, it would target a segment within a segment, or a niche. This decision was made, in part, because Lance was a small firm with limited resources competing with industry giants such as Nabisco, Frito-Lay, Borden, and Keebler. Niching can be profitable since the market nicher learns about the target consumer group so well that it can satisfy needs better than competitors who are casually selling to this niche. Consequently, in the beginning Lance was able to charge a substantial markup over costs because of the added value. Lance had found an ideal market niche since it had growth potential and the market of health-conscious consumers is of sufficient size and purchasing power to be profitable. In the beginning the niche was of negligible interest to major competitors, but eventually this situation did change. A fundamental principal in niching is specialization, but niching carries an important risk in that the market niche might be attacked. The snack food industry is a mature, intensely competitive industry. Lance had entered a market niche and thus was able to achieve profits through high margins.

Niching is a promising option for small companies that are not market leaders, although larger firms have also used this option. White Castle, which basically sells only hamburgers, has used a niche strategy to its advantage. The danger is that the market environment could change, for a variety of reasons. To illustrate, when the granola bar was introduced, it was positioned as a snack or diet food for the nutritionally minded consumer who did not desire to buy a candy bar. Competition grew, and Quaker took a risk by increasing distribution from primarily the southern states to Pennsylvania, New York, the Midwest, Colorado, Nebraska, parts of Arizona, and all of Texas and adjacent states. Chicago and Boston, in the 1990s, represented new markets for Lance. Expansion of geographical distribution represented both an opportunity and a threat for Lance. The store-to-door delivery method was expensive in terms of labor costs and truck expenses.

Lance's marketing strategy revolved around a follow-the-leader strategy for new product development, a focus on marketing a single-serving product size, and no advertising. Costs were low since larger companies developed and marketed new products and Lance merely copied the successful products. Moreover, by not using the traditional media of television, radio, and newspapers, low promotional costs were maintained. Lance was confronted with strong competition, especially from organizations such as Frito-Lay, Borden, and Eagle, all of which had personnel with highly developed marketing expertise.

Another important challenge to Lance was the differences that prevailed in regional taste preferences. Products such as pork skins, salt-and-vinegar potato chips, and moon pies were big sellers in the Southeast, but generated low revenues in other geographical areas. Frito-Lay wrapped its granola bar in chocolate. Soon other competitors added chocolate chips and marshmallows, and the granola bar became a candy bar in disguise.

The heart of the Lance distribution system is its sales force of over 2,000 sales representatives. In the past Lance limited its scope to the southeastern United States and, like Hershey Chocolate of some years ago, used limited traditional advertising. As other major competitors are beginning to serve the nutritionally concerned consumer market, Lance is beginning to widen its geographical area and to use more traditional advertising. Lance is under sharp attack, and profits have been affected.

Lance, in the past, targeted the single-serving customer. This type of consumer is an impulse buyer who wants to enjoy a snack at a particular moment, and the target market is reached through vending machines and rack displays at every possible retail outlet. Lance also serves institutional customers, which include principally school cafeterias, restaurants, and retirement homes. Products are familiar complements to salad bars at restaurants throughout its distribution area and include such products as twin-pack saltines and Captain's Wafers.

Lance broadened its effort to grow in the 1990s by regionalizing its operations. This prompted Borden to target its snack food division for growth by consolidating and acquiring strong regional companies. The regional-market-segmentation approach, developed to a high degree by Campbell Soup, was beginning to take hold in the snack food industry.

Lance has successfully followed a niche strategy that includes a wide variety of packaged snack foods and bread-basket items throughout more than thirty states. The company has developed a marketing strategy based on a follow-the-leader approach. However, caution is warranted as the marketing environment in the snack food industry changes. First, the distribution thrust has been on single-serving product sizes, although more than 70 percent of snack food is sold in supermarkets. Second, Lance has faced intense competition from Frito-Lay and Borden but has found a way to compete in supermarkets. Lance, to its credit, has developed a Home-pak line of products that offers consumers eighteen-count units. Even with this positive change in strategy, it's difficult to imagine how Lance will obtain more shelf space in supermarkets without changing its advertising strategy. Supermarkets desire customers to be presold on snack food brands, and Frito-Lay, Borden, Keebler, and Nabisco have satisfied this marketing need. If Lance wishes to compete with large competitors, then Lance must revise its advertising strategy. Even Hershey changed its no-advertising policy because of a changing marketing environment. Moreover, Lance changed strategies slowly in the past but it may not be able to continue this policy if the company becomes increasingly involved in supermarket distribution. An important advantage of a follow-the-leader strategy has been low cost, but there is a danger that this advantage may be sacrificed with a change in strategy.

There are strong environmental opportunities that are in Lance's favor. Consumption of snack foods is increasing, as is the health consciousness of an aging population. Lance has a strong base in the sunbelt, which is growing. Furthermore, Lance has a strong corporate culture and offers a high-quality, competitive product that is low in fat, cholesterol, and sodium. But regional tastes vary, and large competitors such as Frito-Lay and Borden have been emphasizing regional strategies. Lance is at a strategic crossroads, and a number of strategic decisions must be made in the near future.

Other Competitors: Successes and Mistakes

Competitors in the snack food industry are both national and regional. Borden, Eagle, Keebler, and Mrs. Field's Cookies are among the prominent competitors in the snack food industry. Many regional firms have been acquired over the years by such large firms as Borden. The company has acquired such regional firms as the Snacktime Company and Laura Scudder. Among the regional brands are Laura Scudder's, Geiser's Potato Chips, and Red Seal. Borden's principal national brands are Wise, La Famous, New York Deli, Seyfert, and of course Borden.

Borden has targeted its snack food division for growth in the 1990s. Borden retained the regional brand in most markets but used the distribution strength of the Borden brand to launch the Wise brand of related snacks, which includes corn-based products as well as small cakes and cookies. Borden plans to make the Wise brand of potato chips a national brand. Borden has moved away from centralization of operations to decentralization. Pretzels are marketed under the Seyfert brand name, and nut products are also marketed under both the Seyfert and Guy's brand names.

Borden has become an important player in the low-fat, low-cholesterol, and low-calorie market with the brand of Lite-Line snacks. The Lite-Line brand is targeted at consumers who are motivated by a lifestyle to be in the best of health and at a peak of physical fitness. Fitness-conscious consumers who have dropped snacks from their regular shopping list are provided with more available products and brands. Since Borden is firmly entrenched in food stores, which constitute more than 70 percent of the distribution of snack foods, Borden will be a formidable competitor. Borden is experiencing difficulties in the ice cream industry, but countless opportunities are present in the snack food industry.

Although Eagle, owned by Anheuser-Busch, made significant inroads in the pretzel market, Eagle had not made a profit in seventeen years and therefore became extinct. Snyder's of Hanover, a privately held company, has dominated this market. Private labels are also a significant competitor in this market. Anheuser-Busch saw synergies in beer and snacks and miscalculated. Rather than synergy, Anheuser-Busch was confronted by a logistical quagmire. Distributors of Eagle did not have much product breadth, and costs remained high. Frito-Lay reduced costs and slashed prices. Synder of Hanover sold nothing but pretzels and was able to provide a large variety of flavors. Moreover, many supermarkets had strong private-label operations. Eagle was plagued by fragmented distribution and no cost or quality advantage, and therefore, in 1996, Anheuser-Busch threw in the towel.

Keebler is the second-largest cracker and cookie company in sales and, until 1994, was a sleeping giant. Keebler's efforts to compete successfully with Nabisco through a price war ended in disaster. Not only was price competition a major mistake, but Keebler, through poor execution, launched low-fat crackers and cookies in 1994 and in 1995—much later than its competitors. The story of Keebler's assault on Nabisco was a scenario of the cookies and crackers crumbling. Even the assault on the potato chip market left Keebler adrift. As a result, in 1996 Keebler merged with the Sunshine Biscuit Company with the hope that the addition of well-known brands would facilitate the acquisition of hard-to-get supermarket shelf space. Keebler dates back to 1853 and Sunshine to 1882, and Keebler's brands have been well known to retailers. Included in the company offerings are the following: Town House Crackers, Wheatables, Zesta Saltines, Chips Deluxe, Hi-Ho and Krispy crackers, and Vienna Fingers. Keebler has more than 75,000 distribution outlets nationwide, and while the company has strength in cookies and crackers, it lags far behind in the potato chip market. Keebler entered the low-fat, low-cholesterol market late and needs to overcome both marketing myopia and lethargy.

The scenario of Mrs. Field's Cookies is a modern day success episode in the annals of business history. Debbi Fields, at the age of 20, founded Mrs. Field's Cookies, which eventually became a $150 million company. Mrs. Fields was an innovator inasmuch as retail cookie stores were almost unheard of when her first store was opened in 1977. Another innovation occurred in 1989, when Mrs. Field's Cookies became the first company to streamline operations and production schedules using a state-of-the-art computer system. The program is used at the Harvard Business School and illustrates successful application of technology in business management. In the late 1980s Mrs. Field's Cookies was one of the fastest growing specialty food companies in the United States. By the 1990s there were more than 600 retail units. Mrs. Field's Cookies was to become well known by selling only fresh cookies and removing cookies not sold within two hours. The company's major form of advertising was sampling—giving away cookie samples within the shopping mall. Each store was given an hourly sales quota. Mrs. Field's also made unannounced visits to retail store units to evaluate enthusiasm and sales techniques of store crews and to ascertain product quality. Product quality was an obsession. The computer system aided Mrs. Fields by providing instantaneous information on store performance and by providing a means of store operation.

After years of success, past mistakes caught up with Mrs. Field's Cookies, and everything went wrong. One perspective would be that during dips in the economy, consumers were no longer willing to pay nearly a dollar for a chocolate-chip cookie. Another viewpoint could be advanced that Mrs. Fields expanded too fast, opening 225 new stores between 1985 and 1988 and more than 45 abroad. Many of these new stores were not able to derive revenues that would justify expensive locations. The decision not to franchise or license could be another reason for Mrs. Field's Cookies to amass considerable debt. Slowly Mrs. Field's Cookies began to franchise, but competitors like David's Cookies had already franchised and licensed. Although Mrs. Field's Cookies did diversify by selling yogurt, coffee, and muffins, it was too late. Finally, Mrs. Field's Cookies was bought out, but Debbi Fields remains as chairwoman and an effective public relations representative.

Why Frito-Lay Dominates the Snack Food Industry

- Pledges to replace retailer stock-outs within a 24-hour period
- Systematization of the sales function
- Excellent geographic market segmentation strategies that identify neighborhood purchasing patterns
- Enthusiasm and motivation of sales force
- Shorter distribution routes
- Precise attention to detail and, therefore, excellent execution of strategic planning
- Large product assortment, providing economies of scale to intermediaries
- A highly developed information system, which aids in defining markets and buyer characteristics
- Consumer-driven instead of market-driven company

In summary, Frito-Lay has a highly developed system of sales and distribution in the food industry. Frito-Lay has been cited by Tom Peters, the author of *In Search of Excellence*, for its outstanding, well-developed marketing system, and by Thomas Bonoma, in *The Marketing Edge*, for excellent day-to-day implementation of strategic planning. Frito-Lay leads the snack food industry with an approximately 40 percent market share, and its newest competitor is Borden, with a 6 percent market share.

Marketing Successes in the Snack Food Industry

- Successful use of information systems by Frito-Lay and Borden, effectively shortening delivery time and thereby accelerating service and reducing costs
- Effective niche segmentation by Lance in response to consumer health concerns
- The category-management structure used by Nabisco
- Product innovation by Nabisco and Mrs. Field's Cookies
- Geographic segmentation by Frito-Lay
- Innovation by Mrs. Fields in opening retail cookie stores
- Industry market segmentation for those consumers who desire to consume less calories in snacks
- Effective differentiation of potato chip products
- Strong private labels in pretzels and other types of snack foods
- Borden's brand extension of Wise

Marketing Mistakes in the Snack Food Industry

- Poor execution of strategic planning by Eagle
- Keebler's slow development of low-fat products
- Mrs. Field's Cookies' failure to franchise, and rapid expansion of new retail units
- Eagle's increase in promotional budget without an adequate distribution network
- Lance's concentration for a long period of time on single-serving packages
- Frito-Lay's failure to prevent Lance from seizing a niche in the low-fat, low-cholesterol market
- Brand images that are not distinct

MANAGING CHANGE

Managing change in the snack food industry has centered around distribution and consumer health concerns. The breakable nature of the product and the route method commonly used for deliveries limits the distance that can be reached from the manufacturer's plant. The cookie does crumble and potato chips do break if not handled properly. Union contracts with supermarkets generally state that products will be placed on store shelves by supermarket employees. Exceptions to this union clause are the product categories of baby food and snack food. Supermarket management does not desire to assume responsibility for crumbling cookies or broken potato chips. Snack food sells quickly, and therefore there is a frequent need for replenishment. Frito-Lay has addressed the challenges of high product turnover by pledging to replenish store shelves within a 24-hour period, thus avoiding supermarket stock-outs.

Distribution is a major challenge in the snack food industry. Frequent deliveries to retail stores increase costs and cause high prices. Large food manufacturers, particularly Borden, have acquired many smaller, regional firms with the objective of shortening the distribution route from plant to store. The merger between Keebler and Sunshine was in part an effort to shorten the distribution route and address the complaint of retailer stock-outs. Frito-Lay owes much of its success not so much to brand power, as Campbell Soup and Kellogg do, but to developing a business system that addresses retailer problems.

Another important factor that has caused change in the snack-food industry has been consumer health concerns. These concerns have allowed Lance to develop a marketing niche in the snack food industry. Large firms such as Frito-Lay, Eagle, and Borden were slow to realize the potential of the low-cholesterol, low-fat, and low-sodium market. However, in 1998, Frito-Lay introduced Lay's WOW, a potato chip with half the calories and no fat made with Olean, a brand fat-free cooking oil. Eagle, Borden, Nabisco, and other giant competitors have made significant mistakes by failing to grasp the importance of consumer health concerns.

MANAGERIAL INSIGHTS

The most successful firm in the snack food industry is Frito-Lay. Unlike Kellogg in the breakfast cereal industry and Campbell in the soup industry, Frito-Lay has utilized a systems approach with brand power rather than brand power alone. A systems approach allows the marketer to view the product not as an individual entity but as just one aspect of the customers' total need-satisfaction system. Frito-Lay uses a systems orientation coupled with brand recognition or, hopefully, brand preferences as an integrated whole—functioning or operating in unison with their entire organization.

The system entails, first, identifying market opportunities by determining what retailers and consumers desire. Next, feedback on this information is dispatched to appropriate departments of the firm. In addition to an information system, Frito-Lay has added a service system that permits the company to promote its relationships with retailers before, during, and long after products are delivered. Frito-Lay has been a pioneer in servicing systems by replenishing store shelves with reported stock-outs within a 24-hour period.

Frito-Lay has maximized the efficiencies of a physical distribution system. Naturally, costs are an important consideration, and any system should be aimed at reducing costs. The lesson to be learned is that brand power alone is not sufficient. Witness the inroads that private labels have made in the breakfast cereal industry. A marketing system with sales service as the key component needs to be developed. Brand images are not as highly developed as in the cereal industry. This is a shortcoming that will eventually hurt many of these firms.

CHAPTER 9

THE CANDY INDUSTRY

Strengths
- Use of family brand names
- Intensive distribution
- Important acquisitions
- Blocked introduction of store brands
- Mass market segmentation strategies
- Product differentiation strategies
- Product-line extension strategies
- Occasion market segmentation strategies
- High quality product standards

Weaknesses
- New product development
- Packaging innovation
- Inability to target consumer needs
- Lack of low-calorie, low-cholesterol, low-fat, and low-sodium products
- Lack of proactive strategies in promotion
- Difficulty in getting retail shelf space

Milky Way, Snickers, 3 Musketeers, and M&M's, marketed by Mars; Baby Ruth, Raisinets, and Butterfinger, marketed by Nestlé; and Reese's, KitKat, Oh Henry!, Kisses, Peter Paul Mounds, and Almond Joy milk chocolate bars, marketed by Hershey, are well-known brands that not only have withstood the test of time but have become legends. Although new-product development has been successful, it has not been as successful as in other food sectors such as cereal, soup, or ice cream. The Dove Bar, marketed by Mars, and Symphony, marketed by Hershey, are recent brand success stories. However, brand extensions, such as Milky Way Lite, seem to be even more successful. The trend toward producing a candy bar with fewer total calories and fewer calories from fat is a logical addition to the product line, but sales have not lived up to expectations.

The state of the candy industry in the United States is best characterized by the dominance of the Hershey Foods Corporation, a major manufacturer of chocolate candy and other food products. History indicates that the Hershey chocolate bar has become a household word, even though in the past Hershey utilized a limited retail promotion program. Instead of using mass consumer advertising, Hershey focused its promotional efforts on point-of-sale advertising and other retail promotions. Salespeople were traditionally paid more than the industry average in order to attract personnel of higher caliber. No store was too small, no location too isolated for a Hershey salesperson to approach. Intensive distribution was the key to Hershey's success. Even though these past strategies have changed, Hershey's image has been maintained throughout the 1980s with the aid of considerable advertising. This extensive mass advertising helped to account for its increase in market share from approximately 15 percent in 1980 to 20 percent by 1988. Hershey realized that marketing practices had changed and that strategies would need to reflect these changes. Hershey had lost the number one spot in the candy industry, but the change in strategy to widespread advertising allowed Hershey to overtake Mars in the competitive struggle.

Milton S. Hershey was much like other entrepreneurs, in that he was a fanatic about product quality. Hershey believed in producing the highest quality product at an affordable price, ensuring consumers the best value for their money. This philosophy was to establish the standard for the candy industry.

The history of the candy industry is intertwined with the development of the Hershey Chocolate Corporation, which was later to change its name to Hershey Foods Corporation. Hershey's milk chocolate bar with and without almonds was first produced in 1894. Hershey's Kisses chocolates were first manufactured in 1907, and in 1925 the Mr. Goodbar chocolate bar was introduced. The Krackel chocolate bar and Hershey's Miniatures were launched in the late 1930s.

Acquisitions were to become important to the development of Hershey, and in 1963 the Reese Candy Company, maker of Reese's Peanut Butter Cups, was acquired. Hershey decided to diversify into noncandy areas, and in 1966 acquired San Giorgio Macaroni and Delmonico Foods. Consequently, in 1968 Hershey Chocolate Corporation changed its name to Hershey Foods Corporation. Hershey was experiencing keen competition, primarily from Mars, Nestlé, and other candy manufacturers seizing market share, and in 1970 a dramatic change was made in strategy. Hershey introduced national television and radio advertising, a reversal of its solely word-of-mouth and retailer-promotion strategies. Additional companies such as Procino-Rossi Corporation's pasta-making operation, the Skinner Macaroni Company; the American Beauty Macaroni Company; and the confectionery operations of The Dietrich Corporation, including Luden's, maker of cough drops; Fifth Avenue candy bars, and Queen-Anne, maker of chocolate-covered cherries, were also acquired. An important acquisition to Hershey's candy operation was that of Peter Paul and later the Cadbury operation. As a result of these acquisitions, Hershey became the number one pasta producer in the United States and substantially strengthened its candy operations with brands such as Reese, Fifth Avenue, and Peter Paul. Hershey also assumed the U.S. distribution of the KitKat wafer bars through agreement with Rowntree Mackintosh of England.

In contrast to the early development of Hershey, other major firms in the candy industry, such as Mars, Russell Stover, and Fanny Farmer, did not gain momentum until the 1920s. Although the origins of the Nestlé Company go all the way back to 1867, Nestlé was established in Switzerland and originally marketed milk and infant formulas. It was not until the 1920s that Nestlé, through acquisition, became interested in the candy industry. In the United States, Nestlé is well known as a coffee producer and has acquired such American firms as Carnation and Perrier. Nestlé in 1988 acquired Rowntree Mackintosh of Great Britain, the world's fourth-largest manufacturer of chocolates and confectionery items. In the early 1990s, Nestlé was the largest food company in the world. Around the world Nestlé is well known for its Nestlé Crunch and KitKat brands.

Hershey has been the dominant firm in the candy industry, but for a brief period of time it underestimated Mars's capability, and subsequently Mars became the market leader. Mars was the market leader from about 1980 to 1988, but because Hershey did a lot of things right and Mars made many mistakes, market leadership changed hands. When Mars seemed depleted of new ideas and innovation, Hershey struck. By the early 1990s, it was clear that Mars's product development record was dismal, and some senior managers left, having found the work environment somewhat repressive. Meanwhile, Hershey introduced Hugs, a white-chocolate version of the chocolate Kiss, NutRageous, and Nuggets, a thick chocolate bar. The image of the candy industry firms is positive, especially of Hershey, Mars, Nestlé, Godiva, Russell Stover, and Fanny Farmer. However, the candy industry does not win high marks for market segmentation strategies. Only Hershey has developed an effective strategy for segmenting the adult market, with the Symphony Bar. The candy industry has been late in cultivating product-usage segments, with six-packs of candy bars, and in endeavoring to sell multipackages in addition to single candy bars. The candy industry has done an effective job of using mass-market segmentation with product-differentiation strategies. Physical distribution resources have not played as important a role as in the ice cream industry. However, intensive distribution and inventory replenishment has been important, and these strategies have been used well. The use of human resources has been effective, but not as outstanding as in the soup industry or the snack food industry.

Chocolate is subject to melting and therefore has a relatively short shelf life and is not as appetizing in hot weather. A technological breakthrough that would make chocolate heat resistant has been needed. It is possible that this new technology would result in new products and services not yet envisioned and would lower prices through the development of more cost-efficient production and distribution methods. Recently, this new technological breakthrough has been announced, but it is too early to discern whether or not there can be a positive marketing application. A possible long-range benefit would be the extension of shelf life for the product. The short-range objective would be that consumers have less fear of buying chocolate in hot weather. The issue of taste does arise, and hopefully an analogy can be drawn to the development of diet drinks. After a period of trial and error, diet drinks and their taste have satisfied a certain market segment. Hopefully, the candy industry will develop products that satisfy consumer tastes and will be able to achieve opportunities for extending product shelf life and overcoming consumer resistance to consuming chocolate in hot weather. If this new technological discovery has positive mar-

Table 9.1
An Overview of the Candy Industry in 1996

Manufacturers	Brands
Hershey	Reese's, KitKat, Oh Henry!, Mr. Goodbar, Hershey's milk chocolate with and without almonds, Kisses, Fifth Avenue, Cadbury
Mars	M&M's, Snickers, Mars, Twix, 3 Musketeers, Dove, Bounty, Milky Way, Milky Way Lite, Milky Way Dark
Nestlé	Raisinets, Butterfinger, Baby Ruth, Goobers, Chunky
E. J. Brach and Brock	Brach
Nabisco	Planters Peanuts, Beechnut, Life Savers
Russell Stover (Fannie Mae)	Russell Stover, Barbie Licensee
Fanny Farmer	Fanny Farmer
Campbell Soup	Godiva
Wrigley	Wrigley

Note: Reported are major brands of national significance. Brands that are primarily regional are not reported.

keting applications, the candy industry could be changed as consumers now know it.

MARKET STRUCTURE

Table 9.1 presents an overview of the candy industry in 1996 and depicts chocolate bars, boxed candy, peanuts, and other items that might be classified within the candy market structure. The candy industry is dominated by Hershey and Mars. Although a case might be made to include Nabisco and Wrigley under the candy classification, these firms will be excluded from coverage because chocolate products are not offered.

In the 1990s, Hershey and Mars were battling for the top spot in the candy bar sector of the industry. Hershey has pulled slightly ahead of Mars with about a 30 to 35 percent market share, which fluctuates. Nestlé has about 10 percent, and E. J. Brach has about 9 percent market share. Mars is a privately held company and thus has an inherent flexibility advantage over public owned firms, inasmuch as strategy can be formulated more quickly and in a more concealed environment.

Boxed candy sales experienced a decline in the 1990s. The boxed chocolate industry ranges from large producers to many small organizations with only a single location. Russell Stover and Fanny Farmer, which were purchased by Fannie Mae, are the two leaders. Other prominent firms are See's and Whitman's. The superpremium category is led by Godiva, a division of Campbell Soup; Perugina, based in Italy; and Lindt, a Swiss company. Bloomingdale's distributes not only upscale Godiva chocolates but also Hershey's Kisses. Some boxed candy producers, in both the past and the present, have vertically integrated by opening their own retail stores. For example, Fanny Farmer, Lofts, Barricini, and Barton's have administered a vertical marketing system. Barton's Candy, in the past, gained distribution in over forty states by franchising nearly 3,000 outlets, including department stores, pharmacies, greeting card shops, airports, and candy shops. Barton's also operated some company-owned candy stores, but has fallen upon hard times.

Baking-chocolate brands are dominated by Nestlé, which has more than a 50 percent market share. Baker's and Hershey are the only other firms that have market share in the double digits. The exception would be private labels, which together have slightly more market share than either Baker's or Hershey. Private labels are not significant in either the candy bar or candy box industry, and do not seem to be a future competitive threat.

Supermarkets are the distribution channel that comprise the majority of candy bar sales. Discount outlets are a rising important distribution outlet. Sales in discount stores are bound to increase as such discounters as Wal-Mart sell more food items and the popularity of Sam's Club increases. Consumers making purchases in discount stores have demonstrated a preference for these leading candy brands in the following order: Hershey (17 percent); M&M's (12 percent); Snickers, owned by Mars (10 percent); and Brach's (10 percent). There are, indeed, few products so relatively overpriced, with so much fat and calories and of so little nutritious value that have experienced such healthy growth. Although supermarkets and discount stores are the leading channels of distribution, neither has been able to develop store brands that are competitive with manufacturer brands.

In 1994 E. J. Brach acquired the Brock Candy Company, which specializes in marketing hard candy. The firm will now be better positioned to withstand the assault of Hershey and Mars into the hard and soft candy product lines that Brock and Brach produce. Brock candies are sold primarily through mass merchandisers, with Wal-Mart accounting for approximately 40 percent of total sales. Star Brites, Wild'n Fruity, Twisters, and Special Treasures are the better-known brands.

MARKET CONDUCT

Hershey and Mars, the two leading companies in the candy-bar industry, have launched low-fat, low-calorie products. Mars, for example, introduced Milky Way Lite, which has 32 percent fewer calories (190 versus

280) and less fat content (8 grams versus 11 grams) than the original product. However, most chocolate lovers have not greeted with enthusiasm the opportunity to purchase chocolate with less fat or less calories. The behavior of chocolate lovers would seem to be contrary to the purchase behavior in the snack food industry. However, candy miniatures have given consumers more control over their calorie intake, and this packaging innovation has grown in popularity.

Candy bar firms would be myopic if they focused only on their brand competitors. The real challenge is to expand their primary market rather than to independently fight one another for larger market share. There is a trend for consumers to eat less in general and to eat less candy in particular. Therefore, even though this consumer health concern is not an imminent threat, this trend has to be closely monitored by the candy industry. Sales of dietetic candy are increasing. Failure to exploit opportunities to expand the whole market or at least prevent it from eroding would be a marketing mistake.

The candy industry has failed to take advantage of product-usage segmentation variables. Marketers tend to distinguish between two broad classes of variables: user-oriented and product-usage variables. User-oriented segmentation variables include such consumer characteristics as sex, age, geographic location, and ethnic origin as well as psychographic and lifestyle variables such as motives, attitudes, interests, and opinions. Product-usage segmentation variables involve such factors as the amount of use, time of use, place of use, the user of the product, product benefits, and the occasion for consumption. For example, Halloween is a special occasion, and the focus is on satisfying the children's market for this holiday. The best-selling candy brands during Halloween are Nestlé Crunch Mini Bar, Hershey Chocolate Kisses, Reese's Mini Cups, Hershey mini-assortments, and Brach's Candy Corn. Valentine's Day and Mother's Day are two other important special occasions that the candy industry could emphasize even more. Godiva and other upscale candy producers have done a good job, but for the most part the middle-price range has been relatively neglected.

Consumers have different motivations and receive varied benefits and types of satisfaction from products, depending on the occasion. Candy manufacturers, before applying occasion segmentation, should decide whether they are looking for consumers who are similar across situations or consumers who are seeking to fill only one consumption role. For example, a candy manufacturer could search for people who buy boxed candy frequently or for those who make purchases only on Valentine's Day. Occasion segmentation is probably most appropriate when marketers attempt to identify opportunities for accelerating demand among current markets. The strategy of occasion segmentation would be less effective in reaching new markets. In contrast to psychographic and lifestyle variables, purchase intentions are generally more reliable predictors of behavior. Therefore, product-usage segmentation variables seem worthy of greater attention from candy manufacturers. Moreover, since consumers are complex, it seems reasonable that multidimensional bases are better than one-dimensional bases for segmenting markets.

The key to understanding market conduct in the candy industry is the strategy of product availability. Hershey, Mars, and Nestlé sell their products to all consumption markets. These markets are composed of consumer markets, industrial markets, reseller markets, government and nonprofit markets, and international markets. Hershey, Mars, and Nestlé sell mainly to resellers, retailers, and wholesalers, which in turn sell candy to consumers, either directly or indirectly. Another important group is institutional consumers, namely, schools, factories, government agencies, and other organizations that operate cafeterias for their employees. Candy manufacturers also sell a substantial volume to foreign consumers, producers, resellers, and governments. Each market exhibits specific characteristics that warrant careful study.

Age-group growth trends and their marketing implications are an important variable for candy marketers. Children and youths from ages 10 to 19 years old and young adults from ages 20 to 34 have traditionally purchased candy bars in larger quantities than other age groups, such as retirees over 65. The changing age structure of the population will result in different growth rates for various age groups over every ten-year period and will strongly affect strategies. The increasing attention of consumers to health concerns will be another important variable. Consumers have not yet responded in substantial sales volume to candy products that reduce calories, cholesterol, or fat intake. Although baby boomers are at an age to purchase box candy, sales of this form of candy product have declined in the past decade. Prospects for selling sugar-free candy in bulk should be given greater attention, especially to retailers located in shopping malls. Compared to the cereal industry and the snack food industry, the candy industry has done little advertising to attract the children's market.

The candy industry has done an exceptional job in precluding competition from supermarket store brands. Some factors responsible for this lack of competition might be the prevailing power of well-known national brands, such as Snickers and Hershey, and the relatively low price of the product. Although manufacturer brands are well known both in the cereal and ice cream industries, price is used as a competitive weapon. Brand names in the candy industry continue to command customer loyalty. Brands promoted by Hershey, Mars, and Nestlé have helped to build the corporate image and convey the quality and size of the company.

The candy industry has not been successful in fighting against indirect competition. The snack food and breakfast cereal industries have seized significant market share. The food wars are growing more intense, and marketers must give indirect competition as much importance as they do direct competition.

HERSHEY: THE DEFENDING CHAMPION

Hershey has been established longer than any other prominent firm in the candy industry, and although constantly challenged by Mars, it is still the defending champion. The company is confronted with keen competition, especially from Mars and Nestlé. In the early 1970s, Hershey lost its lead in market share to Mars. Mars has a battery of formidable brands such as Snickers, Milky Way, 3 Musketeers, and M&M's. Another aspect of declining sales is that consumers have deliberately tried to consume less candy. A strong negative, in the early 1990s, was the debate about whether or not chocolate is high in saturated fat, the type of fat that raises blood cholesterol levels. Other health concerns are whether or not chocolate is high in caffeine and in sodium and whether it promotes tooth decay. In order to diminish these objections, a nutrition group engages in basic research projects in areas such as tooth decay, acne, chocolate allergies, and nutrition.

Hershey has been successful with product-development extension strategies. Successes can be noted with Reese's Crunchy Peanut Butter Cups, Reese's Peanut Butter Chips, Hershey's Kisses with Almonds, and the Golden Collection Solitaires. In 1988, Hershey acquired Peter Paul and Cadbury's U.S. candy operations for Cadbury's successful fruit and nut chocolate products and Peter Paul's Almond Joy and coconut Mounds. While Hershey has been successful, most notably in brand-extension strategies, failures have occurred. For example, in the mid-1970s, The Rally Bar, a chocolate, caramel, and peanut candy bar, was deleted from the product line. One of its problems was that the peanuts became soggy on the retailers' shelves. In the early 1990s, Hershey introduced the reduced calorie and fat candy bar, but sales did not live up to expectations.

Hershey is confronted with seasonal demand for its products. Candy sales are generally highest from July through December, due largely to the holiday seasons. Buyer behavior appears to indicate that consumers rarely select the same candy bar twice in a row, preferring a variety for consumption. Therefore, Hershey has developed a variety of product offerings.

Through the years, Hershey has endeavored to maintain high-quality employer and employee relations and has achieved a good reputation for fairness to employees. Hershey has emphasized social responsibility and has contributed heavily to the Milton Hershey School for Orphans and other social causes.

MARKETING STRATEGIES

Hershey's marketing strategy is predicated on consistently superior product quality, intensive distribution, and best possible value in terms of price and weight. The company uses a variety of promotional programs to implement its strategy. Television gets a lion's share of the budget, but magazines and radio are also used. Business folklore informs that Milton Hershey was fanatical about product quality. This fanaticism was carried to the extreme when Hershey would personally carry a large spoon in the factory and personally sample the chocolate. Hershey, like Henry Ford and many early entrepreneurs, demanded a high-quality product that would reflect value for purchasers. Advertising as a marketing strategy was not utilized then, since Hershey believed that consumer word-of-mouth communication concerning product quality would become widespread and would be sufficient.

Milton Hershey believed that no store was situated in a location that was too inconvenient for a Hershey salesman to reach. Milton Hershey also maintained that no store was too small and no potential account was too small to be neglected. This early philosophy was the foundation for what is known as an intensive distribution strategy. An intensive distribution strategy makes a product available at all possible retail outlets. This may mean that the product is carried at a wide variety of different and even competing retail institutions in the geographical area, such as food stores and drugstores. The distribution of chocolate bars, which are low in price and high in product turnover, have mass-market appeal. This is consistent with an intensive distribution strategy. Many consumers purchase chocolate bars on impulse, and therefore it is advantageous to have the product displayed in as many places as possible. This strategy gives the product widespread buyer recognition. The main limitation of an intensive distribution strategy for a firm in the candy industry is that it is difficult to provide any degree of control over a large number of retailers. Moreover, since the product is characterized by a low margin and high turnover, frequent replenishment of stock is essential.

The element of weather is an uncontrollable factor in the marketing environment. Few individuals desire to munch a chocolate bar in hot weather. Consequently, the sale of candy bars may be seasonal in nature. However, appropriate marketing strategies may be able to appreciably diminish this uncontrollable factor in the marketing environment.

The leading firm in the chocolate box candy industry is Russell Stover. Russell Stover, like Mars, is a privately held company with more than 5,000 retail outlets. The company was founded in 1923 by Mr. and Mrs. Russell Stover, who began the candy business in their bungalow home in Denver, Colorado. Russell Stover is the largest producer of boxed chocolates in the United States and has over 40,000 accounts in such outlets as drugstores, card and gift stores, grocery stores, department stores, and mass-merchandising stores. Other firms, such as Fanny Farmer and Barton's, are more prominent in regional locations.

A sizable portion of the boxed candy industry profits are derived from the Christmas, Valentine's Day and Easter selling seasons. Occasion and market segmentation are frequently used marketing strategies. For example, for Halloween Russell Stover has marketed Monster Boxes aimed at the children's market. The Barbie Doll has been licensed from Mattel and Barbie Baskets were designed for the 1997 Easter season. Russell Stover has even ventured into producing bar and bag candy packages for the Halloween season.

Boxed chocolate candy, in contrast to candy bars, can profit much more from market segmentation by occasion and from targeting separate markets, such as the children's market. Valentine's Day boxes segment all three price ranges—low, medium, and high. Godiva, owned by Campbell Soup, targets the superpremium market. The superpremium chocolate market designates someone special as a gift recipient. There isn't really a single way to select a market segment. Different segmentation variables need to be tried, separately and combined, in an effort to target the most appropriate market segment. The boxed candy industry has identified such market segments as adults, children, and special occasions. To some extent benefit segmentation strategies that are closely allied to psychographic and product-usage bases can be profitably employed. The candy box industry has made great use of occasion segmentation strategies used for the Christmas, Easter, and Valentine's Day seasons. Consumers have different motivations and receive different benefits, depending upon the occasion. Occasion segmentation is probably most useful when endeavoring to identify opportunities for increasing consumption among current markets.

Product-Market Strategies

Around the turn of the twentieth century, Hershey maintained that there was no need for advertising, except for word of mouth. Increased competition changed this strategy. At the end of the 20th century Hershey is among the top 100 advertisers in the United States. Companies that have implemented product market strategies are continuously competing with Mars for leadership in the chocolate candy industry. Hershey, Mars, and Nestlé have been able to preclude competition with brand power, acquisition of smaller firms, and a knowledge of consumer markets. Hershey's product line includes Hershey's chocolate bars, Hershey Kisses, Reese's candy, and old-line products such as Mr. Goodbar. New products, such as Symphony, compete with Mars's product line, which includes Snickers,

M&M's, 3 Musketeers, and Milky Way. Nestlé offers Butterfinger, Baby Ruth, and Goobers, but the Nestlé products are not as formidable as either the Hershey or the Mars products.

Traditionally, Hershey targeted the older consumer. This strategy changed in the 1980s as Hershey began to gear its efforts toward advertising to preteens and teenagers. Demographic studies revealed that there would be more than 27 million people between the ages of 13 and 19 by the year 2000, with more money to spend than any previous generation in this age range. The Fifth Avenue candy bar was launched for this market. Hershey also realized that it would be possible to target diverse markets simultaneously. The Hershey Symphony Bar was developed to target the more mature market. An older generation had acquired a taste for almonds, and candy with almonds increased in popularity by the late 1980s. The older generation seems to perceive that more protein and nutritional value is derived by consuming a candy bar with almonds rather than a plain chocolate bar. The Symphony Bar was targeted toward the middle-and upper-class consumer and marketed as a premium bar.

Mars has managed to remain competitive with Hershey with regard to market share by directly producing products that compete with Hershey brands. Mars has not tried to market products that are somewhat different than Hershey's. The target market is the same for both firms. Since Mars is privately owned, new product introduction can be a well guarded secret and thus can carry a strategic advantage. However, skipping the market-testing stage of product development in order to provide a surprise to the competition can produce a decided limitation. The purpose of market testing is to learn how consumers and dealers react to the actual product and to determine the potential size of the market. Most firms believe in test-marketing a new product in small regions that represent the target market. Because of the high costs of test marketing and the risk of giving competitors an opportunity to seize the same opportunity, some firms have decided to abandon the test-market stage or have developed newer, faster, and less expensive ways to test-market their products. It is possible that a competitor willing to assume the risk could quickly produce a me-too product and even enter target markets ahead of the innovating firm. To illustrate, General Foods once test-marketed a snack product known as Toast'em Popups. At the same time, Kellogg, without test marketing, was able to distribute a very similar product known as Pop-Tarts. To eliminate test marketing entirely is a gamble, and in most situations may not be warranted. However, a modified test-marketing technique known as a simulated store can yield valuable information concerning whether or not to launch a product. Hershey, with its research-and-development team, was able to get the jump on Mars by producing the Symphony Bar before Mars could successfully market the Dove Bar.

Hershey uses a variety of packages, such as boxes, trays, and bags, to distinguish and display its product line. Sizes for candy bars include standard, large, and giant. More than thirty brand names are marketed. Candy bars are by far the best-selling form of chocolate. Snickers, made by Mars, and Reese's Peanut Butter Cups, made by Hershey, are the leading candy bar brands. Nestlé, however, cannot be ruled out in candy-bar competition, and markets such formidable brands as Butterfinger and Baby Ruth. The candy companies have expanded their markets principally by producing new chocolate bars, diversifying peanut butter formulas into new forms, and diversifying chocolate into other food types. Hershey's product line has more than doubled in the past decade. However, the candy industry could do a more effective job with packaging, such as aggressively promoting six-packs and multipackages. The chocolate-bar industry seems to be fresh out of ideas. New product development is dismal, with the exception of brand-line extensions, such as Hershey Kisses with Almonds and Mars's Milky Way Lite. There is a genuine lack in industry innovation. Naturally, one firm may be evaluated as more innovative than another, but the candy industry as a whole lacks fresh ideas. Even the launching of low-calorie and fat-free candy bars has encountered numerous snags. The candy industry is marked for low growth, and although acquisitions may resolve some problems, genuine innovation is missing, and yet it is vital for continued success.

Fads are usually adopted with great zeal, peak early, and decline very quickly. Soft and creamy chocolate bars have proved the exception. A new fad has penetrated the candy industry known as crunchiness. Crunchiness may be linked to freshness or even to the relief of stress. Reese's Crunchy Cookie Cups was launched by Hershey, and Nestlé introduced White Crunch, the first line extension to its Nestlé Crunch candy bar. Fads appeal to people who are searching for something different. Fads do not survive because they generally do not satisfy a strong need. It is difficult to predict the duration of a fad. A fad curve can be considered within the framework of the product life cycle. A fad curve represents a product with quick popularity and sudden decline. An extended fad curve is like a fad except that residual sales continue at a fraction of earlier sales. The development of a fad is viewed positively by the candy industry, since change has not been its strength.

DISTRIBUTION STRATEGIES

Distribution strategies by Hershey, Mars, and Nestlé in marketing candy bars employ the services of middlemen. Middlemen are used because the manufacturer cannot perform several marketing tasks as efficiently without them. Manufacturers are primarily interested in producing large quantities of candy bars from their factories. In contrast, the customer is interested in purchasing one bar of candy in a convenient location, at a convenient time, with a related assortment of other goods desired, and with an easy payment procedure. The gap between the interests of the manufacturers and those of the consumer must be closed. Middlemen perform functions to overcome discrepancies in quantities, place, time, assortment, and possession.

Middlemen create place utility by stocking candy bars where customers are situated. Time utility is created by convenient hours of operation. Quantity utility is established by making candy bars available in single bars, bags, and boxes. Assortment utility is accomplished by stocking related goods that can be purchased in the same shopping trip. Impulse buying of candy bars is stimulated by placement near checkout counters and at other strategic locations. Possession utility is provided by developing a simple payment plan. Candy manufacturers would need to develop a network of stores throughout the country in order to perform the same functions as middlemen. Yet the selection of middlemen is not a simple task. Questions arise as to whether only large wholesalers or a balance of small, regional distributors would be advisable. An increasing share of candy distribution is in the hands of large retail corporate chains such as Kroger, Safeway, and Winn-Dixie. These distributors, both wholesalers and retailers, have the power to dictate the terms. The competition for shelf space in food stores is intense and accelerating. The candy industry must learn how to stimulate and satisfy resellers, or face diminishing support or exclusion. For the most part, the candy industry has followed the intensive distribution strategy developed by Hershey around the turn of the 20th century.

Growth in the candy industry has been flat for some years. However, Mars and Hershey share a formidable intangible asset, which is their position as one of the strongest distribution oligopolies in the United States. Competitors are not prohibited from entering the market, but obtaining shelf space is extremely difficult. The cost of establishing a new brand and field support for resellers is quite high. Even Nestlé, with approximately 10 percent of the U.S. market, has been unable to increase its market share significantly after trying to do so for a decade.

OTHER MARKETING STRATEGIES

Although Hershey has been more flexible in its promotional expenditures with retailers and wholesalers, Mars has alienated resellers. Specifically, Mars eliminated its special discounts with a lack of diplomacy, something the company is known for, by simply withdrawing its promotional program without notification. Moreover, former Mars executives maintain that the firm stifles risk taking and innovation.

The Mars culture, however, does stimulate its field organization to excel. The company has sponsored the World Cup soccer championships and other notable sports events. This type of national advertising lends support to the Mars field sales force. Even though resellers have been alienated, the Mars brands are well known and are profitable for retailers and wholesalers.

The price of a product is related to its branding and distribution activities. To illustrate, branding aids consumers in recognizing and evaluating products that can provide a psychological reward by symbolizing status or quality. Godiva is identified as a brand name that symbolizes high-quality chocolates. Premium-priced products are frequently sold in a limited number of stores, whereas lower-priced products in similar product categories may be sold in numerous stores. Godiva and other premium-priced chocolates are distributed through selected specialty stores. In contrast, Hershey and Mars chocolates are distributed through multiple outlets. Mars especially has been known to suffer from periodic stock-outs or capacity problems, difficulties that are not as prevalent with premium-priced chocolate brands.

The varying price of the cocoa bean used in making chocolate has presented problems to manufacturers. The challenge remains as to what to do when prices of the cocoa bean increase. Some producers may decide to offer the chocolate bar at the same price but give less of the product. In this way vending machine operators and other resellers are placated. Consumers, however, may feel cheated, and company image may be tarnished by this pricing strategy. On the other hand, in 1990 Hershey raised candy-bar prices by approximately 12 percent for the first time since 1985. Hershey's arch rival, Mars, immediately responded with an identical price increase. Consumers reacted by reducing their consumption, and Hershey's volume decreased by 6 percent in the second quarter of 1991 and by 3 percent in the third quarter. Consumers did adjust, and finally Hershey and Mars regained lost ground, but a powerful lesson was learned.

Nestlé has drummed up sales with its Disney tie-in pact in advertising, and Hershey has introduced new products such as Nuggets and extra creamy chocolate bars. Mars has sponsored the World Cup program and increased expenditures for M&M's, Milky Way, and Snickers. National advertising spending will probably accelerate in the future.

Candy bars are impulse products. Impulse products are items that the consumer does not plan to purchase on a specific trip to a store. The purchase of candy bars, even though an impulse item, can be done on a rational basis. Self-service and open-display selling presentations strategically placed at checkout counters have brought about a situation where buying may be postponed until the consumer reaches the retail store. Emphasis by candy manufacturers must be placed on promotional programs designed to get customers into the store. Displays must be appealing, since the brand name and the package wrapping will serve to trigger impulse buying. The candy industry excels in developing point-of-purchase displays.

WHY HERSHEY IS STILL THE CHAMPION

Hershey has not been content with the status quo and has proceeded to innovate, especially with product development and revised advertising strategies. Hershey abandoned its nonnational advertising policy in 1970 and decided to advertise nationally for several reasons. First, there was increased competition in the candy industry, and heavy competitive advertising was making inroads into established market share. Second, there was the need to better acquaint consumers under age 25 with Hershey products. According to the census, this target market under age 25 comprised half of the U.S. population. Mass advertising, it was maintained, would promote mass distribution, which would, in turn, lead to mass production. Hershey envisioned future problems with this revised advertising strategy and should be praised for taking necessary precautions. Preparations were satisfactorily made to defend its advertising directed toward children and to counter claims that chocolate may promote tooth decay. With careful advertising and public relations programs, Hershey was able to avoid and reduce much potential criticism.

Hershey, after losing ground to Mars, became the leading candy manufacturer in the United States in 1988. Mars has experimented with new product development, but unlike the case with Hershey, many of its new candy products have not been too successful. Mars has extended itself into the ice cream market with frozen Snickers ice cream bars, but new candy bar brands such as Balisto and P B Max have met with poor results. The Bounty candy bar brand has been only moderately successful. Hershey, however, in recent years successfully launched such new brands as Fifth Avenue and Symphony, and acquired the Cadbury product line along with Peter Paul's Almond Joy candy bar. In contrast, Nestlé has tried for years to significantly increase its market share in the U.S. chocolate candy bar industry without much success. Nestlé Crunch and Bon Bons have been moderately successful, but the old standbys of Butterfinger and Baby Ruth are still the mainstays. Nestlé is known for its coffee brands, including Taster's Choice and Hills Brothers, but has been unable to make significant inroads into the candy bar industry.

Hershey has been able to surpass competitors such as Mars and Nestlé for the following reasons:

- Successful intensive distribution strategies

- Strong brand recognition and preference

- Successful acquisition of candy firms such as Reese, Peter Paul, and Cadbury, and of the distribution of KitKat wafer bars in the United States

- Successful market segmentation to both adults and children
- Maintenance of high-quality product standards
- Exceptional services to resellers

MARKETING SUCCESSES AND MISTAKES

Brand power and intensive distribution strategies are the two most important reasons for success in the candy industry. The chocolate bar candy industry, because of strong brand power, has been able to prevent inroads from store brands. Branding provides advantages to consumers, distributors, and producers. Brand names such as Hershey and Snickers help consumers identify and select products with confidence. Consumers are assured of product quality levels. Loyal consumers are less vulnerable to competitive promotional programs. Distributors generally gain higher profit margins from well-known brands and benefit from customer brand acceptance. Producers are better able to establish a market niche, and the brands symbolize the reputation and quality of the organization.

Hershey has achieved success by using a family brand name. This is also true of Nestlé to a more limited extent. Mars, in contrast, has used the family brand name but also has developed individual brands. There is an inherent danger that too many individual brands can dilute the company's marketing resources. Both Hershey and Mars have successfully used brand-extension strategies. Brand extension is a strategy of applying successful brand names to new products, for example, Hershey's Kisses Chocolates and the brand extension of Hershey's Kisses with Almonds Chocolates, Reese's Peanut Butter Cups and the brand extension of Reese's Peanut Butter Chips, and Mars's Milky Way and the brand extension of Milky Way Lite and Milky Way Dark. A brand is more than just a method to prove ownership. Hershey's brand image and Mars's brand image are made up of a multitude of impressions and values conveyed in their advertising and slogans. Brand power is an intangible that has real rewards. A well-known brand name represents added value to consumers. The more well-known the brand name, the stronger the competitive advantage.

The candy bar industry, with the leadership of Hershey, has successfully applied the strategy of intensive distribution. Hershey, Mars, and Nestlé each implement an intensive distribution strategy by using a large number of wholesalers and retailers to obtain widespread market coverage. Intensive distribution is a strategy aimed at reaching the greatest number of consumers. The marketing emphasis is on mass advertising and convenient locations within the retail store. Candy displays within the retail store situated near checkout counters and at other strategic locations have been especially successful in promoting impulse buying.

The candy industry has not been very successful in competing with indirect competition. Indirect competition can be defined as competing with alternatives in other product categories. Defining the competition depends on how narrowly the product category is defined. Snickers could, for example, define its competition only as chocolate candy, but this would constitute an important mistake. The indirect competition from snacks such as cookies, popcorn, nuts, raisins, and fruits has caused a contraction in sales volume for the candy industry. The snack food industry has done a much better job of developing low-salt, low-fat, and low-calorie products. The candy industry has tried but has been unsuccessful in addressing consumer health concerns.

The candy industry has not used the strategy of market segmentation very well. Market segmentation refers to efforts to group potential buyers by demographic characteristics, geographical region, lifestyle, usage patterns, and behavioral factors. Market segmentation strategy based upon occasion, such as Valentine's Day, has been done well, but segmentation based upon lifestyle, gender, and/or income are strategies not fully explored. The marketing of the Symphony Bar by Hershey was a beginning. In contrast, the strategy of product differentiation has been used successfully by the candy industry. The successful application of the strategy of product differentiation should result in an increased horizontal share of a generalized market. Product differentiation refers to marketing efforts that distinguish a basically homogeneous product from competitors' products. Methods used to accomplish this include altering the product's physical characteristics, brand, and advertising, and packaging that is targeted to the stimulation of the individual's five senses. These promotional appeals can be especially successful in an affluent society. The candy industry demonstrates strength in branding and advertising strategies, but differentiation through packaging, with six-packs and multipacks, is only in its beginning stages. Premiums have not been fully explored. Godiva, in the box candy industry, has successfully targeted packaging and has been a leader in successful market-segmentation strategies. Since growth is a problem in the candy industry, strategies that reflect weakness must be explored. On the other hand, Mars's strategy with line extension in the development of Milky Way, Milky Way Lite, and Milky Way Dark can be viewed positively.

MANAGING CHANGE

Whether the marketing activity is product planning, pricing, promotion, or distribution, change dominates the environment. Change is a driving force that pervades the dynamics of the candy industry. Therefore, contingency planning is both a necessary and a vital function for marketing executives.

Strategy is always surrounded by uncertainty, and contingency planning helps to limit exposure to adverse risks. Projecting the marketing environment five or more years into the future is a difficult task, since environmental change has accelerated in the latter half of the 20th century. For example, the sales of box candy have not fared well. Firms such as Barton's, Lofts, and Barricini are either nonexistent or just a shadow of what they were in the past. For example, Barton's Candy in the 1970s had distribution in over forty states, and its products were sold through nearly 3,000 franchised outlets, including department stores, pharmacies, greeting card shops, airports, franchised stores, and company-owned stores. Barton's had also entered into an agreement with Macy's in California to lease and operate the entire candy department in ten stores. Although Barton's does have a presence in the Northeast, its former extensive distribution network is now limited.

The question remains as to how marketing executives in the candy industry can develop differential-advantage strategies while coping with a changing environment. One method is to develop good environmental forecasts. For example, it is difficult to predict the future price of the cocoa bean in world markets. While specifics do change, experience does indicate, however, that most of the broad trends can be predicated within a useful range. Reactions to the increase or decrease in prices of the cocoa bean may take the form of giving consumers either more product or less product. Changes in strategy may involve price increases, price decreases, or price stabilization. A range of reactions can be developed based upon the magnitude of the cocoa bean's projected price increase or decrease.

Another approach is to limit the exposure to adverse risks. For example, consideration of the impact on distribution would be an important consideration. What would happen to vending machine operations if price increases or decreases were implemented? Would risk be more limited if, instead, more or less of the product were given to consumers? Contingency strategies are a device for limiting losses. Contingency plans provide a fallback alternative if the main goal is unattainable. Alternative approaches develop a wider range of alternatives, and thus a lower risk can be achieved.

A progressive revision of strategy based upon new knowledge can be an effective way of managing change. For example, environmental forces were such that the price of cars and commodities were rising. Inflation had taken its toll. Godiva chocolates marched in and made a superpremium brand of box chocolate that conveyed status and social prestige. Consumers were willing to "splurge" and reward themselves without overextending their pocketbooks. Godiva has not only revised its strategy in the box chocolate industry but has taken advantage of a market opportunity by differentiating its product. Godiva aimed its product at the self-indulgent consumer and the consumer who desired to enjoy a special occasion by spending much more than usual. Godiva chocolates were shown nestled in jewelry boxes.

In a period of runaway inflation, Godiva focused on the market opportunity of helping consumers reward themselves at relatively low prices compared to prices for other items, such as automobiles. Economic and social change was largely responsible for the success of Godiva.

MANAGERIAL INSIGHTS

Hershey, Mars, and Nestlé have achieved a virtual status-quo equilibrium. As these three firms battled for market share, other candy producers were unable to make significant inroads into the candy market. Sales of box candy are declining, and sales of chocolate bar candy remain flat. This lack of growth can be perceived as an ominous warning. Hershey, Mars, and Nestlé attained dominance through brand power and intensive distribution strategies, but the marketing environment has stifled growth. Hershey, Mars, Nestlé, and the boxed candy firms such as Russell Stover and Fanny Farmer have not developed proactive strategies to combat this lack of sales-volume growth.

Perhaps the absence of proactive strategies to combat the lack of growth can be considered a small mistake. Certainly the viability of the leading firms in the candy industry has not been jeopardized. The candy industry appears to be in a state of hesitation. Competition within the candy industry has been considered, but indirect competition, which has not been considered, has caused sales-volume erosion and loss of market share to other product categories.

The lack of innovation in the candy industry is glaring. Although the candy industry has differentiated the candy product with dark and light chocolate, nuts, and raisins, this innovation is minor compared to those in other food sectors, notably ice cream, breakfast cereal, soup, and snack food. Hershey has targeted the adult market with the Symphony Bar and children with Halloween candy, but this is only the tip of the iceberg. The candy bar industry could give away premiums such as baseball cards in order to stimulate sales. The candy wrapper itself, in many instances, hasn't changed in years.

Cooperative advertising or joint advertising is any advertising for which the cost is shared by two or more organizations, each of which should benefit from the advertising. The Mars Company has joined forces with the Kellogg product Special K to advertise their Milky Way Lite product. The Milky Way Lite candy bar is advertised on the back of the Special K cereal carton, and the consumer is able to cut out a price-reduction coupon. The Milky Way Lite candy bar features 50 percent less fat than the regular candy bar. The Special K product highlights its nonfat characteristics. This type of alliance made by the candy industry represents a beginning to more creative strategies for an industry that is experiencing a decline in consumer demand.

In summary, the candy industry needs to develop a much higher degree of creativity in initiating marketing activities. Other industries such as the snack food industry and the ice cream industry are diverting demand from the candy industry. A lack of innovation, regardless of the rationale, will cause the entrance of substitute products. Compared to the soft-drink and snack food industries, the candy industry was late in product packaging development and in introducing new products.

CHAPTER 10

THE SOFT-DRINK INDUSTRY

Strategies in a Changing Market
- Anticipate changing market segments
- Place products in new locations
- Strong development of national brands
- Strong market segmentation and product differentiation strategies
- Clearly defined objectives
- Effective pricing and promotion strategies
- Broadened product line
- Packaging innovation
- Position image and product offerings to stand apart from competitors

Strategies in the Maturity Stage of the Product Life-Cycle
- Maintain profit margins
- Psychological appeals to loyal customer core
- Emphasize the expansion of location strategies
- Make the vertical system more efficient
- Eliminate marginal items
- Target precise market segments

The soft-drink industry in the United States is an integral part of daily life. Competition in the soft-drink industry could easily be labeled the "soft-drink wars." The wars have continued into the 1990s, and the battle for shelf, aisle and vending machine space has reached staggering dimensions as the colas receive competition from bottled water, iced tea, fruit juices, lemon-lime drinks, and private labels. The world of the one perfect soft drink for everyone is gone as strategies of market segmentation and product differentiation are used separately and together.

The development of the U.S. soft-drink industry started in the early 1800s, when numerous mineral waters were sold by druggists. Druggists often flavored mineral water with various extracts, such as root beer or ginger ale, to please customers at their soda fountains. By the late 19th century, most soft drinks were local in origin, and while there was some attempt to distribute beyond local trading areas, these attempts were insignificant.

Coca-Cola was developed by Dr. John Pemberton, a pharmacist in Atlanta, Georgia, in 1886. Eventually the rights to the soft drink were sold to Asa Candler. Although Coca-Cola was first sold as a headache cure, a modification of the formula was soon unveiled and distributed to soda fountains in used beer bottles. In 1919, Ernest Woodruff purchased the Coca-Cola Company, and in 1923 his son, Robert W. Woodruff, took over; he was to become the most important figure in Coca-Cola's history.

Gaining national distribution was an important factor in the success of Coca-Cola. There were many obstacles in this venture. The product sold for only a nickel, and therefore profitability depended upon volume sales. Moreover, its ingredients were heavy and bulky. If repeat sales were to be generated, the product needed widespread distribution. This meant that the product had to be available in all types of retail outlets. Coca-Cola quickly established a strong trademark with high consumer identification that was able to withstand competitors.

Pepsi-Cola was created in 1893 by Caleb Bradham, a pharmacist, when he developed a unique mixture of kola nut extract, vanilla, and rare oils. Originally called "Brad's drink" by his customers, it is now known as Pepsi-Cola. Pepsi-Cola was officially registered with the United States Patent Office in 1903, and a franchise system that depended upon local bottlers was constructed. Originally all soft drinks were available at fountains or pharmacies, and manufacturers had to develop methods to bottle soda and make it portable. Pepsi's first bottling plant was built in 1905, and bottling operations continued to expand. After 1933, Pepsi began to bottle its soda in 12-ounce bottles priced at five cents. Competitors were selling their products at 6 ounces for five cents, and therefore Pepsi gained a differential advantage, though this was later diminished as other manufacturers met Pepsi's competitive threat. Innovation and entrepreneurial vision were the keys to Pepsi's growth.

Dr. Pepper can trace its beginnings to 1885 and is the oldest soft drink in the United States. Dr. Pepper is a uniquely flavored drink based on a combination of juices. Historically, Dr. Pepper had been a regional producer in the Southwest, but by 1930 distribution had spread throughout the South and the Midwest. By 1960 Dr. Pepper had become one of the major soft-drink brands in the United States. A major obstacle to growth was removed in the 1960s when a U.S. court ruled that Dr. Pepper was not a cola and consequently Coca-Cola or Pepsi-Cola bottlers were able to carry it. Dr. Pepper was launched in New York City in 1970 and thus developed from a regional southern-based soft drink into a national product. In the early 1980s, Dr. Pepper acquired Welch's Foods' line of soft drinks as well as Canada Dry. Dr. Pepper became the third-largest soft-drink producer in the United States. Although Dr. Pepper is the oldest soft drink, lack of vision precluded the establishment of a bottling network. The lack of an efficient vertical system has diminished its growth potential through the years.

The 7-Up Company was founded in 1920, and the 7-Up soft drink was introduced in 1929. 7-Up is not a cola, but faces fierce competition from the colas. 7-Up has a variety of competitors in the lemon-lime market, but the most formidable is Sprite, promoted by Coca-Cola. Pepsi-Cola markets Slice. A major problem of 7-Up is that many of its bottlers also distribute Coke, Pepsi, or Royal Crown. This is viewed as a threat to its bottlers' business; in addition, Coke and Pepsi are able to give bottlers larger discounts. Philip Morris acquired both Dr. Pepper and 7-Up and since has been acquired by Cadbury-Schweppes. 7-Up has targeted a narrow market segment and its promotions have been successful, but its growth potential is limited.

Royal Crown Cola was first introduced in 1935 and is currently confronted with a considerable challenge as a distant runner-up to Coca-Cola and Pepsi. Royal Crown's top brands are RC Cola and Diet Rite. The company has fallen behind private-label entries in the cola market. Royal Crown Cola at one time was considered to be an innovative producer since the company introduced the first diet cola, the first salt-free diet cola, and the first caffeine-free cola. Royal Crown's troubles can be traced back to 1984, when its advertising budget was slashed drastically because of a buy-out. Efforts have been made to revitalize Royal Crown by increasing its presence in restaurants. For example, Royal Crown serves about 12 percent of the more than 2,500 Arby's restaurants, and greater potential is in sight. Royal Crown Cola faces formidable opposition, and its best bet is to serve retailers by selling direct instead of allowing its formula to be repackaged as a private label. Triarc owns both Arby's and RC Cola, and each should benefit from this relationship. However, Royal Crown has limited access to distribution and low brand recognition compared to Coca-Cola and Pepsi. Since Royal Crown by comparison does not have an effective vertical marketing or bottler system, its growth potential is limited.

The early history of Coca-Cola, Pepsi-Cola, and other soft drinks is closely tied to a scenario of innovation. Innovation was present with the development of the bottler network and even the development of the sizes and shapes of the bottles. This network and the successful image of brand identity was developed by the early pioneers of Coca-Cola, who had entrepreneurial vision—John Pemberton, Asa Candler, and later Robert Woodruff. The strategy of the soft-drink industry from the mid-20th century was market-segmentation and product-differentiation as diet drinks and caffeine-free drinks were developed. The soft-drink industry became successful not only in the United States but throughout the world. Physical resources emphasized intensive distribution, with salespeople going everywhere and bottlers in convenient locations. The soft-drink industry has been successful in the implementation of a vertical marketing system, brand identity, and making product purchases convenient for customers.

The main criticism of the soft-drink industry is complacency, and this has plagued Coca-Cola. In 1933 Pepsi-Cola developed the 12-ounce bottle and priced it the same as Coca-Cola's 6-ounce bottle. Pepsi-Cola previously had been no more successful challenging Coca-Cola than ginger ale. The "Pepsi Generation" campaign made further inroads. From the mid-20th century to the present, 7-Up and the bottled water industry have also made successful inroads into the cola market share. Coca-Cola and even now Pepsi-Cola, to some extent, have been slow to recognize the advent of potential competition. Pepsi-Cola made the mistake of committing major financial resources to restaurants. These resources may have been better allocated to their primary soft-drink business. Therefore, to some extent Pepsi shares the modern day complacency of Coca-Cola to the advent of potential competition.

Table 10.1
An Overview of the Soft-Drink Industry in 1996

Manufacturer	Selected Brands	Market-Share Range
Coca-Cola	Coke, Diet Coke, Tab, Sprite, Fresca, Mr. Pibb, Minute Maid, Hi-C, PowerAde, Barq	37%-43%
Pepsi-Cola	Pepsi, Diet Pepsi, Mountain Dew, Crystal Pepsi, Pepsi-Lipton Tea, All-Sport	27%-33%
Cadbury-Schweppes	Dr. Pepper, 7-Up, A&W Root Beer, Sunkist, Schweppes, Crush, IBC Root Beer, Welch's, Squirt, Canada Dry	15%-17%
Triarc	Royal Crown Cola, Diet Rite, Nehi, Mistic Ice, Snapple beverages	2%
Seagrams's	Bottled water	-
Dr. Brown	Dr. Brown	-
Quaker Oats	Gatorade	-
Yoo-hoo	Yoo-hoo	-
Country Time	Country Time	-
Arizona Iced Tea	Arizona Iced Tea	-
Nestlé	Perrier, Arrowhead, Poland Spring	-
Private Store Brands	Private Labels	-

Note: Reported are major brands of some national significance. Market-share range figures
are approximate.

MARKET STRUCTURE

Table 10.1, An Overview of the Soft-Drink Industry in 1996, shows
selected brands and market-share range of important manufacturers. Private store brands and manufacturers of bottled water, iced teas, and other
types of drinks constitute approximately 10 percent to 20 percent market
share. Coca-Cola and Pepsi-Cola dominate the soft-drink industry. Table
10.1 depicts other brands that are sold in supermarket chains in the soft-
drink grocery aisle. The placement of bottled water, iced teas, and citrus
drinks will vary from supermarket chain to supermarket chain and across
geographical regions. Cadbury-Schweppes is prominently in third place in
the soft-drink industry and has a product line with high brand-name recognition. Dr. Pepper is the oldest nationally distributed soft drink in the
United States. Welch's fruit-flavored carbonates consist of a variety of flavors, and the Welch's Grape brand has become the leading grape-flavored
carbonated soft drink.

Coca-Cola and Pepsi-Cola dominate the cola market. A direct challenge to the cola market is the lemon-lime segment of the market. The 7-Up brand has presented an "Uncola" challenge, but Coca-Cola owns Sprite, so the impact of this assault has been diminished. Such has been the competition from Sprite that Cadbury-Schweppes is planning to reformulate its 7-Up drink by making it less sweet and giving it a crisper taste. One problem for Cadbury-Schweppes is that some of the licensed bottlers of their product line also distribute Coca-Cola and Pepsi-Cola products.

Although Triarc with Royal Crown Cola has only a 2 percent market share, Snapple was acquired from Quaker Oats in 1997, and therefore Triarc may be in a position to increase its market share. Triarc plans to reduce costs by jointly marketing Snapple with brands such as Mistic, RC Cola, Diet Rite, and Nehi. Triarc's relationship with distributors is strong, and its marketing program has improved in recent years. Triarc also has an alliance with Saratoga Bottled Water and Celestial Seasonings.

Cadbury-Schweppes is one of the largest British-owned confectionery and soft-drink companies in the world. The company has been better known in the past for its ginger ale and its Schweppes and Canada Dry products. Dr. Pepper and 7-Up are more recent acquisitions. The dominant position of Canada Dry and Schweppes in the soft-drink market has made the task of obtaining shelf space somewhat easier, since these product lines are not confronted with keen competition. However, the Dr. Pepper and 7-Up product lines face heavy competition, and adequate shelf space for these product lines is more difficult to obtain.

Coca-Cola and Pepsi-Cola dominate the soft-drink industry. Coca-Cola in the middle of the 1970s became an aggressive competitor. Diet Coke became successful in 1982, Caffeine-Free Coke and Caffeine-Free Diet Coke were added in 1983, and Cherry Coke was added in 1985. The Coca-Cola name and logo were even franchised for use by apparel and other manufacturers. Pepsi-Cola launched the "Pepsi Challenge." However, Pepsi was still the follower rather than the leader. In recent years Pepsi has marketed Pepsi-Lipton Tea, Mountain Dew, and Crystal Pepsi, and these brands have been moderately successful. However, Pepsi is still number two and Coke remains number one in the soft-drink industry. In 1995 Coca-Cola acquired Barq, a root beer, as part of its strategy of diversification, and Barq now competes directly with A&W Root Beer for market leadership. Coca-Cola has also achieved a differential advantage due to the Coke brand name and a strong-bottlers network.

One of the important changes in the soft-drink market has been the decline of diet drinks. One reason is that many consumers are becoming more health conscious and favor drinking bottled water. Another reason for the decline in the soft-drink market is that baby boomers are getting older and many of them no longer seem to be as concerned as previously about maintaining their weight or losing extra pounds. As a result, in 1996 diet drinks accounted for less than 24 percent of carbonated soft drinks, a decline of market share from 30 percent in 1990. Soft-drink sales increased only a little over 1 percent in 1995 and appear to have plateaued.

MARKET CONDUCT

The bottler network has been largely responsible for the success of the soft-drink industry. Bottling operations for Coca-Cola began before the turn of the 20th century. The bottlers did essential work in market development, and Coca-Cola motivated the bottler system by granting perpetual licenses. If Coca-Cola approved the purchaser, bottlers had the right to sell their franchises or to extend them to their children. A number of franchises encompassed four generations by 1960. The bottler system at that time was the best way to achieve the nationwide intensive distribution that was essential to success. As time progressed, however, Coca-Cola realized that more profitable arrangements could be made. Coca-Cola now sells syrup directly to the bottler system through an independent organization known as Coca-Cola Enterprises.

Conflict does exist in the bottler system. The basic objective of the distribution system is the compatible objectives of both manufacturer and bottler to sell Coca-Cola. However, for the manufacturer, profits result from soft-drink sales in the glass as well as in the bottle, but the bottlers depend upon sales only from the bottle. Thus bottlers desire to sell bottled drinks and try to discourage customers from fountain sales. On the other hand, bottlers can handle noncompeting products such as Dr. Pepper.

Intensive distribution has been the key to the success not only of the soft-drink industry but to candy, snack, and other food industries as well. The objective is to place the product with as many potential sellers as possible. Buying habits of consumers are predicated on convenience of purchase. The dominant factor is place utility. Since brand insistence may be relatively weak, maximum exposure is critical. Consumers may request Coke, but they feel that substitutes are acceptable. Although intensive distribution is required, it is unlikely that the manufacturer will be able to depend upon the retailer for much promotional assistance. The manufacturer often assumes most of the responsibility and cost of advertising and point-of-purchase materials. In the case of marketing soft drinks, important retailers are food, drug, and discount stores. In this situation, soft drinks are one of several thousand items sold by the retailer, so strategic shelf placement and other merchandising aids cannot necessarily be expected by the manufacturer.

A decision to use as many resellers of a particular type as possible to distribute the product is usually based on a combination of factors. Generally, distribution saturation is attempted if the product price is relatively low and if buyers frequently purchase the product but are willing to accept a substitute product. The soft-drink industry uses multiple outlets, especially differentiated by type of retailer, to saturate the market with the product. Therefore, intensive distribution gives the soft-drink manufacturer wide coverage, customer recognition, and high brand turnover. Intensive distribution is often accompanied with fierce price competition.

Another aspect of market conduct has been the strategies of market segmentation and product differentiation particularly emphasized in the cola industry. Coca-Cola has been the universal cola, and consequently Pepsi needed to develop a new basis for competition. The Pepsi Generation campaign developed the modern guidelines for market conduct in the soft-drink industry. This campaign targeted the young and consumers with a certain lifestyle and attitude toward life. Use was made both of demographic segmentation and psychographic segmentation. The image of the Pepsi Generation was young people, both men and women, participating in physical activities or sports. This campaign had little possible connection to the product, but Pepsi-Cola was endeavoring to inform customers about itself. Modern segmentation strategies composed of demographic and psychographic factors are an outcome of the later half of the 20th century. Product differentiation has been used, as in developing caffeine-free products, and is tied to a market-segmentation strategy in the soft-drink industry.

The Mistakes of Coca-Cola and Pepsi

Coca-Cola in 1985 made one of the most memorable mistakes in marketing history. Based upon information gathered from blind taste tests, a decision was made to change the original formula to a sweeter type of formula. Reasons for this change were the growing popularity of Pepsi, especially with young people, as a result of the Pepsi Generation campaign, and Coca-Cola bottlers' desire for the company to take a more aggressive position in its competition with Pepsi. What Coca-Cola never anticipated was the negative public reaction. The product failed miserably, and it never got out of the introductory stage of the product life cycle. There is a high failure rate during the introductory stage of the product life cycle in the food and beverage industry, but Coke never expected such consumer anger and demand to change back to the original formula. Thus New Coke was removed from the shelves and the original Coke was marketed again in less than a year under the name of Coca-Cola Classic. Through hard work, Coca-Cola eventually regained its lost market share.

The background of this infamous decision to change the formula of Coca-Cola was that Pepsi was significantly increasing its market share with a Pepsi Generation campaign that captured the imagination of the baby boomers with its idealism and youth. The association with youth and vitality favorably enhanced the image of Pepsi. Furthermore, taste tests revealed that consumers liked the taste of Pepsi better than Coke. Pepsi was beginning to close the gap in market-share sales, and Coca-Cola was becoming alarmed, especially since Coca-Cola was outspending Pepsi in advertising and dominated fountain and vending machine sales. Since Coke's market share had declined in the late 1970s into the 1980s despite superior promotion and distribution, the belief was maintained, supported by the taste tests, that taste was the most important factor in the decline of Coke's market share. Thus in 1985 the decision was made to reformulate Coke. Critics were to label this decision "the Edsel of the 1980s" and the marketing blunder of the decade.

The marketing-research design had been flawed. Taste tests are subject to inconsistencies. Unless the flavor difference is extreme, brand image can be a more powerful sales stimulant. Brand image is important if it is an inherent part of the culture and societal values. Coke had been around for a hundred years, and consumers did not take kindly to tampering with tradition. The marketing of two Cokes—"the New Coke" and "Classic Coke," caused confusion not only among consumers but retailers as well. Pepsi had launched effective campaigns with the Pepsi Challenge and the Pepsi Generation. Greater advertising expenditures alone would not change this circumstance. Coca-Cola needed an effective campaign to counter Pepsi's strategies. This mistake turned out well for Coca-Cola, since free publicity was generated, and soon market share was recovered and even increased.

Coca-Cola's mistakes were counterbalanced by Pepsi-Cola's mistakes. Pepsi-Cola invested heavily in Pizza Hut, Kentucky Fried Chicken, and Taco Bell, and incurred a shrinking profit situation. Pepsi-Cola's financial resources could have been better used elsewhere to strengthen its product line. There was a battle for fountain accounts when Wendy's and Burger King switched their fountain accounts from Pepsi to Coca-Cola in 1990. Pepsi's strength in the restaurant sector, with competing chains, caused this change in policy on the part of Wendy's and Burger King. Pepsi found that diversification into other areas unknown to management can be a disadvantage.

The Mistakes of Perrier

Perrier is the leading marketer of bottled water in the United States. The main competition is from soft and diet drinks, juices, and domestic sparkling waters. The target market consists of upscale, well-educated, health-conscious adults. The Perrier Group's competitive advantage is that it markets nine brands, many of which are best-sellers. Among the brands are Perrier, Arrowhead, Calistoga, Oasis, Great Bear, Ice Mountain, Ozarka, Deer Park, and Poland Spring. Poland Spring and Arrowhead are considered major brands. The main competitors in the bottled water market are Evian, which is carried in gym bags and comes in unbreakable plastic bottles, and San Pellegrino, targeted toward upscale bottled water drinkers and distributed in upscale restaurants.

In 1990 traces of benzene were found in Perrier bottled water. Although at first glance, reaction to this unexpected crisis seemed appropriate, marketing mistakes of major proportions surfaced later. Perrier increased its promotional efforts from $6 million annually to $25 million for a concentrated sixteen-month relaunch program. Reaction of competitors to the recall was surprising, since the industry maintained a low profile so as not to frighten consumers from purchasing bottled water.

The company announced that they believed that contamination occurred when an employee mistakenly used cleaning fluid containing benzene to clean production-line machinery that fills bottles for North America. The product was to be withdrawn for two to three months. This time frame was criticized by marketing experts. During this period Evian and San Pellegrino made inroads on market share. This long time frame was viewed as unnecessary by some marketing experts and allowed the Adolph Coors Company to introduce Coors Rocky Mountain Sparkling Water and Pepsi to introduce H_2 Oh!

A second mistake by Perrier was for company officials to acknowledge that benzene occurs naturally in Perrier water and that the current problem developed because workers failed to remove filters designed to remove it. This second statement was a critical reversal of the first announcement and destroyed credibility. Suspicions grew that a health risk might be present. The biggest problem of Perrier seemed to be the false impressions that Perrier itself had generated.

Perrier's recovery after the recall was attributed to its other brands, such as Arrowhead, Poland Spring, and Calistoga. Executives granted media interviews and behaved apologetically. Perrier made changes in its labeling and production-line monitoring. These changes were viewed positively and accelerated Perrier's comeback. Moreover, rivals were afraid to exploit the Perrier turmoil because public suspicions might transfer to their brands and because many competitors did not have the financial or logistical resources to capitalize on Perrier's situation. Perrier's recovery was also caused by consumer demand for bottled water, which was the fastest-growing category in the United States beverage industry.

Perrier was fortunate that other competitors were not in a position to take advantage of its mistakes. To withdraw from the competitive playing field for a long time frame invites takeover. Retailers also found it necessary to make new purchases to fill shelf space. Furthermore, it is vital that public announcements are consistent, or credibility will be questioned. An industry catering to health is particularly vulnerable to public scrutiny. Perrier should have established a crisis-management team so mistakes could have been avoided. Perrier was acquired by Nestlé in 1992. Nestlé, known for marketing coffee (Nescafé, Taster's Choice, and Hills Brothers) and candy (Butterfinger, Baby Ruth, and Chunky) in the United States, has a lot of marketing power in supermarkets.

Consumers' concerns over their water supply is increasing, and thus bottled water will be in greater demand in the future.

The Challenge of the Bottled Water Industry

Perrier has successfully used a product-positioning strategy to capture a larger market share of the soft-drink industry. Perrier "positioned" its product in consumers' minds as an alternative to soft drinks. A product's position is the complex association of perceptions, impressions, and feelings that consumers maintain for the product as compared to competing products. For Perrier to accomplish its objectives, the product had to be sold to supermarkets and displayed in the same aisle as soft drinks. Previously, Perrier was sold only in health food and gourmet shops. Perrier managed to overcome obstacles to motivate independent soft-drink bottlers and beer distributors throughout the United States to distribute Perrier and continually replenish store shelves.

Perrier is now marketed with natural essence flavor in varieties of lemon, lime, orange, and berry. The product is calorie-free and natural. Thus, Perrier is competing with soft drinks by offering flavored water. Perrier has met the consumer need for convenience by making the product available in cans that can be easily taken to picnics or consumed at poolside. Perrier is environmentally responsible by providing glass and plastic bottles that are recyclable. The bottled water industry has come a long way since Canada Dry responded to the fear of water-system pollution by marketing pure water as a mixer in other drinks in the early 1980s.

Evian and San Pellegrino, Perrier's main competitors, have seized the advantage since Perrier's difficulties in 1990. Evian is in direct competition with Perrier's leading brands—Arrowhead and Poland Springs. San Pellegrino is Perrier's main competitor in upscale restaurants. Both Evian and San Pellegrino have increased their market share of the bottled water industry to the detriment of Perrier.

Pepsi and Coca-Cola entered the bottled water industry late. Coca-Cola has tried to revive Fresca with a sleek, 9-ounce, light green bottle positioned against Perrier. Nordic Mist, a clear, carbonated soft drink, has also been introduced. Pepsi has launched Crystal Pepsi. Crystal Pepsi, Fresca, and Nordic Mist are part of the soft-drink market and are not considered to be part of the bottled water industry. Intense competition is coming from the Adolph Coors Company with Coors Rocky Mountain Sparkling Water. The Pepsi entry H_2 Oh!, introduced in 1989, has been only moderately successful. On the other hand, the marketing of iced tea has presented another dimension. There is no doubt that the marketing of "alternative" beverages such as iced tea and bottled water has taken away market share from the soft-drink industry. Pepsi has recognized the potential of alternative beverages by marketing the Pepsi-Lipton brand tea. The ready-to-drink tea category grew by 60 percent; Pepsi is number one in this industry and thus profited from its decision to enter this market. Bottled water comprises approximately 15 percent of Pepsi's beverage categories, and while not as profitable as its iced tea entry, the bottled water segment is growing, and in 1994 Pepsi introduced AquafinA.

Coca-Cola does not believe that its real future lies in marketing alternative beverages, according to its 1996 corporate report. Coca-Cola does market PowerAde, Fruitopia, and Minute Maid, but does not have a serious entry in the bottled water industry. The fact remains that sales of diet soda have declined slightly and the sales of soft drinks appear flat. Although soft-drink growth is not apparent, Coca-Cola is pushing its products into retail outlets such as beauty shops, nail salons, and tanning parlors.

Triarc has developed an alliance with Saratoga Beverage Group to market its bottled water. Royal Crown and Pepsi have entered the bottled water industry. Since 1992 Perrier has been a subsidiary of Nestlé, and sales have increased by 50 percent and operating profits by 100 percent. The growth rate of the bottled water industry was 7 percent in 1996, in contrast to a flat growth rate in the soft-drink industry. Perrier has made the product more accessible by using direct delivery of bottled water to homes and offices. In 1996 Perrier grew by a 14 percent rate. The alliance with Nestlé has added more momentum to Perrier.

The small, convenient package of bottled water that Evian pioneered was the fastest-growing subsegment of the beverage industry in 1996. This target market segment grew by approximately 24 percent. The small, convenient package of bottled water constitutes about 18 percent of sales of the bottled water industry. Soft drinks and beer sales have increased only slightly, and the bottled water industry represents explosive growth potential by comparison.

MARKETING STRATEGIES

Coca-Cola has been the acknowledged leader in the soft-drink industry. Pepsi did mount a formidable offensive with its "You're in the Pepsi Generation" campaign. A fundamental in marketing strategy is not to attack the industry leader with an imitative strategy. The inherent advantages in the industry's leader's position will probably overcome such a challenge and exhaust the resources of the challengers. In order to successfully attack the market leader, the challenger must have a sustainable competitive advantage in either cost or differentiation. Independent bottlers are crucial to differentiation. Coca-Cola and Pepsi-Cola expend much attention and considerable financial resources endeavoring to upgrade bottlers and improve their effectiveness. Coca-Cola has been arranging the sale of less efficient bottlers to stronger organizations.

The 7-Up Company tried to dislodge both Coke and Pepsi by using a product-differentiation strategy. When 7-Up was positioned away from competitors as the "Uncola," it became the number three soft drink. Later, 7-Up positioned itself from competitors as the soft drink without caffeine. Unfortunately for 7-Up, the company lacked the physical resources—a network of bottlers to compete. Moreover, 7-Up lacked the financial resources to sustain a long-term effective challenge. Eventually Sprite, owned by Coca-Cola, was to take away market share from 7-Up, and both Coke and Pepsi were able to offer caffeine-free products.

No firm is invulnerable to competition. From 1950 to 1960 Pepsi-Cola increased its market share from approximately 17 percent to 31 percent. The product's taste was inconsistent from bottler to bottler, so a uniform formula was adopted. Packaging and packaging size became competitive. The target market was shifted away from the poor to a growing and affluent middle class. Vending machine operations were more quickly cultivated by Pepsi than by Coca-Cola. The bargain image of the product was changed to make it compatible with its new target market. Distribution was greatly improved by committing company funds to the support of dealer activities. In the 1950s the promotional theme of "the light refreshment" worked wonders. All of this was accomplished because of the complacency of Coca-Cola. Coca-Cola had not changed its bottle size nor its promotional strategies in years. Coke was content to do things without making any changes. The importance of dealer-bottler relations cannot be underestimated. Pepsi motivated its dealers to contribute heavily to advertising, increased vending machine operations, expanded geographical presence through new plants, and maintained strict product quality control.

Target-Market Strategies

Market segmentation is the strategy of dividing a market into groups of consumers with relatively similar characteristics, wants and needs, and purchasing patterns. These submarkets based upon market attributes would include the size of the market, the geographic location, and the demographic description of purchasers or potential buyers. Each submarket is evaluated by size, accessibility, behavioral differences, and degree of current need fulfillment. An analysis of consumer behavior will determine those customer market segments that can best be served by the firm. Lifestyle segmentation strategy attracts customers by demonstrating that the firm's products fit with customer's activities, interests, or opinions. Product-differentiation strategy in a broad sense helps consumers perceive the product as being different and better than competing products. These perceived differences may involve physical features such as adding or deleting sugar from the product or nonphysical ones such as image or price. Coca-Cola and Pepsi-Cola have used strategies of market segmentation, lifestyle market segmentation, and product differentiation either alone or in consort.

There are some target-market strategies that are used for attaining competitive advantage. For example, Coca-Cola's introduction of Tab, the original diet soda, prompted Pepsi to introduce Diet Pepsi. Tab was originally targeted for the female market, and eventually Coca-Cola desired to broaden its base by appealing to men and the entire family. Therefore, Diet Coke was introduced to satisfy these objectives, but it damaged the Tab brand in the process. Many marketing professionals would contend that this was a sound strategy, although the impact of the Tab brand was diminished.

Pepsi, with a strategy of targeting a core market instead of the total market, demonstrated the opportunities created by narrowing the target market. Coke's strength was its tradition, which meant that older consumers had a stronger attachment, whereas younger consumers would more easily switch brands. In many instances, younger customers would want to drink something different than older consumers. The Pepsi Generation campaign capitalized on younger consumers' desires to drink something different. Teenagers drink more soft drinks than any other market segment. All age groups purchase substantial quantities of soft drinks, and this appeal also attracted consumers who perceived themselves as young and physically active. Thus Pepsi was able to close a wide gap between the market leader and itself by effectively using a lifestyle-segmentation strategy.

Diet Coke and Diet Pepsi with and without caffeine use strategies of market segmentation and product differentiation to reach their target markets. Tab was introduced in 1963 as a diet cola positioned for women, and in 1983 caffeine-free versions of Coca-Cola, Diet Coke, and Tab were positioned for health-oriented consumers. Coca-Cola also launched Minute Maid soda as a fruit-based drink in reaction to Pepsi's introduction of Slice. Minute Maid is positioned to attract a market segment that likes fruit juice as well as to health-and nutrition-conscious consumers. 7-Up popularized the appeal of the health-oriented market segment with a lemon-lime entry positioned to consumers who like a lemon-lime flavor. Coca-Cola fought back with Sprite for the lemon-lime market.

Royal Crown Cola used a focus competitive strategy that failed. This strategy rested upon the choice of a narrow competitive scope within an industry. In this case, the objective is to tailor the firm's strategy to serve a segment or group of segments within the industry to the exclusion of others. Since the strategy is optimized, the hope is to attain a competitive advantage even though the firm does not possess a competitive advantage overall. Royal Crown attempted to focus only on cola drinks, but Coca-Cola and Pepsi-Cola have broad product lines and enjoyed the economies of having a broader line. Moreover, retailers had a wider product line to offer their customers. Royal Crown offered nothing that was different or better to resellers or consumers.

Product-Management Strategies

The consumer does not consider the product important enough to give a great deal of thought or consideration when making low-involvement purchases. In many instances, the purchaser tries a number of brands to create interest in the purchase and avoid the boredom of routine. The chocolate candy bar industry and the snack food industry could be cited as making products available that are low-involvement purchases. Some purchasers might envision enough differences between brands of cookies to warrant seeking information about alternatives and to evaluate them. In contrast, other consumers may seek relatively little information about competing brands of cookies simply because they do not believe it's worth the time or trouble.

The soft-drink industry emphasizes low-involvement purchases, but this was not the case with Coca-Cola and its plans to change the traditional formula for its flagship brand. However, in many soft-drink purchases, consumer low involvement would probably be true. There would be many occasions when soft drinks would be purchased on impulse and substitute brands would be accepted willingly. Consumers may purchase either the most familiar product on the shelf, the lowest-priced brand, or a leading brand that is offered at a lower price than the competition.

Brand loyalty is usually the result of the continued satisfaction of the consumer and results in repeat purchases. Brand loyalty is usually based upon careful deliberation and is a high-involvement purchase decision. It is somewhat surprising to note that the outcry over Coca-Cola's decision to eliminate the original formula for its leading brand caused such consumer dissatisfaction. Obviously, for some consumers Coca-Cola was not just another soft drink; it had become a symbol of the culture and environment of their youth and current preferences. The change of formula resulted in a change of taste, or a change in product-differentiation strategy, that was unacceptable to those consumers who were loyal to the brand.

Innovation has been a characteristic of product management in the soft-drink industry. For example, Pepsi in the 1950s introduced its product in 8-ounce and 32-ounce bottles, which contributed to its successful operation. Cans as a means of packaging were introduced in 1959. In the late 1970s, 64-ounce plastic bottles made of a plastic called polyethylene terephthalate were introduced. These innovations made it easier for consumers to purchase soft drinks. Packaging innovation continued into the 1980s and 1990s, with the introduction of twelve packs and two-liter bottles.

Although many authorities maintain that the soft-drink industry has reached the maturity stage of the product life cycle, new products are constantly introduced. To illustrate, Crystal Pepsi is a new product innovation. Another innovation of the soft drink industry has been the introduction of juice-added soft drinks such as Slice. Triarc is marketing Mistic Iced Tea. Pepsi has formed an alliance with Lipton to offer Pepsi-Lipton Tea. In addition, sport drinks such as PowerAde have been launched.

Competition in the soft-drink industry is fierce. Two firms, Coca-Cola and Pepsi-Cola, dominate an industry where growth is slowing. Coca-Cola has approximately 41 percent and Pepsi-Cola has approximately 31 percent market share. The diet soft-drink market has actually declined in the last few years. However, the images of Coke and Pepsi are clear and distinct, reflecting a culture and environment that is well remembered by consumers. Soft drinks are not really an essential product. Profits have been maintained through volume and entrepreneurial vision. Product management has exercised a marketing imagination that has promoted and fostered corporate images and cultivated appropriate consumer market segments.

DISTRIBUTION STRATEGIES

In the soft-drink industry, the bottler is an important intermediary. The bottler buys the concentrate from the brand owner and is responsible for manufacturing, quality standards, packaging, and distribution of the finished product. The brand owner, for example, Coca-Cola or Pepsi-Cola, licenses the brand to the bottler and supplies the concentrate. The brand owner develops new products and is responsible for promotion. The bottler, in turn, sells to the retailer. Many bottlers act independently of the producers of the syrup. The Coca-Cola Company has had only a few restrictions in its contracts. The Royal Crown Cola Company, now owned by Triarc, has taken advantage of the lack of contractual constraints on the bottlers of Coca-Cola by designing a distribution system to include these bottlers for its Dr. Pepper soft drink, and the courts have held that Dr. Pepper is a noncola and therefore a noncompeting brand. Bottlers for Coca-Cola were attracted to Dr. Pepper because of its vertical cooperative advertising program and free product sampling in geographical areas where Coca-Cola and Pepsi-Cola are firmly entrenched. From the Coca-Cola Company's standpoint, two negative factors are apparent. First, less attention by these multicompany bottlers will be paid to Coca-Cola and other brands of soft-drink syrups produced by the firm, and second, the Coca-Cola Company has introduced Mr. Pibb, a direct competitor on taste with Dr. Pepper, a situation that can create even more divided loyalties in the bottlers. All of this transpired in the 1980s, and as time progressed into the 1990s, Coca-Cola made a distribution strategy to buy out independent bottlers as circumstances warrant.

Soft-drink bottlers can be divided into principally four types of operations. First, there are independent, privately owned bottlers. Many of these bottlers are small in size, but others have achieved substantial growth by purchasing other franchises in contiguous geographical locations and by distributing secondary brands such as Dr. Pepper or 7-Up. A second group of bottlers is based in major metropolitan areas such as New York City; this group consists of multibrand franchise firms. The third category of bottlers consists of companies owned by diversified firms; these are mainly Coca-Cola and Pepsi-Cola franchises. The fourth category of bottlers consists of those owned by producers such as Coca-Cola. Coca-Cola and Pepsi-Cola purchase independent bottlers as they become available for sale.

The key to the distribution system for the soft-drink industry is product availability. Soft drinks are available in just about every location. The list ranges from bowling alleys to colleges, gasoline stations, hospitals and hotels, parks and places of amusement, restaurants, and transportation depots. More recently, efforts have been made to place vending machines in nail salons and beauty parlors. This strategy of widespread distribution is known as intensive distribution and is especially appropriate to the marketing of soft drinks. Soft drinks have a relatively low unit cost, need constant replacement, and can be sold to a mass market. The objective is to provide saturation coverage of the market, enabling the consumer to purchase soft-drink beverages with a minimum of effort. There are tens of thousands of outlets where soft drinks can be purchased. The buyouts by Coca-Cola's bottler allow the firm to consolidate operations in order to improve production and distribution to widespread markets as well as to gain better control over the market.

The major reason for the continuous sales and prompt availability of soft drinks is the effectiveness of the franchise system. Recent trends are for the consolidation of single ownerships into multifranchise groups because of escalating production, distribution, and packaging costs. The ability to maintain high price margins has made Coca-Cola and Pepsi-Cola profitable operations. High profitability in the soft-drink industry means high volume, which must be achieved through promotion and intensive distribution. Coca-Cola Enterprises is a separate organization designed to administer the bottling system of Coca-Cola. The trend is for consolidation of bottling operations. Pepsi-Cola has the same objective, but has not yet been able to spin off a separate organization to administer its bottler system, a move that is considered advisable.

PROMOTION AND PRICE STRATEGIES

Promotional support by the brand owner, whether it be Coca-Cola, Pepsi-Cola, Cadbury-Schweppes, or Triarc, is an important motivator for bottlers and retailers to carry their products. Consumers are stimulated by advertising and encouraged by consumer promotions to continue buying or to switch brands. Although 7-Up did make some inroads with their Uncola promotional campaign, the soft drink promotional wars have been mainly between Coca-Cola and Pepsi-Cola.

Coke and Pepsi are continually battling in promotional efforts. Coke was way ahead in market share but grew complacent, and Pepsi has emerged from a weak second to a strong second place in the soft-drink industry. Each company has used a different approach in its promotional campaigns; however, Pepsi has on many occasions ranked higher in advertising recall. Pepsi's creative and imaginative campaign has captured many in a new generation. Pepsi has altered its image from marketing what consumers perceived as a bargain product to marketing a product of quality.

Pepsi's advertising budget in 1939 was substantially less than Coca-Cola's, with an allocation of approximately $600,000 compared to $15 million. In 1942 Pepsi targeted the concept of offering consumers twice as much for their money. The jingle emphasized a larger size bottle:

> Pepsi-Cola hits the spot.
> Twelve full ounces, that's a lot.
> Twice as much, for a nickel, too.
> Pepsi-Cola is the drink for you.

The jingle was translated into fifty-five different languages, and in 1949 *Life* magazine called it immortal.

In 1955 Pepsi-Cola was reborn by Alfred Steele, who married Joan Crawford, a well-known movie actress. Steele was a flamboyant showman who had a gift for promotion and whose wife, actress Joan Crawford, added a glamorous image to the Pepsi-Cola brand. Bottlers and their wives were enchanted by meeting Joan Crawford at numerous social gatherings, and these events became a strong tool for gaining bottler loyalty and participation in promotional events.

Steele innovated by directing Pepsi to introduce bottles of various sizes: 8-, 12-, and 6 ½-ounce categories. Price strategy allowed Pepsi to provide much more of the product than Coca-Cola. Coca-Cola bottlers had invested millions in the 6 ½-ounce bottle size, so a change in bottle size would have meant that much of that investment would have been lost. When Coca-Cola finally did change bottle sizes, it was perceived as copying Pepsi.

Pepsi used promotional campaigns to segment the market by age. The Pepsi Generation campaign was a strategic move. Implicit in the message was that Pepsi was the beverage of the young at heart. This strategy was quite different from the Coca-Cola strategy of portraying itself as timeless and ageless rather than trendy. Pepsi had effectively used lifestyle segmentation to appeal to middle and upper-middle classes in advertisements.

Pepsi had dramatically changed its image from a bargain product for the lower classes to a more metropolitan, sophisticated drink.

Although Coca-Cola's product-development program, with such new brands as Diet Coke, Sprite, Cherry Coke, Fanta, Fresca, Mr. Pibb, and Minute Maid Orange Soda, broke new ground and effectively increased market share, Pepsi's success had been extraordinary. Coca-Cola through the years had a virtual monopoly in the soft-drink industry, but by 1985 Pepsi-Cola had succeeded in giving Coca-Cola all the competition it could handle. Pepsi had turned the market situation into a duopoly. Effective promotion and pricing strategy by Pepsi had dramatically modified the structure of the soft-drink industry.

WHY COCA-COLA SUCCEEDS

There are many reasons why Coca-Cola has been successful, including brand identity, access to distribution, and the development of new markets with new products. Coca-Cola has one of the most recognizable trademarks in the world, and it is a powerful marketing tool for selling soft drinks. This brand identity protects Coca-Cola's equity in goodwill created for its products, and has been extended across national boundaries. When diet soft drinks were still viewed as specialty products for people with special needs, Coca-Cola used the brand Tab to give its product legitimacy. Eventually, when diet drinks were viewed as assets, the trademark was used in conjunction with the new product—Diet Coke. Successful trademarks are built over time. Diet Coke with and without caffeine was used for successful brand positioning. Coca-Cola is a brand with strong consumer loyalties, and consequently, it tends to win distribution support more easily.

Coca-Cola has strong access to distribution. Coca-Cola was the earliest innovator in developing a bottler distribution system that promoted profits through volume. Coca-Cola immediately captured the drugstore market share. Initially the syrup was shipped to the druggist, who in turn mixed it with carbonated water. Coca-Cola is supreme in the fountain sales market. For some years, Coca-Cola franchised bottlers and developed a highly efficient network. Vertical integration is now the vanguard in the 1990s, and proposed acquisitions include purchasing Coca-Cola Bottling of New York, the dominant bottler in the Northeast. This transition reflects the strategy of consolidating bottling operations into large "anchor bottlers" that enjoy economies of scale.

Vertical integration is the process whereby the firm acquires another firm at a different level of distribution. For example, the manufacturer might acquire a wholesaler, or a wholesaler might acquire a retailer. This is called forward vertical integration. If the retailer acquires a wholesaler, then this would be known as backward vertical integration. Vertical integration is an effective means of securing increased coordination, integration of effort, and commitment. It is an old axiom of marketing that it is possible to eliminate the wholesaler, but it is not possible to eliminate the functions performed by the wholesaler. Initially Coca-Cola shifted several functions, including packaging, transportation, and selling to retailers, to their bottlers. For Coca-Cola this was a cost-saving measure, as efforts were made to enlarge the market for their product. In the 1990s, Coca-Cola is engaged in the strategy of vertical reintegration. This means that in purchasing bottlers, Coca-Cola will itself need to perform functions such as storage, transportation, packaging, and marketing to retailers. The problem is that Coca-Cola will now assume the costs of distribution that were previously assumed by the bottlers. If marketing functions can be performed efficiently, then cost savings can accumulate. The end objective is control over the entire distribution network. Because of increased intense competition, technological innovations, and a shortened product life cycle, reallocation of marketing functions may further strengthen the competitive position of Coca-Cola. While the end product is not changed, Coca-Cola now operates at additional levels and recent acquisitions include Wichita Coca-Cola Bottling and Coca-Cola Bottling based in Billings, Montana.

Coca-Cola has been outstanding in its development of new products for different markets and also has efficiently enlarged markets. Classic Coke and Diet Coke are targeted to different markets and are the best-sellers in their categories. Through acquisition, Barq, the number one root beer, has been added to the product line. Mr. Pibb was developed to offset Dr. Pepper, and Sprite is positioned against 7-Up. All of these brands have been successful in their target-market segments. A successful strategy has been the ability of Coca-Cola to locate its products in multiple places, such as beauty and tanning parlors, and to enlarge upon its primary market. Starting in the middle 1980s, Coca-Cola convinced consumers to drink Coke in the morning instead of coffee. This new market is composed primarily of young people. Coca-Cola is selling a brand with universal appeal and has been placed in accessible locations.

In summary, Coca-Cola has been successful because of its high brand identity, and profits have been derived through volume sales. Distribution strategies have made the product convenient and accessible, and vertical integration has been wisely employed. Moreover, new markets have been penetrated by developing new products that satisfy the needs of these new markets.

Marketing Successes in the Soft-Drink Industry

- Profits generated through volume
- Successful market-segmentation and product-differentiation strategies, developed especially by Coca-Cola, Pepsi-Cola, and 7-Up

- Product innovation by Coca-Cola
- Product accessibility spearheaded by Coca-Cola and Pepsi-Cola
- Strong brand power, which serves as protection against private labels
- A strong bottling network developed by Coca-Cola and Pepsi-Cola
- Maintenance of relatively low product prices
- Effective promotional campaigns, especially by Pepsi-Cola

Marketing Mistakes in the Soft-Drink Industry

- Allowing Perrier and the bottled water industry to gain a foothold in the soft-drink industry
- Reactive strategies instead of proactive strategies confronting 7-Up
- Complacency about the rise of alternative drink sales
- Pepsi-Cola's heavy investment in restaurants when financial resources could have been better allocated to its soft-drink products

MANAGING CHANGE

New product introductions have been an integral part of managing change in the soft-drink industry. Coca-Cola developed a new products group in 1989. The new products group reformulated Fresca and introduced the sports drink PowerAde. Moreover, Caffeine-Free Coca-Cola Classic was introduced to address the health concerns of a specific market segment. Coca-Cola reformulated Cherry Coke and Diet Cherry Coke, again demonstrating a flexibility in satisfying the needs of a specific target market. Pepsi demonstrated a pronounced interest in the development of alternative drinks by developing AllSport, a new sports drink, and single servings of Ocean Spray juices in stores and vending machines, and by forming an alliance with Lipton to distribute tea. Pepsi also developed Crystal Pepsi. The alliance to distribute Ocean Spray was discontinued in 1996 as Pepsi wanted to give its own fruit juice brands more attention.

The soft-drink industry from the 1980s to the present focused upon lifestyle product positioning. Pepsi concentrated on creating advertisements to make Pepsi a respectable drink for middle-class consumers to serve guests. Coca-Cola developed Tab to satisfy the needs of women for a low-calorie drink. Diet Coke was introduced to meet the needs of the entire family and simultaneously satisfy health concerns. 7-Up shook up the entire cola industry with its Uncola campaign. In response, caffeine-free colas were launched. In the 1990s, alternative products such as bottled water, sport drinks, tea, and fruit juices have gained increased momentum. However, the core of the soft-drink market still remains the traditional beverages of

Coca-Cola Classic and Pepsi-Cola. Dr. Pepper; 7-Up; bottled water, marketed especially by Perrier; and Gatorade, marketed by Quaker Oats, have all made inroads into the soft-drink market, but the core cola market still exhibits strong loyalties.

Growth in the soft-drink industry has contracted in the 1990s compared to rapid growth in the 1980s. Soft-drink firms are constantly developing new products and other areas for growth. Coca-Cola has been especially adept at convincing consumers in certain age groups to drink Coke in the morning instead of coffee. Another strategy for expansion has been to increase consumption in nonconventional locations, and position products in new and different ways. Pepsi has spun off its fast food restaurants, Pizza Hut, Taco Bell, and Kentucky Fried Chicken into a new company called Tricon Global Restaurants. This allows Pepsi to concentrate on the soft-drink business.

MANAGERIAL INSIGHTS

There are two strategies in effect in the soft-drink industry that have intensified in the 1990s and should continue into the 21st century. Vertical-integration strategies have developed in full force in the 1990s and should prove advantageous to both Coca-Cola and Pepsi-Cola. Second, a further refinement of product life-cycle strategies for products in the maturity stage should renew interest in soft drinks and should continue for at least another decade.

Vertical integration represents a potential growth direction for Coca-Cola and Pepsi-Cola in an industry where sales have plateaued in the United States. Both Coca-Cola and Pepsi-Cola have made various moves toward integrating their corporate systems. Coca-Cola has provided an offer to purchase Coca-Cola Bottling of New York, the largest bottler in the Northeast, and Pepsi-Cola has announced that a separate unit will be formed from the bottling business—and it is anticipated that a spin-off will materialize. Vertical integration can result in possible benefits and costs. One benefit of vertical integration is certain operating economies such as economies of scale, allowing the sharing of warehouses, accounting, operations, computer facilities, and such staff activities as marketing research. Moreover, savings can result in handling, transportation, and inventory costs. A second benefit would be more and better control of the product system. A third possible benefit would be enhancing technological innovation. Information may be more freely exchanged, and the selling job needed to implement innovations or new-product introductions may be facilitated.

Vertical integration, if not implemented correctly, could create potential operating costs that outweigh operating economies. The management system could become strained, as precise coordination of functions will be necessary. Moreover, the classic method of reducing risk is to diversify, but vertical integration tends to increase commitment and investment. Vertical integration may also mean reduced flexibility. Coca-Cola sells concentrate to bottling companies, which in turn add carbonation, bottle, and distribute the product. Pepsi-Cola, while purchasing bottlers, may spin off its acquisitions.

The soft-drink industry is in the market-maturity stage of the product life cycle. The first clue as to its arrival is evidence of market saturation. This means that sales grow about on a par with the population. Price competition becomes intense. Coca-Cola is aggressively aiming price competition at the fountain-sales market. Competitive strategies to maintain brand preference involve finer differentiation in the product, customer services, and promotional practices. A concentrated effort is made to secure more intensive distribution. Manufacturers such as Coca-Cola and Pepsi-Cola, instead of relying on retailers, are communicating directly with consumers. Appeals to users are made on the basis of price, product distinctions, or both. The soft-drink industry is promoting fine product differences through packaging and advertising and appealing to special market segments. Extension strategies have helped to stabilize forces. The soft-drink market in the United States is in danger of a gradual but steady per-capita decline, as in the case of beer.

The soft-drink industry has had a successful record in the past of achieving profit through volume, intensive distribution, and innovation. Strategies of market segmentation and product differentiation have been a model for the entire food industry. It will be interesting to observe how the soft-drink industry will meet the challenges of the 21st century.

SELECTED BIBLIOGRAPHY

BOOKS

Bruce, Scott, and Bill Crawford. *Cerealizing America: The Unsweetened Story of American Breakfast Cereal*. Boston: Faber and Faber, 1995.

Chetley, Andrew. *The Politics of Baby Foods: Successful Challenges to an International Marketing Strategy*. New York: St. Martin's Press, 1986.

Collins, Douglas, and Nathalie Dupree. *America's Favorite Food*. New York: Harry N. Abrams, 1994.

Florman, Monte, and Marjorie Florman. *Fast Foods: Eating In and Taking Out*. Mount Vernon, NY: Consumers Union, 1990.

Funderburg, Anne Cooper. *Chocolate, Strawberry, and Vanilla: A History of American Ice Cream*. Bowling Green, OH: Bowling Green State University Popular Press, 1995.

Graf, Ernst, and Israel Sam Saguy. *Food Product Development: From Concept to the Marketplace*. New York: Van Nostrand Reinhold, 1991.

Lager, Fred. *Ben & Jerry's, the Inside Scoop: How Two Real Guys Built a Business with Social Conscience and a Sense of Humor*. New York: Crown Trade Paperbacks, 1995.

Michman, Ronald D. *Lifestyle Market Segmentation*. New York: Praeger, 1991.

Porter, Michael E. *Competitive Advantage: Creating and Sustaining Superior Performance*. New York: Free Press, 1985.

U.S. Bureau of the Census. *Statistical Abstract of the United States: 1995* (115th edition). Washington, DC, 1995.

Van Every, Phillip Lance. *History of Lance*. New York: The Newcomen Society in North America, 1974.

Wojahn, Ellen. *Playing by Different Rules*. New York: American Management Association, 1988.

ANNUAL REPORTS

Borden 1995 Annual Report.
Campbell Soup 1995 Annual Report.

Coca-Cola 1995 Annual Report.
Dreyers 1995 Annual Report.
Food Lion 1995 Annual Report.
General Mills 1995 Annual Report.
Grand Metropolitan 1995 Annual Report.
Hershey 1995 Annual Report. ˙
Kellogg 1995 Annual Report.
Kroger 1995 Annual Report.
Lance 1995 Annual Report.
McDonald's 1995 Annual Report.
Nestlé 1995 Annual Report.
PepsiCo 1995 Annual Report.
Quaker Oats 1995 Annual Report.
RJR Nabisco 1995 Annual Report.
Unilever 1995 Annual Report.

PERIODICAL ARTICLES

Alwitt, Linda, and Paul R. Prabhaker. "Identifying Who Dislikes Television Advertising: Not By Demographics Alone." *Journal of Advertising Research* (Nov.–Dec. 1994), p. 17.

Benezra, Karen. "Burger Warriors Call Truce on Price: Marketing of Fast Food Chains." *Brandweek*, June 17, 1996, p. 9.

———. "Can This Monarchy Be Saved? Royal Crown Soft-Drink Brand." *Brandweek*, Jan. 15, 1996, p. 31.

———. "Keebler, Eagle Rev Up New Product Engines vs. Frito." *Brandweek*, Feb. 27, 1995, p. 9.

———. "PepsiCo's Enrico: Mustering Brands Beyond Cola Wars into Star Wars." *Brandweek*, May 20, 1996, p. 10.

———. "Roger Enrico: Pepsi Chief Executive Officer." *Brandweek*, Oct. 7, 1996, p. 56.

Berss, Marcia R. "Biscuit Wars." *Forbes*, April 26, 1993, p. 47.

Burke, Bill. "Brand Indentity's New Math: New Coke Campaign Adds Up to a Well-Focused Effort." *Advertising Age*, April 4, 1994, p. 32.

Cortez, John P. "Subway Builds Its Way to No. 2." *Advertising Age*, July 5, 1993, p. 32.

Cropper, Marie. "Bringing Up Baby with Its Parents on the Sideline; Heinz Aims to Make an Organic Brand Part of Its Family." *The New York Times*, May 5, 1996, p. F1.

Elitzak, Howard. "Food Marketing Costs Increased in 1994." *Food Review*, May–August 1995, p. 20.

Fisher, Christy. "Line Extension No Recipe for Success in Candy." *Advertising Age*, Jan. 31, 1994, p. 3.

Fisher, Christy, and Ira Teinowitz. "Kisses Lead to Hugs at Feisty Hershey." *Advertising Age*, May 17, 1993, p. 3.

"Fizz Bang." *The Economist*, July 1, 1995, p. 63.

Green, Corliss L. "Media's Exposure's Impact on Perceived Availability and Redemption of Coupons by Ethnic Consumers." *Journal of Advertising Research* (March–April 1995), p. 56.

Greenwald, John. "Cereal Showdown." *Time*, April 29, 1996, p. 60.

Haran, Leah. "Promos Go Soggy as Co-Marketing, Intros Freshen Cereals (Market Share Statistics for Ready-to-Eat Cereals)." *Advertising Age*, Sept. 29, 1993, p. 6.

Hollingsworth, Pierce. "Oh, Baby (Increase in Sales of Baby-Foods and Baby-Formulas)!" *Food Technology*, June 1993, p. 42.

Judge, Paul C. "Is It Rainforest Crunch Time?" *Business Week*, July 15, 1996, p. 70.

Liesse, Julie. "Cereal Giants Get Crunched: Private Labels Post 5.1% of Dollar Sales." *Advertising Age*, July 19, 1993, p. 3.

———. "Häagen-Dazs Spoons Up a Revival. By Taking on Ben & Jerry's, Ice Cream Marketer Gains Edge." *Advertising Age*, August 22, 1994, p. 38.

Martin, Justin. "Mars Has a New Center." *Fortune*, Feb. 5, 1996, p. 38.

McDermott, Michael J. "Marketers Pay Attention! Ethnics Comprise 25% of the U.S. Minorities, Are Majorities in One of Every Six U.S. Cities." *Brandweek*, July 18, 1994, p. 26.

McManus, John. "Sweet Times Become a Bitter Lesson When Mars' Domos Pull the Plug." *Brandweek*, Feb. 27, 1995, p. 16.

McMath, Robert. "Playing with Breakfast Cereal Is the Whole Marketing Idea." *Brandweek*, Nov. 8, 1993, p. 58.

Melcher, Richard A., and Greg Burns. "How Eagle Became Extinct." *Business Week*, March 4, 1996, pp. 68–69.

Mogelonsky, Marcia. "Baby Food Is Growing Up." *American Demographics*, May 1993, p. 20.

Morgenson, Gretchen. "Denial in Battle Creek: Its Market and Profit Margins Narrow, but the Management of Cereal Maker Kellogg Remains Unperturbed." *Forbes*, Oct. 1, 1996, p. 44.

"New Look for Campbell's." *Advertising Age*, April 25, 1994, p. 58.

Pollack, Judann. "Cereals to Pare Ad Plans: Purse Strings to Tighten After Push for Price Cuts." *Advertising Age*, June 24, 1996, p. 1.

Rosin, Hanna. "The Evil Empire: The Scoop on Ben & Jerry's Crunchy Capitalism." *The New Republic*, Sept. 11, 1995, p. 22.

Saporito, Bill. "The Eclipse of Mars." *Fortune*, Nov. 28, 1994, p. 82.

———. "Parched for Growth: Pepsi Had a Grand Plan for Global Expansion." *Time*, Sept. 2, 1996, p. 48.

Schmuckler, Eric. "A Multiplicity of Ethnicity: Ethnic Media Just Keeps On Growing." *Brandweek*, July 17, 1995, p. 22.

Schori, Thomas R. "Getting the Most Out of Image: An Example from the Fast-Food Industry." *Psychological Reports*, June 1996, p. 1299.

Sellers, Patricia. "How Coke Is Kicking Pepsi's Can." *Fortune*, Oct. 28, 1996, p. 70.

Skow, John. "They All Scream for It." *Time*, Aug. 10, 1981, p. 52.

Sloan, A. Elizabeth. "Why New Products Fail." *Food Technology*, Jan. 1994, p. 36.

Spethmann, Betsy. "Barq's Budget Makes Root Beer Float." *Brandweek*, Jan. 30, 1995, p. 18.

———. "Keebler Heavies Up: It's Elves vs. Nabisco." *Brandweek*, June 6, 1994, p. 1.

———. "New Mood Among Retailers: Don't Just Vend—Let's Talk Marketing." *Brandweek*, May 15, 1996, p. 14.

Stanley, T. L., Betsy Spethman, Terry Lefton, and Karen Benezra. "Brand Builders: Examination of Several Excellent Brand-Building Companies and the Techniques They Used." *Brandweek*, August 7, 1995, p. 20.

"Storm in a Bottle." *The Economist*, August 6, 1994, p. 54.

Sullivan, Lee. "Leaner Menus: Fast-Food Restaurants." *Forbes*, March 13, 1995, p. 154.

Taylor, Charles R., Ju Yung Lee, and Barbera B. Stern. "Portrayals of African, Hispanic, and Asian Americans in Magazine Advertising." *American Behavioral Scientist*, Feb. 1995, p. 608.

Underwood, Anne. "The King of Cream Returns." *Newsweek*, Nov. 1, 1993, p. 48.

Warner, Fara. "Upscale Chocolate's Not Hot, so Godiva Does a Makeover: The Chocolatier Gets a New Look and Ponders Coffee Bars." *Brandweek*, July 4, 1994, p. 21.

Weisz, Pam. "The Candy Bar of the '90s?" *Brandweek*, May 29, 1995, p. 21.

Whalen, Jeanne. "Chicken Chains Try to Stoke Sales: Industry Overview." *Advertising Age*, Dec. 12, 1994, p. 12.

Index

About the Authors

RONALD D. MICHMAN is Professor Emeritus of Marketing, Shippens-burg University, Pennsylvania. Widely published in professional journals and a member of several editorial boards, he is the author or coauthor of seven books including *Retailing Triumphs and Blunders* (Quorum, 1995), *Lifestyle Market Segmentation* (Praeger, 1991), and *Marketing to Changing Consumer Markets* (Praeger, 1983).

EDWARD M. MAZZE is Dean of The Belk College of Business Admin-istration and Professor of Marketing at the University of North Carolina, Charlotte. Former Chairman of the Board and Chief Executive Officer of the William Penn Bank (now part of Mellon Bank), he is author, coauthor, or editor of eight books and more than 150 articles. He serves and has served on the Board of Directors of several companies and on the editorial board of several journals. He has also been a consultant to a number of companies in the food industry.